GEOPROPERTY

GEOPROPERTY

Foreign Affairs, National Security and Property Rights

GEOFF DEMAREST

FRANK CASS
LONDON • PORTLAND, OR

First published in 1998 in Great Britain by
FRANK CASS PUBLISHERS
Newbury House, 900 Eastern Avenue
London, IG2 7HH

and in the United States of America by
FRANK CASS PUBLISHERS
c/o ISBS, 5804 N.E. Hassalo Street
Portland, Oregon, 97213-3644

Copyright © 1998 Geoff Demarest

British Library Cataloguing in Publication Data:

Demarest Geoff
   Geoproperty: foreign affairs, national security and
property rights
   1. Right of property 2. International relations 3. National
security
   I. Title
   323.4'6

ISBN 0-7146-4854-X (cloth)
ISBN 0-7146-4475-7 (paper)

Library of Congress Cataloging-in-Publication Data:

Demarest, Geoff.
   Geoproperty : foreign affairs, national security and
property rights / Geoff Demarest.
      p.   cm.
   Includes bibliographical references and index.
   ISBN 0-7146-4854-X (cloth). − ISBN 0-7146-4475-7 (paper)
   1. International relations − Economic aspects.
   2. International relations − Psychological aspects.
   3. International relations − Social aspects. 4. Property.
   I. Title.
   JZ1252.D46   1998
   320.1'2 −dc21   98−11815
                                                                       CIP

All rights reserved. No part of this publication may be reproduced, stored in or introduced into a retrieval system or transmitted in any form or by any means, electronic, mechanical, photocopying, recording or otherwise, without the prior written permission of the publisher of this book.

Printed in Great Britain by
Bookcraft (Bath) Ltd, Midsomer Norton, Avon

To my family and to our faith in God

Contents

Preface ix

Acknowledgements xiii

1 The Concert of Rights and Duties 1

2 Sovereignty: 'Who Owns This Place, Anyway?' 30

3 Technology and the Modernity of Conflict 69

4 Power and Proprietors 110

5 Strategy, Access and Extortion 149

6 Operational Law and Law Enforcement 188

7 New Things, New Owners, New Rules 215

Bibliography 255

Index 267

Preface

The word 'property', especially as it connotes private property, has been a Cold War prisoner, distorted by the left and evaded by the right. We make better use of the word herein, applying principles of domestic property theory on a global scale. The objective is a changed mental landscape regarding conflict generally. Property ownership has been missed or dismissed in most descriptions and explanations of international or foreign violence. Only under the rubric of land reform, or in cases where there has been obvious and exceptional private property arrogance, has property been given an explanatory status in international relations writing. If a Vanderbilt or a Rhodes intercedes in the affairs of state to build a rail empire – or if Zapatista rebels invoke indigenous rights against capitalist hegemony – or if the Dulles brothers cook a coup to protect private interests in a banana plantation – only then has the essential struggle for property been admitted. Students of conflict, informed positively or negatively by writings such as Harold Jacobson's *Networks of Interdependence*, Paul Kennedy's *The Rise and Fall of the Great Powers*, Daniel Moynihan's *Pandaemonium*, or the Tofflers' *War and Anti-War*, might want to look again at Robert Ardrey's *The Territorial Imperative*. It is curious that the notion of property has been so lightly regarded and so under-used outside the dense confines of Marxist theory. Curiouser still considering the surprise, indignation and sanctimony that often accompanies the uncovering of some secret interest in land. While investigating processes and systems, levels of conflict, game theory and motivators of violence, we presumed the object of human struggle into invisibility. An intellectual fig leaf was dangled over a powerful word. Now it is time to peek back under there; and that is the mission of this book. With it the reader is invited to consider a property-based appraisal of human struggles.

The method looks broadly at property rights (especially rights in land), the identity of claimants, and at systems of ownership rules. These subjects are the what, who, and how of what can be called the ownership environment. A look at technology and its effect on property follows. This leads to a property assessment of strategic power and strategy. Power becomes the ability to gain or protect property – and strategy the rational use of available resources to gain or protect property. The final chapters indulge in suggesting a few foreign policy consequences exposed by this new approach. The United States, for instance, is advised to form a distinct expeditionary police force to help protect the gamut of its property rights (national interests) around the globe. More sweeping is the conclusion that foreign policy emphasis on human rights is a concession to crisis thinking, a treatment of symptoms, and a prospective failure. If the imbalances in human relations that cause violations of basic human rights are to be managed and anticipated, then the focus of foreign policy attention must shift to property rights. Furthermore, the book suggests that important international property struggles are about to impinge directly on United States territory.

Subjective remarks about United States policies are parochial in tone, but the book's central theme is about the manner by which any country might go about deciding what it needs to protect, promote, and oppose. It assumes that American material success has some basis in the qualities of its political principles and cultural character, but emphasis in this writing on American national benefit can be read as an aside. The book's property-focused explanatory model is as applicable to the interests of one country as it is to those of another. It will be noted as well that handling state sovereignty as property does not create zero-sum games in which one nation gains at the expense of others or fails as a result of their gain.

Using property as an explanatory keystone (instead of economics, politics or class) brings some abstractions of political science closer to the field marshal's doctrinal realm of taking and holding terrain. It helps bridge the gap between lofty political philosophy and more mundane preoccupations like force structuring and contingency planning. A nod must be made in this regard to Francis Fukuyama (*End of History and The Last Man*). Fukuyama couches his discussion about the flow of human political history in philosophic terms, but his description of the dialectic competition between liberal democracy and communism carries a message for the strategist. Fukuyama is talking about why people fight, what they fight for, and the future of why they fight after the Marxist–Leninist demise. He suggests that the victory of liberal democracy threatens to leave Western man without the condition of slavery against which to battle. Thereby, an essential need of humanity to struggle against his chains is frustrated in the very condition of liberty attained. According to Fukuyama, the big ideological villains are discredited, and we as liberal democrats may be reduced to policing up the boring details until a worthy challenge comes along to generate cultural resolve.

Property analysis hints that we are not so far along the path of political history as Fukuyama suggests, and that humans will continue fighting for ownership and against being owned much the same as always. An irony of our post-Soviet world is exposed. More international and transnational organizations, more non-governmental organizations, more groups and individuals of every kind are gaining voice. We are witnessing the continuing diffusion of property rights and duties. Part of the diffusion comes from improvements in organizing and communications that increase the opportunities for shared, and challenged, ownership. Central governments and international forums control, represent and influence some ownership identities increasingly well. But other ownership types are thriving – types that defy the state system and in so doing make irrelevant or unresponsive many of the theories of diplomacy and security otherwise operative within the state system. It is in answer to this failure of concepts that geoproperty claims space.

Acknowledgments

There is not enough space or time to name all the people whose help I welcomed, or whose ideas I gladly incorporated. I appreciate them all. I wish, however, to make special note of the assistance provided me by members of the Foreign Military Studies Office at Fort Leavenworth, Kansas – all of whom were patient and supportive in their editing and re-readings. I produced most of this book as part of my military duties while serving in that research unit. Particular gratitude is owed to two colleagues there. One is Dr Graham Turbiville, a foremost expert on ungovernability and on transnational crime. The other is strategist and military author Colonel (R.) William Mendel. These two men saw the unique value of the idea for this text and invested much of their own time supporting its development. Both gentlemen appreciated the originality of a game for ordering international affairs that does not revert to standard economics, *realpolitik* or human rights. I would like to call them disciples of geoproperty, but they have been my mentors, not vice versa. Precursors, catalysts, instigators – these are better descriptors.

1

The Concert of Rights and Duties

INTRODUCTION

> So strong is this propensity of mankind to fall into mutual animosities that where no substantial occasion presents itself the most frivolous and fanciful distinctions have been sufficient to kindle their unfriendly passions and excite their most violent conflicts. But the most common and durable source of factions has been the various and unequal distribution of property.[1]
> (James Madison)

The icons of modern political philosophy, including and especially 'sovereignty', do not represent timeless or universal ideas. They are inventions, condemned to their own historical contexts, causes and effects of human history, in the same way that physical inventions are. They vary in their endurance, and their limits should come as no surprise. Sovereignty, self-determination, nationalism, communism – all are simply expressions about property ownership. They and their similars can be reduced, examined, compared and judged as such.

This contention, patent to many, carries an argumentative consequence that is unattractive for some students of international relations. Logically, if sovereignty is but the ownership of property, then national sovereignty, like the bundle of rights and duties associated with any parcel of domestic realty, is infinitely divisible. Just as we distribute the various rights to a piece of suburban land by easements, municipal bonds, specialized leases and a hundred other instruments, so we can detail the rights and duties accruing to a national state. Following this logic we can simplify the description of foreign affairs. Strategic power becomes the ability to keep and acquire ownership rights around the world. National, sub-, supra- or transnational strategic power can be measured accordingly. The process allows us to outline almost any conflict anywhere using a common vocabulary that exposes interests and suggests the kind of power that might be brought to bear to protect those interests. It simultaneously implies the public reasoning for doing so.[2]

Standard political science definitions of sovereignty embrace the idea of a *summa potestas*, a unified authority supreme in internal affairs and independent with respect to external affairs. Although this essay does not reject that tradition outright, it is handled a bit disrespectfully. The author's contention – that almost without exception the use of the term 'sovereignty' is either a reference to the ownership of property or an argument for ownership – de-mystifies sovereignty. Treated as infinitely divisible ownership, the idea of sovereignty is stripped of weight in determining the limitations of international influence and intervention. Demotion of sovereignty admits new arguments for interstate meddling, and undermines organizations founded on the supremacy of the sovereign state. Given this danger in trifling with the stature of state sovereignty as an organizing principle for world order, Chapter 2 pays special attention to the subject. There, the status of state sovereignty is presented as being more arbitrary and less valuable a quantity than is often supposed. It is not dismissed, but it becomes one among many identities of preferential ownership.

Regardless of the honor paid to state sovereignty, there are at least two advantages of a property-focused approach to international studies. First, the effects of technological change on sovereignty are easily incorporated. As in domestic society, key inventions create new sets of rights and duties that rearrange international relations, often causing conflicts in the process. Second, property analysis can prove equally useful to the understanding of international, sub-national or transnational conflict. It offers a theoretical common denominator for interstate wars, insurgencies, tribal struggles, separatist movements or even international criminal enterprises. In the process, it can expose connections among the causes of these various phenomena.

One disclaimer is necessary – property analysis may prove a neat vehicle for the orderly description of human conflicts, but by itself it is superficial. Religious, economic, psychological and other interpretations of human relations provide a richness of understanding that this model does not discredit or attempt to replace. Nevertheless, a property-focused approach to international affairs can reconcile themes like interdependence, human rights, self-determination, geopolitics, or world order.[3] For instance, many political and military analysts frame the world in terms intended to promote advantageous decisions in support of national interests.[4] Theirs might be referred to as a geopolitical, realist or *realpolitik* approach. Others begin from intentions tied less to national advantage and more to moral principle, founding arguments about the international application of national resources on explicit human rights grounds.[5] We see considerable overlap of the two constructs – sophisticated policy interpretations proclaim both *realpolitik* advantage and moral imperative – but the two perspectives often polarize debate. Property analysis can provide a dispassionate reconciliation of the 'geopolitical' and 'moral' connotations of policy. National interests of a geopolitical nature can be framed in terms of property rights, specifying the identities and claims of would-be owners and the rules of ownership that should or should not apply. Human rights issues can be described and ordered in the same terms.

The chapters that follow define property and argue the conceptual relationship of property to sovereignty. International examples find their way into the initial discussion of property theory, but the application of property concepts to strategic analysis does not really begin until later in the writing. The logic of the descriptive model, including the assertion that sovereignty is ownership of property, depends on acceptance of the theoretical meaning of 'ownership' as preferential rights associated with things (including and especially, land).

Since the object of ownership is commonly called 'property, ' the terms 'ownership', 'property', and 'property ownership' are almost synonymous. Property ownership environments can be broken into three parts. Nameable rights and duties make up the first part. (In relation to a piece of domestic realty, these rights and duties might include the right to deny access, the right to free use and enjoyment, or the duty to protect visitors.) The second subject is the identity of owners and would-be owners, that is, the identities of everyone with competing claims of ownership. The third part of the ownership environment is the regime of ownership rules. This regime, or system of rules, may or may not be codified and may exist in forms as simple as a landlord tenant statute or as complex as Marxist ideology. Of course, the three subjects – rights, people, and rules – are not separate one from another. Separating them is merely an artifice to allow an orderly consideration of competition over property.

Property analysis places sovereignty and human rights on the same conceptual plane. Both involve rights and duties relating people with places. To see this more clearly, it is helpful to look at one of the staples of modern legal education. In 1913 and 1917, a Yale law professor named Wesley Newcomb Hofeld published a pair of short articles titled *Fundamental Legal Conceptions as Applied to Judicial Reasoning*.[6] In the first article he provided a matrix of what he claimed were fundamental conceptions in terms of which he believed all legal problems could be analyzed. His goal in presenting his analytical framework was to provide a scheme for the practical unraveling of day-to-day legal claims. The crux of his approach was to order legal rights along with legal 'no-rights' as opposites, and with legal duties as correlatives. Associated with every right, Hofeld identified 'no-rights' and duties. The existence of a right implies the existence of an opposite (no-right) and a correlative (duty). For instance, an individual can have rights in real estate such as the right to enter or the right to deny entry. Other persons, who do not share in the ownership, have a no-right. That is to say, they logically have no right of entry. Along with owners' rights come correlative duties, such as the duty to keep visitors safe.

Hofeld wanted to create a rights–duties cookbook useful in a specialized legal context, and his cookbook approach is still used as a prompt for recognizing competing legal claims and their merits. It works not only in property law issues, but more broadly in other legal conflicts, and the same pairings of 'right, no-right (or non-right)', and 'right, duty' can be applied to treat international sovereignty issues. With Hofeld in mind, every discussion in this book about sovereign rights implies the existence of correlative duties and opposing non-rights.

While the first chapters of this book describe the nature of ownership environments with a view toward applying property theories on an international scale, later chapters carry property theory to the realm of strategy. Simply defined, national strategy is planned effort to gain or protect identifiable property rights on behalf of a people. Every cubic inch of land, sea, sky and space on and around the earth bears some identifiable right belonging to the British. It might not be much – in some places maybe little more than the right to physical integrity while visiting – but it is hard to imagine a place where a Briton has no claim to any rights. The British government, correspondingly, formulates and implements, in varying degrees of formality, specificity, clarity and effect, an attempt to guard the rights of Britons around the world. These rights may be individual, corporate, common, express or implied, but some of their bits of ownership related to the billions of cubic inches of earth's geography must be underwritten by the use or threat of the use of physical force, so a military strategy evolves in support of the overall strategy.

Military strategy refers to only one part of the set of methods and resources available to the state to help guarantee property rights around the world. Governments also apply diplomatic, economic, and propagandistic strategies, but it is, after all, military strategy that supposes the management of violence. We may have become overly confident in the moral and even physical superiority of the nation-state as a political entity, and about the national military that goes with it. The United States military, at least, has ordered its concept of what is militarily professional around the idea of being a nation-state army. This is noteworthy from a polity whose founders were interested in creating the least central government and the least national army feasible. Over time, many American military leaders have assumed an attitude that ethnic, sub-national, insurgent, religious, tribal, Mafia, political party conflicts and their ilk are out of the ordinary, less important and less worthy of professional military attention than wars between nation-states. This mindset has to be excused in view of the danger posed by nation-state wars and the sheer power of nation-state militaries since the late nineteenth century. Interestingly, early glories of the American military are rooted as much in civil war, Indian war, pirate punishment and revolution as they are in interstate rivalry. Also noteworthy is that United States military members do not swear to defend American terrain or sovereignty. They swear to uphold a social contract ordering ownership – they promise to defend the Constitution of the United States.

The nation-state is not going away soon, but the twenty-first century is going to see more competitions, including military, between entities and about issues only indirectly or partially related to nation-states. The parties to these conflicts will, nevertheless, be fighting for the same substance, a substance that may be best analyzed as property.

WITHOUT TITLE OR DEED

> Dosn't thou 'ear my 'erse's legs, as they canters awaäy,
> Proputty, proputty, proputty – that's what I 'ears 'em saaäy.
> Proputty, proputty, proputty – Sam, thou's an ass for thy paaïns;
> Theer's moor sense i' one o' 'is legs, nor in all thy braaïns.[7]
> (Alfred Tennyson, from *The Northern Farmer* [new style])

The index of Reinold Noyes' pre-World War II scholarly classic, *The Institution of Property*, does not contain the words 'sovereignty', 'international', or even 'nation', since he did not address the application of his findings to international studies.[8] Noyes' contribution to the present essay is his elaborate observation regarding the psychological concept of property. Purists of legal theory have long held property to be merely a concert of rights, and Noyes expanded on this view with an interpretation of the early evolution of Roman legal terms. Words leading to the very ability to consider property as a substantive thing were, in the days of the early Republic, descriptors of legal or pre-legal court actions.[9] In other words, an early Roman might have pleaded, 'He hunted where only I may hunt', or 'he took grain from land where only I may harvest'. These claims of violated rights led to the idea of 'property' as a separate class of complaint and then as a special class of thing. According to Noyes, prior to the recognition of preferential rights in courts, the noun 'property' could not exist to encompass legally owned things. Vocabulary leading to the notion of property as a thing was legalistic, so Noyes made a semantic investigation of mishaps in Roman and English legal interpretations. He discovered, in effect, that the invention of property law came before widespread usage of the noun. Furthermore, much of the early semantic debate about the property concept revolved around fundamental, abstract and prehistoric distinctions between 'law' and 'power', 'power' and 'right', 'right' and 'claim'. In other words, at some point in our Western jurisprudential past, distinctions between human and property rights, and the act of asserting them in court, did not exist, or at least could not be formally expressed. From this perspective on the less-than-essential quality of the term, Noyes concluded that modern legal protections afforded to real property could be expanded to include every right associated with things in general. In the half-century since Noyes' treatise was published, US courts accepted an ever-growing list of theories of protectable rights litigated as property. It has been a later trend to litigate the violation of human rights as a separate category of public action.

So can or should human rights be re-defined as property today? At the time of his writing, Noyes felt he had to argue almost the opposite – that the legal regime would be improved if human rights did not have to be protected under property theories. Domestic property law concepts are a tool whose usefulness in analyzing human conflict can be exceeded. Classifying serious human rights abuses as property questions could routinize the presentation of such crimes and diminish urgency in confronting them. Nevertheless, even in relation to the most serious human rights abuses, property issues will often be identified as causes. Few abuses are not rooted in competitions for property. Unfortunately, when dealing with international human rights, the problem becomes one of metering the status of human beings not only to the extent that their property rights are being protected, but to the extent that they themselves are being treated as property.

Some property concepts applied in the following presentation will reflect the development of ownership rules within a Western belief system, more specifically of Britain and the United States. However, looking back as Noyes did at the ancient psychological development of the property concept, the terms 'ownership', or 'property', or 'property ownership' can all be understood as referring to some concert of rights. In this light, we can apply a property-based analytical approach to conflict regardless of the varying nature of belief systems. The same three-subject (rights, owners, rules) reduction of the property environment works irrespective of the culture-specific relationship between man and land.[10] Consideration of the system of ownership rules must include inspection of incompatibilities between competing systems, but the property analysis method does not require application of solely Western notions of property ownership. The analytical framework encompasses any cultural variation regarding ownership, even if some perhaps purely Western property theories appear in the explanation of the model.[11]

Although 'geoproperty' alludes to a broader set of preferential interests than just those associated directly with land, we are most immediately aware of struggles relating to land. Differences in land ownership practices (culture-to-culture and age-to-age) are well documented, but this body of observations does not support a conclusion that the ownership principles and ethics of one culture are difficult to comprehend from within the ownership regime of another culture. It is quite reasonable to devise theories about the relationship between ownership regimes and conflict. John Powelson, respected economist from the University of Colorado, produced a fascinating work entitled *The Story of Land*.[12] Powelson puts together, in one place, a survey of the history of land tenure and reform in past centuries. In contemplating the similarities among land tenure histories he proffers the hypothesis that 'customary land tenure, nonliterate society, trend migrations, slavery, and continuous warfare (conflicts not expected to be resolved) all go together; they contrast with fixed tenure (land registration), literacy (written contract) settled existence, free wage labor, periodic peace, and the expectation that contracts will end'. He further hypothesizes that 'negotiation and compromise are a last resort, to be employed only when war and conquest have failed over centuries and only when land shortage prevents enemies from escaping each other any more ...'. Powelson's theorizing fits within what we would like to call geoproperty theory, though we would expand the scope of ownership and the meaning of property to include concerts of rights and duties not associated or only indirectly associated with land. The specifics of Powelson's hypotheses are compelling, but the following observation needs making: additions to the amount and types of property worldwide, brought about mainly by technological change, are as much a cause of conflict as are shortages of property.

Powelson makes another hypothesis that is immediately relevant: 'I hypothesize that economic development requires a culture in which individuals and corporate bodies are clearly bounded and identified; in which rights, duties, and obligations with respect to property, also well defined, are clearly assigned to those individuals and corporate bodies, including the state; and where the distribution of rights and resources is not unduly concentrated in any of these bodies, including the state.' It is currently out of fashion to rate cultures as more or less primitive, more or less advanced – but the cultural progress to which Powelson refers is a degree of civilization. Civilizations are advanced that order and protect property rights. To remain civilized, and to remain in being, the regime of property ownership must be able to cope with changes brought about by three simultaneous and interrelated trends. One is environmental change, the second is technological advancement, and the third is population growth. The importance of all three lies in the stress put on the ability of regimes of property ownership to peacefully reconcile competing claims.

RIGHTS AND OBLIGATIONS

> It should be remembered that the foundation of the social contract is property; and its first condition, that everyone should be maintained in the peaceful possession of what belongs to him. (Jean-Jacques Rousseau, from *A Discourse on Political Economy*)

As proposed in the introduction, the first subject for analysis in the ownership environment is the concert of rights and duties itself. It is easiest to begin with a discussion of real estate. Real estate ownership involves all the variety of rights, non-rights and duties that can be associated with a piece of land or a structure on it. Under the system of property concepts generally shared by the states of the United States and rooted historically in English common law, the practical ownership of a piece of real estate can be infinitely subdivided. A 'life estate' can be granted that gives certain elements of ownership to a person only for the life of that person. A remainder might be bought or sold that gives rights in the property only after the death of the holder of the life estate. Possible subdivisions of the total ownership of real estate include the right of current use and enjoyment (such as an apartment rental) subsurface mineral rights, or an easement for running a community sewer line. A usufruct, or usufructuary right, gives use, enjoyment, and profits from property 'belonging' to someone else. All these rights are associated with correlatives and opposites. Obviously, if the apartment renter owns the current use of the apartment space, other individuals, even including the landlord, have no right to enter without consent (or a warrant). In addition, the law enforcement system has a duty to protect the renters' rights as well as those of the landlord. Potential horrors of landlord–tenant relationships are familiar to most of us, as is the rocky history of landlord–tenant laws in most jurisdictions. Citing landlord–tenant problems would alone be sufficient to assert the complexity of the rights of ownership in land, but the division of real estate ownership involves intricacies that go well beyond this relationship.

Going further to establish the nature of the ownership of real property, consider a piece of ground on which a corporation owns a condominium building in a zoned part of suburban land controlled by a municipal corporation. Assume there are various easements on the property (telephone cable, other utilities, and various access easements), there are four sets of taxes being paid, and one of the condominiums has been turned into a health spa. Title to the subsurface rights is in doubt because the majority shareholder in that corporation (who had made a contract not to exert claim of the subsurface value) has died and bequeathed his shares in the property via a life estate to his mother. Children have walked to school for years over one corner of the property, an ancient burial site and some mammoth bones are found under another corner, and the property overlaps four state and federal voting districts (probably gerrymandered).

This hypothetical case does not present such an uncommonly complicated division of property rights for a modern piece of American real estate. So who is the real owner of the land? Who has the title? And so what, if pieces of ownership are evidenced in various deeds, contracts for sale, municipal codes, wills, and court orders? There may be no 'real owner' even though everyone mentioned is the real owner of some part. Additionally, every element of ownership in this complicated web involves more than just rights. Each element involves non-rights and duties, some of which are even less apparent than the ownership rights. The 'owners' of the property across which the school children walk have a duty to make sure the children are safe while there. Identifying the 'owners' with that specific duty becomes a very important financial question for a tort lawyer when one of the children falls and gets hurt. The lawyer will 'find' the owner based on the injury, and we can bet that he will start looking for rich owners first. He will attempt to convince a judge or a jury to 'find' an unmet duty. Many other people, with very small slivers of ownership in the suburban property, will have non-rights associated with the land as well. A burglar has no right to enter the apartments. He will anyway, and hopefully he will be caught. Designated individuals, including police and prosecutors will then meet duties related to the apartment dweller's right to deny access, and will try to punish the trespasser. More complicated still is the non-right of persons living hundreds of miles away to pollute the property with acid rain. But it is obviously possible that someone could make legal demands respecting even this type of non-right.

Under ancient English common law, if someone were to own all the various rights in a piece of land, it would be said that the land was owned in 'fee simple absolute' or that the owner 'held the fee'. Of course, no piece of land is really held in fee these days. The government always finds the right to tax the value of the land, overfly it, zone it, or condemn it to put through a railroad. The best a would-be total 'owner' can do is to hold a clear title to a remote piece of dirt outside any school district or municipality, insured by a reputable and solvent title guarantee company. Not many of us can afford to live on such a plot, however, or would care to. If we did, we would find that complete ownership of the land still entails some public and private duties. A restraining order could be slapped on us at the request of the neighbors if we waste the land or despoil it in some way that endangers neighboring lands or even that endangers some species of animal. An owner really cannot do just anything he wants.

The community is going to hold rights in otherwise private property no matter how dear a price is paid for the dirt. In addition, the worth of land and the market measure of its worth are intimately related to personal priorities consciously or subconsciously assigned to various kinds of rights in land. As we gain a greater control of some rights related to a property, we find that the value of the property (probably reflected in its market price) is very limited in relation to other rights. In other words, if we escape city water easements we must dig our own well. If we want land as a vehicle for earnings, we will have a different sense of the attractiveness of the market price depending on its exposure to shared rights. The hermit and the used-car dealer relate to a piece of land differently because of the relative importance of distinct, definable rights and duties associated with the land. While in possession, the hermit will place greatest emphasis on the right to exclude access. A gentleman's club might be another example of the same emphasis. Obviously, the potential for expressing and enjoying one type of right as opposed to another rests greatly on geographical location. In determining if we should buy a piece of land, location is usually the most important factor besides price.

PROPERTY OWNERS AND THE REACH OF IDENTITY

> Bourgeois means an owner of property. The bourgeoisie are all the owners of property taken together. A big bourgeois is the owner of big property. A petty bourgeois is the owner of small property.[13]   (V.I. Lenin)

Identifying all the owners of rights associated with a single piece of land can be a complicated task. That is why title search firms do so well; but beyond the simple identification of owners is a problem involving the coherence of owner identity. In the example of the confused condominium property, rights associated with the occupation of the apartments may be enjoyed by families that vary widely in their sense of identity, unity of purpose, and feelings toward their rights and duties. One group may be closed, jealously protective of their privacy, and proud of their home, while the itinerant prostitutes next door might be a tad more gregarious and not nearly as proud of their residence. Ownership documents only hint at the descriptors and determinants of ownership identity, even while they state who the owners supposedly are. The otherwise unrelated mothers of the children in the suburban real estate example could form a powerful group argument to protect that single right of access. Their appeal might only have to influence a group of city council members who are in turn responsive to a vague sense of equity within a general electorate. The appeal of the mothers could ultimately be manifested by a city ordinance, a lawsuit or other court action, or the outright purchase of a property right. Owner cohesiveness can be strong in relation to even a single right associated with land, while no cohesiveness exists otherwise. Where there is a strong sense of shared ownership, where the sense of 'we-ness', or cohesion of identity is strong, it follows that such owners are more likely to express and defend the rights they have as a group. The selling price of what they consider their share of the property is going to be higher.

The ownership status of individuals can be credited to multiple owner identities. One of the mothers of the children mentioned in the suburban example might fit all of the following groups: mother of children who cross that piece of land on their way to school, citizen of Overland Park, Kansan, Black, Dominican, owner of ten shares of Texaco, property tax payer, Republican, speedboater, female, Baptist, wife, Irish, short person, twin, lefty, kids hockey team representative, mother against drunk drivers, and alcoholic. Each descriptor can be matched to a right related to land that the mother is variably willing to defend or attempt to obtain. As a Black person, she may be fiercely opposed to badges of racism. As a mother of school children and payer of property taxes, she may be just as opposed to allowing illegal immigrant Mexicans from attending school in the district. Other identities may be at odds with one another as far as property rights are concerned. For instance, she may find it difficult to vote for a proposed ordinance against serving alcohol. She is both an alcoholic and a member of Mothers Against Drunk Driving.

We must add more to the confusion regarding which of her identities is momentarily operant. Many of her listed identities may be individually less stable or substantive than one might think. Almost all of our Kansan's identities are artificial to some degree. As Arthur Schlesinger ably discussed, American identity is being decomposed and dispersed according to the most actionable sub-identities, racial labels being perhaps the most divisive. Quoting Ishmael Reed, Schlesinger points out that even Black identity is as much the subject of creative industry as it is genetics. 'If [Alex] Haley [author of *Roots*] had traced his father's rather than his mother's bloodline, he would have traveled 12 generations back to, not Gambia, but Ireland.'[14]

Our hockey mom could even look forward to having one of her kids be a member of a nearby Indian tribe. 'It generally holds that to be accepted into a tribe, at least one parent has to qualify as a tribal member. But because of low populations, some tribes accept members with only one qualifying grandparent.'[15] The need to maintain tribal membership is directly linked to legal recognition, which is in turn connected to preferential property rights. Our

Kansan (until she moves across the river to Missouri) will pick and choose which identities apply, and to what intensity, depending on which issues she decides to shoulder.

The foregoing paragraphs make it apparent why the emotional intensity of ownership claims can be so situation specific. An individual may feel intense group solidarity in relation to competition over one right associated with a piece of land, but may feel little sense of common identity in respect to another right associated with the same land. This is one reason why many analyses of international conflict can mislead. They often treat blocks of people and pieces of land in a way that does not allow for variable weighting of identities based on the specific rights in question. In domestic property adjudication, courts focus on specific rights, and plaintiffs' and defendants' lawyers are attentive to the cohesiveness of identity of all would-be owners. In addition, most ownership conflicts involve human characteristics such as capriciousness, ambivalence, error, and ignorance. Analyses of international behavior, especially those that focus on state decisions, sometimes underplay these human vagaries.

OWNERSHIP RULES

> The theory of the Communists may be summed up in the single phrase: Abolition of private property. (Karl Marx and Friedrich Engels, from *The Communist Manifesto*)

Besides fixing the division of rights associated with property and then defining the owners, we must gain understanding of the regimes of ownership rules. The systems of ownership rules may be manifested in formal, written laws or may be expressed in other dimensions of belief systems that are more difficult to specify. These might include religious beliefs regarding the relationship between humans and land. Whatever their form, ownership rules are the 'how' in the calculus of who owns what and how. In the examples of United States domestic real estate, a legal regime exists as statutes, regulations, ordinances and court decisions. Even within this formalized legal regime of real estate rules, broader social influences play in the ownership environment for land. For instance, if a would-be landlord gives an eviction order to an occupier, and the occupier does leave, the event shows an exercise of ownership. Perhaps the changed possession is the product of coercion or fraud. If the power and arrogance of the taker are sufficient that others do not care to somehow challenge the taking (or cannot), the new possessor (even having taken possession illegally) may eventually become the legal owner of the land. This possibility serves as a reminder that legal ownership is related to the force necessary to support a claim.

This is not a cynical declaration that might makes right, but an observation that the enjoyment of rights associated with domestic property is not perfected without some basis of enforcement. Legal ownership, whether by title, contract, deed, government regulation, will, or court order, can be lost in even the most formalized and maintained system of laws if the supposed owners do not assert their ownership in some way. In a country where the legal system is less respectable, formal legal ownership is more easily lost, often to a tyrannical government mechanism or to private interests enjoying the conspiracy of the government. Landlord–tenant relations were already mentioned as an example of ownership competitions that involve various rights associated with a single piece of geography. In geography with matured legal jurisdiction, if the owner of an apartment complex wants a tenant to evacuate, the owner must follow certain laws, usually statutory. At times it annoys the owner that the tenant does not treat him like the possessor and it annoys the tenant that he is not being treated like a full owner. To ease the potential for violence in these situations, legislatures try to enact precise landlord–tenant laws. In some jurisdictions, the laws favor tenants, while in others the laws seem to help landlords repossess.

At the global or international level, systems of ownership rules may be referred to as customs, mores or ideologies. The terms are more glorious than 'ownership rules', but the effect is the same. Conflict often occurs as competition between distinct ownership systems, or as rebellion against existing preferential rules.

PROPERTY VALUE

> Mine is better than ours.[16] (Benjamin Franklin, from *Poor Richard's Almanac*)

The sections above outlined three aspects of the ownership environment that can be individually considered in terms of their influence on ownership conflicts. Some challenges to ownership – which involve property rights, the identity of owners or the system of ownership rules – are most easily described in terms of property value. Thinking of the market for real property, we ask, 'What is the value of that property, who owns it, how do they own it, and how do they protect what they think they own?' Finally, 'How do we get a better piece of it?' Getting a piece of it does not have to mean reducing the value of what is left. The value of certain rights in land increases as other rights are relinquished. For instance, if visitors enter our restaurant freely, the possibility of making a profit from the property increases. In giving up an exclusive right to entry and by not enforcing the right to deny access, we increase the value of the right to profit from the product of the land. We also incur a duty to protect our visitors while on the property. A change in the mix of rights and duties associated with our real estate can increase its value, but only if we have enough control over the changes to ensure that the new mix of rights fits our priorities. The hermit may not be well compensated by the added income generated by a restaurant. In addition, property adjoining the restaurant may increase in commercial value, but may decrease in value as residential property. In the aggregate, property values can be measured by sale prices, taxes assessed, average local insurance appraisals, municipal bond ratings, commercial loan rates, stock quotations, or even the number of tourist visits.

In order to understand all the influences that might bear on the value and therefore the price of a piece of land, we need more than a listing of owners and corresponding rights. We also require a grasp of the coherence of identity of the owner groups. It may be more expensive to induce a group with a strongly cohesive identity to compromise and to share their ownership portion. It may also be harder to get them to meet duties implied by their ownership and associated with whatever rights they enjoy. Thus an analysis of value and price of a set of property rights must go beyond two-dimensional identification of rights and related 'owners'. The analysis must also consider the nature of the identity of those owners. Finally, no complete price and value analysis is competent without including relevant aspects of the system of ownership rules – the market value of a restaurant will be greatly influenced by a pending change in zoning laws.

Almost every law influences the market value of property. In places where the legal emphasis is on protection of the rights of a tenant (and ignoring all other market factors), the prices of apartments would logically tend to be higher. After all, the value of possession is made greater by the greater security provided by the legal regime. It might be supposed, then, that the market value of rental property as an income-producing investment would go down since there would be more risk involved in owning the complex. Curiously, given additional protection of the tenant by the legal system, the value of the apartment complex as an income producer may go up, since the rents may be higher and the clientele may, in turn, be more solvent. Of course this depends on other market factors. It is possible, however, that the owner of the apartment building would see the profitability of his rights increase even after what seems an erosion of his property rights in favor of the tenant. This is evident after further detailing the identifiable rights. The landowner has a right to gain income from the rental of other rights. That is to say, he receives payment for renting the right to possess space in his building. While he wants to retain the right to eject renters because he feels this ensures the collection of his rental income, the government limits his right of repossession once the landlord–tenant relationship has begun. Government has supported the tenant's claim to sole possession, but the value of another landlord right (the collection of income) has gone up with the value of the tenant's possession. The value of property ownership is often increased when rights in the property are dispersed and shared. International zero-sum games can be exposed as unreasonable in light of this particular real estate observation. Sharing sovereignty, like dispersing rights in domestic real estate, can increase the value of a nation's aggregated owning. Of course, this is not necessarily so. Value can be decreased when ownership is dispersed too much. Gottfried Dietze, in one of the most compelling and thorough arguments on the subject, argued that eroding respect for private property in favor of common property (a result of the assaults of socialist philosophy and decadent living) is a principal threat to the cause of freedom.[17]

COMMON PROPERTY

> No man made the land. It is the original inheritance of the whole species. Its appropriation is wholly a question of general expediency. Public reasons exist for its being appropriated. But if those reasons lost their force, the thing would be unjust. It is no hardship to any one, to be excluded from what others have produced. They were not bound to produce it for his use, and he loses nothing by not sharing in what otherwise would not have existed at all. But it is some hardship to be born into the world and find all nature's gifts previously engrossed, and no place left for the new-comer.[18] (John Stuart Mill, from *Principles of Political Economy*)

Common property is owned as a specialized set of rights. A city park serves the common good by providing open space, psychological relief from the urban landscape, a place to play outdoors, to meet, to birdwatch, to breathe. The community of owners has an understood set of rights that is clearly distinct from the rights they have over their apartments or offices. These rights amount to easy access to and limited use and enjoyment of a few very expensive commodities. A related and instructional issue involves the use of city parks by the homeless. Many non-government organizations, such as the ACLU (American Civil Liberties Union), have argued on behalf of the homeless. They claim that city governments should not have the power to eject the homeless from city parks, that their homesteading falls within their rights and engages a duty owed by the public at large to house them. In essence, the ACLU argues a claim for a set of private property rights in specific pieces of land, on behalf of a select group of people, with a single public identity. The outcome of such arguments is predictable except in the most exotic jurisdictions. The ACLU and the homeless will lose due to the relationship of the homeless' claim to the concert of rights associated with real estate, and especially with urban real estate. ACLU lawyers claim the kinds of rights owned by apartment dwellers, but city parks already provide rights to their owners that are incompatible with the apartment type rights. To give apartment rights to the homeless in parks requires that the common property value associated with its original intent be greatly diminished. Prospects for future parkland would dim, since the public will not buy property rights that will be traded by a vocal minority and a forfeiting court.

Efforts to work in favor of property rights for dispossessed individuals gratify the constituencies of organizations such as the ACLU. Nevertheless, the same constituencies will ultimately reject the disintegration of rights in rare common property except in the most compelling situations. Cities such as Boulder, Colorado, for instance, have invested heavily in public control of open parkland protected by draconian use limitations. Boulderites may support charitable, sensitive treatment of the downtrodden, but they will not greatly alter the rights of ownership associated with most public lands. There as elsewhere, a regime of stiff fines for littering and unauthorized use of motor vehicles does not reconcile well with an invitation to squatters. Also, philanthropy toward the homeless will show hidden costs when insurance has to be purchased, lawsuits answered, or night supervision provided in response to responsibilities to provide security.

Of course, activist courts may seek greater investment by communities in public shelters and may use the threatened degradation of public rights in parkland as leverage to force community commitments to greater individual property concessions for the poor. Still, events involving city parks must be seen for what they are. A park given over to the homeless simply ceases to be a park and becomes instead a public shelter with a new set of rights, duties and division of ownership. In this example, one identity of owners that we might label 'those in solidarity with the homeless' argues a fixed set of private rights against owners that we might label 'supporters of the green common'. The argument takes place under a unique regime of property rules. We see the problem of identifying would-be owners of specifiable rights and the influence of the regime of ownership rules. Sorting out owner identity and cohesiveness is complicated when the same individuals can attach competing owner identities. The same person can be a member of 'those in solidarity with the homeless' and of 'supporters of the green common'. Furthermore, those who provide the greatest strength of cohesiveness and willpower in a competition over property rights need not be members of the group most likely to exercise the rights being argued. The ACLU is a champion in the homeless example, its support coming from a diffuse population of benefactors.

The distinction between private and public land is not clear-cut either. Returning to the suburban restaurant, the system of ownership rules holds that the proprietor has no right to exclude patrons based on race. That is to say, everyone in the general public has a right to enter the restaurant whatever their race. The decision to own property as a restaurant means, as a result of acceptance of or acquiescence to the legal regime, that the private right to deny access is diminished. An invitation to the public creates an expectation in the public and that expectation creates a new duty on the part of the restaurateur. With the invitation, the public 'owns' a slice of the restaurant. Since the cohesive identity of the American public (at least in the context of the formal regime of ownership rules) includes no distinction based on race, the correlative duty requires that everyone, regardless of race, be served. Note also that this and many other interpretations of ownership have not been historically constant, but have changed over time.

Characteristics of the ownership environment for domestic real estate may be obvious enough, but they are presented here with a view toward preparing the analogy to international sovereignty. Oddly, individuals seemingly in exercise of the fewest domestic rights of ownership often exhibit the most fervor for defending its sovereignty. Others, who have apparently benefited the most materially, sometimes have a reputation for reluctance in defending their nation. The reason for this annoying incongruity may be associated with communal experiences and the relatively higher use of common property among the less well-heeled. Many persons know little more private real property ownership than the rights of a slum tenant or a peon. They nevertheless share ownership, identifying with the emotive 'we' that is so often more powerful than the material value of the rights. Although the apartment dweller may have enjoyed few of the ownership slices in private property, this may cause him or her to spend more time on the street, in the park, on the riverfront or, if a country dweller, enjoying the landscapes and seasons. He may identify more thoroughly with emotionally satisfying aspects of land ownership and with the people who immediately surround him. The internalization of a sense of community cannot be correlated with the weight of material value in land. This is one of the messages that Robert Ardrey conveys in *The Territorial Imperative*. To understand how human identity is associated with a place, one must in every case go beyond the legal formalities of ownership, even while these legalities reflect a great deal. On the other hand, many persons and peoples become disaffected because of their unfulfilling status in the ownership environment. The emotional hold of a beloved homeland is, for many, not enough.

Most of us are familiar with the theory of adverse possession that grants title in property to squatters if they dwell openly on land for a fixed period (17 years is a typical domestic statutory wait). These statutes reflect a broadly held notion of equity that land somehow belongs to him who gets some use out of it and who asserts a commitment to stay on it. An opposing cannon of law holds that equity (that is, the court's common sense of justice) abhors a forfeiture (a loss by an existing owner). Thus domestic court cases on adverse possession indicate that the original owner must not have complained officially about the trespass in order for the squatter's interests to become perfected. We see similar confrontations in international issues. For instance, during the 1980s, the United States pressured the Soviets to grant greater freedom to their citizens to emigrate. Simultaneously, the United States clamped down on visa extensions to Soviet émigrés. It occurred to pundits that it was incongruous to insist on the right to emigrate on one hand and to deny the right to immigrate on the other. Why leave if you cannot go anywhere? There is a consistency: if we really own land, one of our basic rights is to leave and enter it as we desire. Another basic right is to deny entry to others. Free travel and emigration does not necessarily mean one can go or stay where one pleases. If we are the owners, we can abandon if we wish, and if we keep, we do not have to share. Unburdened by inconsistencies, we support the right to emigrate, deny the right to immigrate, and support the right of due process to foreign residents whom the government wishes to repatriate.

When we speak of common property, we have to ask – common to whom? It is sometimes puzzling for Americans traveling abroad, and yet a point of pride, that so many people feel they have a right to come to the United States. They think they own part of the United States no matter who they are or where. Denial of a United States visa, or worse – the withdrawal of a US visa – is a serious matter in many countries. United States history, myths, national pride, and manner of ownership are wrapped up in immigration and opportunity. By having created a worldwide expectation, some kind of duty to service that expectation seems to have been created. Has the United States in fact presented a rudimentary right of ownership in its lands because it so enthusiastically exports the ideas that constitute the rules of ownership generally? Like it or not, the answer appears to be yes; and the problem becomes how not to lose track of who the owners are, and of what.

Émigré problems are often characterized as human rights issues, but as the scale of the migration changes, the mix of debated rights and the make-up of interested constituencies changes. Cross-border mass migrations are becoming increasingly common and are changing the global map of nations. These instant migrant populations influence the ownership environment of host geographies and often continue to influence the ownership environment in the losing areas.[19] Property analysis looks at such relocations in terms of disparities in rights, owner identities, and the regimes of ownership rules. The three parts are not really separate one from another, but salients of inequality in any aspect of the ownership environment correlate to instability and often to violent readjustments. Disparities in the concert of rights held by one group as opposed to another, great distance between identities of competing owners, or great differences in competing regimes of ownership rules – these are the sources and symptoms of conflict. They may be labeled ethnic, tribal, national, irredentist, religious, or ideological. We could call all of them human rights problems.

HUMAN RIGHTS

> In every civilized society property rights must be carefully safeguarded; ordinarily and in the great majority of cases, human rights and property rights are fundamentally and in the long run, identical; but when it clearly appears that there is a real conflict between them, human rights must have the upper hand; for property belongs to man and not man to property.[20]
> (Theodore Roosevelt)

The subject of human rights is omnipresent in international matters. In one form or another, United States foreign policy has always been conducted in light of or in spite of a hefty measure of human rights concern. Specific use of the term 'human rights', and integration of the term into policy, has been a more recent phenomenon. 'Property' rights have not seen such a fashion. The moral challenge made by communism and manifested by the Russian Revolution to the idea of private property contributed to the reluctance to discuss rights in property terms. When, in recent decades, international defense of human rights was targeted at Soviet treatment of its citizens, the elemental philosophical differences between the American and Russian revolutions were newly bared. A Soviet treatise on international law written by Soviet jurist and Marxist ideologue G.I. Tunkin in the early 1970s is indicative.[21] It was presented as the official Soviet academic statement on the principles of international law. Many sections of Tunkin's indoctrinated tome are eyebrow raisers, and some are ironically portentous – betraying seeds of the Soviet demise. (For instance, Tunkin's explanations of the right to self-determination seem tailor-made as arguments for the various republics to separate themselves from the Soviet Union.) More to the point are references to the Soviet theoretic understanding of the relationship of the Soviet, as a central government, to the rights of its citizens. 'Conventions on human rights do not grant rights directly to individuals, but establish mutual obligations of states to grant such rights to individuals.'[22] Tunkin's comments about international protection of human rights were made in view of American President Jimmy Carter's defense of the rights of Soviet Jews to emigrate, and also in view of potential defections of Soviets while traveling abroad. Considering subsequent historic events and the contextual problems of translating politically charged abstractions, perhaps we should be charitable. However, the drift of Tunkin's description, with its complete, tacit rejection of natural rights, makes the Soviet citizen appear part of national sovereignty in almost the same way that cattle belong to ranch land.

There is nothing new to the observation that systems of ownership can incrementally approach the state of slavery. Tunkin's description of the state–individual relationship encouraged this author to present certain human rights in terms of property ownership. If we are the full owners of our land, we can do what we please on it, including speak as we please, worship as we please, or leave. The importance of the right to leave property is so obvious when referring to domestic property rights that it is disregarded unless forced under pedantic analysis. Even a prisoner holds some property rights in 'his cell', but it would clearly be more valuable to him as property if he could come and go as he wished. Internationally, we have seen the value of this right reflected in the desperation of peoples whose poverty in the ownership of their native lands has led them to dare dangerous escapes.

Tunkin's expression of the Soviet relationship of the individual to the state suggests how we can treat human rights in property terms, but the link between individual liberties and property rights is already scarred into the American cultural experience. Nothing more clearly proves the point than the agonizing debate of man as chattel that led to the American Civil War. Few understood better than Abraham Lincoln the continuous weave of property and human rights. Lincoln himself equivocated over interpretation of the constitution's respect for private property and the 'peculiar institution' that allowed treatment as property of beings supposedly endowed by the creator with the right to liberty.[23] It is useful to remember that black slaves were held often enough by other Blacks or by Indians.[24] More than a historical novelty, ownership of Blacks by other Blacks shows that the acceptance of property rights as defined by the regime of property laws had consumed recognition of human rights as argued by the nature of humanity. The point is that civil or human rights have often been organized and understood intuitively as property. Basic human rights concepts can be placed on the same plane of analysis as other rights associated with ownership. The historical references are not comfortable ones, but it is instructive in some situations to highlight human status in property terms. The 14th Amendment to the United States Constitution, ratified in 1868, not only prohibits that any state 'deprive any person of life, liberty, or property, without due process of law; nor deny any person within its jurisdiction the equal protection of the laws', the writers of the amendment felt it necessary to specify that financial claims for the loss or emancipation of any slave were illegal and void.

It is safe to say that to one degree or another human rights performance has always figured as an element of the United States' relationships with other lands. Violations of human rights most decried by our government, or by private citizens working through non-governmental organizations, include lack of habeas corpus, torture, organized rape, extrajudicial execution, forced exile, disenfranchisement, and genocide. Less heinous, but more typically practiced abuses abound, and these can be usefully described in property terms. An exclusionary government might exercise property ownership in disregard of what should be the ownership rights of populations within its geographic reach. A government can represent the ownership arrogance of the majority of citizens against a minority population or against another nation. In other cases the government is unable or unwilling to enforce the property rights of citizens that do identify with it. The combinations are many, and each can be detailed in terms of three elements of ownership – rights and duties, owner identities (and cohesiveness of identity), and the systems of ownership rules. This will be demonstrated in more depth further on, but here the point is made that violations of human rights can be subsumed under the idea of failed or missing ownership. Any situation involving the violation of human rights could be expressed in ownership terms, but with reference to the most serious violations, the use of property terminology might sterilize or routinize descriptions. At that point, the relative utility of a property-based description of events and conflicts might be exceeded. What is perhaps most important in defending broad attention to property rights in the analysis of national and international security affairs is observation of the close linkage between denied property rights and evolution of basic human rights abuses.

Concern about human rights inspires or modifies United States foreign policy almost daily. The human rights performance of a small country's government may come to decide the likelihood of United States financial, diplomatic or military assistance. Violations of rights, duly publicized, can become the most important reason for involvement of American forces in areas otherwise lacking strategic interest for the United States. Perhaps all US policies are based on human rights to the extent that rights of ownership are in one way or another tied to almost every conceivable foreign policy problem. Failure to acknowledge relationships between human rights and property ownership can mistakenly force human rights into a category apart from standard policy. Not all violations of human rights are as morally gripping as government-sponsored mass rape or the organized disappearance of dissidents. The right to do business on equal terms with other foreigners, or to expect that the natural environment will not be abused, or to expect a patent to be respected are all ownership rights. They do not have the same psychological urgency as rights associated with the physical integrity of a person. Like all rights, they are associated for policy purposes with geographies, group identities, and systems of ownership rules. The United States government has created policy positions on the treatment of dissidents 'in the Soviet Union', or the alleged abuse of Palestinians 'in Israel', or the cause of majority rule 'in South Africa'. Policy, and any military force imputed to back it, will have a geographic reference, and usually an explicit or implicit reference to owner groups. They will also be made in the context of some kind of system of ownership rules (also at times explicit, at times not). Observers can find what appear as inconsistencies, partiality, or even hypocrisy in the application of human rights standards in many countries' foreign policies. But when we define basic human rights together with rights more commonly interpreted as property rights, we can more easily identify and reconcile strategic priorities. Perhaps more important, human rights abuses, like international wars, can all be traced back to property conflicts.

NOTES

1. James Madison, 'Publius, "The Federalist X"', *Daily Advertiser* (New York), 22 November 1787, reprinted in Bernard Bailyn, ed., *The Debate on the Constitution, Part 1* (New York: The Viking Press, 1992), p. 406; Madison's importance as an intellectual contributor to the American ideological revolution regarding property and the role of government is well established: 'Madison's resolution of the conflict, real or apparent, between Jefferson and Locke adds up to a political doctrine that is so radically revolutionary that I do not believe it is possible to go beyond it. Many revolutions since the American rebellion at the end of the eighteenth century have failed or feared to go so far. Even the Russian Revolution, no matter how far-reaching its social and economic reforms, failed to take the final step that Madison said was imperative for the United States, that it "equally respect the rights of property and the property in rights". The Soviets, in this century, have turned the first kind of property upside down, giving it to those who had nothing, taking it from those who had everything. There is a kind of simple justice in that, although economically it is dreadfully misguided. But no man's, woman's, or child's rights have been secure in the Soviet Union during this century, as they are mostly secure in Madison's country today. To succeed in their revolution, the Soviets believed they had to abolish all private property. Perhaps they meant to abolish only the private property that Locke had claimed governments are instituted to protect. But they also abolished that other property, property in rights. Their revolution has therefore so far failed. It can succeed only when they understand and rectify this view.' Charles Van Doren, *A History of Knowledge: Past Present, and Future* (New York: Carol Publishing Group, 1991), p. 227.
2. See Ronnie D. Lipschutz, *When Nations Clash: Raw Materials, Ideology, and Foreign Policy* (New York: Harper & Row, 1989). Lipschutz is one of few international relations writers to directly address property as a central conflict issue. Lipschutz applies a different construct of property than that used in the present work, and he focuses on the geopolitical tendency to define national interest in terms of

resources. Here property rights are defined more inclusively, but it is worth repeating Lipschutz's argument about why property questions are valuable: 'Clearly, the answers to these questions are of more than just academic interest. They relate after all to the sensitive issue of "truth in advertising" in official explanations of US foreign and military policy; to the validity of suppositions underlying those policies by people who formulate them; to the nature of the military forces the country needs to buy; and to the possibilities of avoiding major military conflicts in the years ahead. Of course the answers are not easily uncovered, for these issues lie at the center of a tangled web whose strands include geology and technology, economics and politics, domestic and international relations, subjective perceptions versus "objective" realities, and the proper interpretation of historical experience in a changing world.' Ibid., p. xix.
3. Compare property analysis to the Microsoft Windows® program on a personal computer. Windows® is not exactly an operating system, not exactly a computer application (though it is both) – perhaps it is better described as an operating environment. It orders what for many computer users are the confusing protocols and instructions of other (nevertheless valid) programming approaches. Many people found that the user-friendly approach of Windows® made the computer psychologically more available as a tool. Others, familiar with the pre-existing DOS commands, were not as enthusiastic. A property-based explanatory approach in international studies is analogous.
4. It is not universally agreed that national interests are a stable and identifiable quantity, or even that the idea of national interest is the essential starting point for development of policy. 'People have grown numb to claims of "national interests" or "vital interests" when in actuality far less is at stake.' Richard N. Haass, *Intervention* (Washington, DC: A Carnegie Endowment Book, 1994), p. 69; see also Thomas L. Friedman, 'It's Harder Now to Figure Out Compelling National Interests', *The New York Times*, 31 May 1992, p. 5; see also Charles A. Beard, The *Idea of the National Interest* (New York: Macmillan, 1934). Beard argued that the national interest of the United States was actually the interests of whatever group controlled the national government at the time.
5. See Torbjørn Knutsen, 'Re-reading Rousseau in the Post-Cold War World', *Journal of Peace Research*, 31, 3 (1994), pp. 247–62; see also William C. Olson and A.J.R. Groom, *International Relations Then and Now: Origins and Trends in Interpretation*, pp. 42–3 (London: HarperCollins Academic, 1991). Describing the recurring theme of idealism v. realism, the authors relate a debate on the Balkan Question between Prime Minister Gladstone and Benjamin Disraeli in the 1870s. The former appealed for the use of force in defense of innocent lives while the latter insisted that the matter was not one of sentiment, but that urgent and enormous British national interests were at stake. It is interesting that in this case both perspectives favored intervention and war. On the intimate historical relationship between geopolitics and the realist school of international relations theory see William Fox, 'Geopolitics and International Relations', in Ciro E. Zoppo and Charles Zorgbibe, eds, *On Geopolitics: Classical and Nuclear* (Boston, MA: Martinus Nijhoff, 1985).
6. Wesley Newcomb Hofeld, *Fundamental Legal Conceptions as Applied to Judicial Reasoning* (New Haven, CT: Yale University Press, 1919) reissued 1964. Also reprinted in Edward Allen Kent, ed., *Law and Philosophy: Readings in Legal Philosophy* (New York: Meridith Corporation, 1970).
7. Alfred Tennyson, *Alfred Tennyson, Selected Poetry: Edited, with an Introduction by Douglas Smith* (New York: Random House, 1951), p. 307.
8. Reinold Noyes, *The Institution of Property* (New York: Longmans Green, 1936).
9. Noyes states: 'the idea of the right of property – the central concept of the legal institution, grew out of the right of action; was in fact the right of action and to some extent still is in legal theory. In early law, property was the legal means of

securing it. Only later did it come to be conceived as something which existed independently of the action or transaction and which the law merely confirmed', ibid., p. 159. By 'right of action' Noyes refers to a complaint that a court would normally be willing to hear.
10. At the root of the definition of property we arrive at the idea of claims for valuable relationships between persons regarding things. If a people, whatever the nature of their belief system, makes a competitive claim against a rival group or culture, it is logically a claim of ownership. One may say, for instance, that the belief systems of many North American Indian tribes were completely distinct from that of the arriving White man, and that most Indian belief systems contemplated no private ownership of land. However, the Indian belief systems obviously included an understanding of land ownership at some level. Otherwise, what logical complaint could the Indian make that land was taken from him? What could be taken away if not rights, at least shared rights, to access, use and enjoyment, or preservation? If it were not for a perceived loss of something, there could be no complaint. For the practical purpose of examining conflicts – if there is no complaint, there is no conflict.
11. The most vigorous theories of international human rights, as well as most geopolitical theories, are Western inventions. It would be picayune to accuse a property interpretation of human rights or of geopolitics as being ethnocentric. The terms of reference are no more or less universal than the term being questioned.
12. John P. Powelson, *The Story of Land: A World History of Land Tenure and Agrarian Reform* (Cambridge, MA: Lincoln Institute of Land Policy, 1988).
13. V.I. Lenin, from *Selected Works*, Vol. 2, p. 254 (cited in a *Dictionary of Economic Quotations*, Comp. S. James, 2nd edn [London: Croom Helm, 1984], p. 18).
14. Arthur M. Schlesinger, Jr, *The Disuniting of America: Reflections on a Multicultural Society* (New York: W.W. Norton, 1992), p. 85.
15. Carl Waldman, *Atlas of the North American Indian* (New York: Facts on File, 1985), p. 199.
16. Benjamin Franklin, *Poor Richard's Almanack*, with a foreword by Phillips Russell (New York: Rimington & Hooper, 1928), p. 19.
17. Gottfried Dietze, *In Defense of Property* (Chicago, IL: Henry Regnery Company, 1963).
18. John Stuart Mill, *Principles of Political Economy with Some of Their Applications to Social Philosophy* (2 vols) (Boston, MA: Charles C. Little & James Brown, 1848), Vol. I, p. 275.
19. See Myron Weiner, ed., *International Migration and Security* (Boulder, CO: Westview Press, 1993).
20. Theodore Roosevelt, speech at the University of Paris, 23 April 1910 in Daniel B. Baker, ed., *Political Quotations* (Detroit, MI: Gale Research, 1990), p. 201.
21. G.I. Tunkin, *Theory of International Law*, translated by William E. Butler (Cambridge, MA: Harvard University Press, 1974).
22. Ibid., p. 83.
23. See Noah Brooks, *Abraham Lincoln and the Downfall of American Slavery* (New York: G.P. Putnam's Sons, 1898). 'Not at once did he throw in his fortunes with those who were to be the leaders of the new Free Soil party. He always moved slowly and with deliberation that deceived many and annoyed not a few. They thought him too slow, over-cautious, even waiting to see which was to be the winning side ... But the time came when he took his final stand and declared that he must thenceforth be the champion of freedom against slavery', ibid., p. 152; see also Robert W. Johannsen, *Lincoln, the South, and Slavery: The Political Dimension* (Baton Rouge, LA: Louisiana State University Press, 1991).
24. See Annie Heloise Abel, *The American Indian as American Slaveholder and Secessionist* (Cleveland, OH: The Arthur H. Clarke Company, 1914). 'With them [Indians who had been transplanted to lands south of the Mason–Dixon Line] it had

been a familiar institution long before the time of their exile. In their native haunts they had had negro slaves as had had the whites and removal had made no difference to them in that particular. Since the beginning of the century refuge to fugitives and confusion of ownership had been occasions for frequent quarrel between them and the citizens of the Southern states.' Ibid., p. 22.

2

Sovereignty: 'Who Owns This Place, Anyway?'

> One result of identifying sovereignty with might instead of legal right was to remove it from the sphere of jurisprudence, where it had its origin and where it properly belongs, and to import it into political science, where it has ever since been a source of confusion.[1]   (J.L. Brierly)

As has been argued in Chapter 1, the term 'property' is an abstraction that may not be needed except as a comforter to bring the principles of ownership within a familiar mental framework. As for the term 'property rights', property does not have rights, humans do. Both prefixes, 'human' and 'property', can be considered superfluous.[2] Depending on the context, it can be useful to present human rights in property terms, but generally when we speak of property rights, we are talking of the human rights held in relation to material objects like land (or quasi-material objects like patents and other intellectual property). As if applicable to a 'superproperty' or an extensive and specially owned area of land, the term 'sovereignty' provides a higher level referent for a set of rights associated with a specifiable geographic area. Diplomats and scholars may claim technical content for the term, but most people use 'sovereignty' to instill emotion in the defense of challenged ownership or national honor. Technical or emotional, 'sovereignty', like 'self-determination' or 'nationalism', is shorthand for the assertion of preferential rights.

In a chapter on sovereignty in *Politics Among Nations*, Hans Morgenthau notes that 'there is much confusion about the meaning of the term, and about what is and what is not compatible with the sovereignty of a particular nation'.[3] Morgenthau complains:

> We have heard it said time and again that we must 'surrender part of our sovereignty' to an international organization for the sake of

world peace, that we must 'share our sovereignty' with such an organization, that the latter would have 'limited' sovereignty while we would keep the substance of it, or vice versa, that there are 'quasi-sovereign' and 'half sovereign' states. We shall endeavor to show that the conception of a divisible sovereignty is contrary to logic and politically unfeasible, but that it is a significant symptom of the discrepancy between the actual and pretended relations existing between international law and international politics in the modern state system.[4]

J.L. Brierly, a Morgenthau contemporary, takes almost the opposite tack in *The Law of Nations*. Brierly, in a definitive section on sovereignty, reflects on the political scientist's sovereignty:

> so strong had the hold of sovereignty upon the imagination of political scientists become that when it became obvious, as it soon did, that the personal monarch no longer fitted the role, they started to hunt for the 'location' of sovereignty, almost as if sovereignty, instead of being a reflection in theory of the political facts of a particular age, were a substance which must surely be found somewhere in every state if only one looked for it carefully enough.[5]

An excerpt from Noyes' *The Institution of Property* suggests why political scientists have been even less supportive of the lawyers' scholarship:

> We must at once admit that, in the distinction between *res corporales* and *res incorporales*, the Roman legal theory, whatever it meant by *ius* and *res*, had clearly begun the perennial error, which still persists, of confounding ownership with its object. If it had not done so, the distinction between the two classes would not have been based on the criterion of corporeality. If, in attempting to fit these categories to the modern notions of 'rights' and 'objects,' we translate *jus* as 'a right,' and *res* as an 'object,' then clearly there should be a *jus* associated with the *res corporales* exactly as well as with the *res incorporales*.[6]

On the surface, this quotation looks to be exactly the kind of impenetrable mumbo-jumbo that for some political scientists verifies why the concept of sovereignty is best kept out of the sphere of jurisprudence. In its full context though, Reinhold Noyes' observation about the development of Roman law delivers something important. It says that many distinctions in our conceptual universe between property and human rights are founded in identifiable quirks of semantic history, not in substance. The inconsistent departures and incorporations of English law from Roman law are greatly to blame. Significantly, whatever political scientists would like to do with sovereignty, its impure conceptual lineage began as a legalistic one, burdened by all the same semantic confusions that surrounded rights in property and rights of people during the Middle Ages. It seems that today, as public and private law (and law enforcement) slowly entangle more international relations, the jurisprudential perspectives on sovereignty will overtake political science perspectives.

According to Brierly, the first explicit formulation of the concept of sovereignty was written in 1576 by Jean Bodin in *De Republica*. The context of Bodin's expression, as understood by Brierly, was one of anarchy born of feudal rivalries and religious intolerance. Bodin thought sovereignty's essential manifestation was the power to make the laws, and since the sovereign made the laws, he clearly could not be bound by the laws he made.[7] Today, this suggestion is repugnant to egalitarians. An often-heard slogan is that no one is above the law, but the principle still has at least limited validity. For instance, within the US government, we make soldiers and civilian employees very aware of the penalties for disclosing or losing classified documents or pieces of classified information. While cases of treason are as rare as they are spectacular, many members of the armed forces (and civilian employees, especially in the intelligence agencies) have damaged or ruined their careers over minor security violations. The president of the United States, Commander in Chief of the Armed Forces, is logically and legally immune from prosecution when it comes to national secrets. National secrets are essentially his, and in the act of disclosure by the president, the information is by logic legally declassified. If we were to define sovereignty today based solely on the possession of state secrets, it would seem that we still had a personalist sovereign. Of course, this is a vestigial example, but notice also that the United States Congress had for years written labor laws of every kind and proceeded to exclude itself from them. In a way this provides modern support to Bodin's logic.[8] Anyway, Bodin apparently felt that the essence of statehood was unity of government. A state, to be a state, needed, in Bodin's view, a *summa potestas* as a single guide. He defined the State as 'a multitude of families and the possessions that they have in common ruled by a supreme power and by reason'.[9]

Considering this idea of a *summa potestas*, it seems that an essential notion of the American political experiment has been to avoid, prevent, or limit the existence of any *summa potestas*. The presidency has a clear constitutional preference for dealing on the nation's behalf in international matters, but even this hint of unity was purposefully handcuffed at the outset of the republic. Evidently the constitutional restrictions created to balance power were rejections of unitary sovereignty. So is the United States a sovereign nation? Yes, the United States is a sovereign nation because a single regime of ownership rules guides the assignment of rights and duties within a fixed geography on behalf of people that share a common identity.

The status of the United States as a sovereign entity does not require that we exalt the status of sovereignty as a concept.[10] The value of sovereignty is not static. Sovereignty began small. Noyes' appreciation in his treatise on the history of Roman law is one of sovereignty residing in the head of a tribal-familial household.[11]

> The paterfamilias also had power over guests, as well as a duty to protect them while in Rome. The patriarch was, in effect, sovereign, and was referred to by the term *herus* or *erus*, which has been translated as 'lord and master'.[12]

Power held by the patriarch can be considered possessory or in the nature of ownership. Noyes calls it 'prepossession', since the idea of property as we know it did not exist in Roman law, at least not until well after the establishment of the basic *familia* and the powers associated with the patriarch. The rights admitted to the lord or master constituted the power he held within his domain until such a time as old age or a progenitor overtook him. He owned in every practical sense of the power by right that he held over land, chattels, slaves, and relatives. He did not yet possess property in the modern sense because the idea of property apart from rights of the lord had not been developed and clarified.[13] This interpretation of the history of Roman law serves the purpose of this book nicely. Roman paterfamilias were in sovereigns, conceived of in terms of rights, and though the terminology for legal consideration as property did not exist, these rights were nevertheless proprietary in nature. The proprietary essence of sovereignty has not changed, but the rules of ownership and the identities of owners have. The sweep of egalitarianism has broadened the expected categories of owners to an extent that definitions of sovereignty themselves delimit acceptable ownership systems.

POPULAR SOVEREIGNTY AND LEGITIMACY

> As typically conceived and in terms of international law, a state is a territorially defined political unit the government of which is supreme in internal affairs and independent with respect to external affairs. The government of a state has this authority because the inhabitants of its territory accord it legitimacy.[14]
> (Harold K. Jacobson, from *Networks of Interdependence*)

Jacobson's definition of sovereignty represents a standard in political science that recounts a basic expression of sovereignty in international law and then glues on something extra, here a notion of legitimacy. Neither the basic legal theory of sovereignty nor many political science interpretations require moral legitimacy. Successful coercion suffices. That is to say, the connotation of moral sufficiency may be absent. A cowed and semiconscious population of chattel property is as good as a hall of senators as far as the basic legal theory is concerned. The device of 'popular sovereignty' was put to effective use by England's American colonies in support of revolution. It has been mustered around the world ever since alongside the emotion of nationalism or in relation to egalitarian principles.[15] Popular sovereignty involves a contradiction, however, between power to the people and a single supreme secular authority. It normally assumes unanimity of purpose and depends on emotional solidarity. National ownership draws on national fervor, but such unity of emotion is no guarantee against tyranny, as the French Revolution attests. Still, popular sovereignty was an essential invention because the individual in a free society is conceived to be an owner and not property. That is to say, however diminutive the scope of the individual's ownership portion, the free citizen is not part of the property owned. As can be seen in the excerpts below, the 1993 Russian Constitution provides one of the freshest and clearest connections between property, sovereignty, and basic civil rights.

We, the multinational people of the Russian Federation, united by a common destiny on our land, asserting human rights and freedoms and civil peace and concord, preserving historically established state unity, proceeding from the generally recognized principles of the equality and self-determination of peoples, revering the memory of our forebears who passed down to us love and respect for the Fatherland and faith in good and justice, reviving the sovereign statehood of Russia and asserting the immutability of its democratic foundations, seeking to ensure the well-being and prosperity of Russia, proceeding from responsibility for our homeland to present and future generations, recognizing ourselves as part of the world community, adopt the CONSTITUTION OF THE RUSSIAN FEDERATION.

ARTICLE 3

1. The repository of sovereignty and the sole source of authority in the Russian Federation is its multinational people ...

ARTICLE 4

1. The sovereignty of the Russian Federation extends to the whole of its territory.

2. The Constitution of the Russian Federation and federal laws are paramount throughout the territory of the Russian Federation.

3. The Russian Federation ensures the integrity and inviolability of its territory ...

ARTICLE 6

1. Citizenship of the Russian Federation is acquired and terminated in accordance with federal law and is uniform and equal irrespective of the basis on which it is acquired.

2. Each citizen of the Russian Federation possesses all rights and freedoms on its territory and bears equal obligations stipulated by the Constitution of the Russian Federation.

3. A citizen of the Russian Federation cannot be deprived of his citizenship or of the right to change it.

ARTICLE 8

1. In the Russian Federation the unity of the economic area, the free movement of goods, services, and financial resources, support for competition, and freedom of economic activity are guaranteed.

2. In the Russian Federation private, state, municipal, and other forms of property enjoy equal recognition and protection.

ARTICLE 9

1. The land and other natural resources are utilized and protected in the Russian Federation as the basis of the life and activity of the peoples inhabiting the corresponding territory.

2. The land and other natural resources can be in private, state, municipal, or other forms of ownership.

ARTICLE 35

1. The right of private ownership is protected by law.

2. Each person is entitled to own property and to possess, utilize, and dispose of it both individually and together with others.

3. No one may be deprived of his property except by court decision. The compulsory expropriation of property for state requirements may be carried out only if full compensation is paid in advance.

4. The right of inheritance is guaranteed.

ARTICLE 36

1. Citizens and their associations are entitled to hold land in private ownership.

2. Owners freely possess, utilize, and dispose of land and other natural resources provided that this does not damage the environment and does not violate the rights and legitimate interests of others.

3. The conditions and procedure for the use of land are defined on the basis of federal law.

ARTICLE 61

1. A citizen of the Russian Federation cannot be expelled from the Russian Federation or extradited to another state.
2. The Russian Federation guarantees the protection and patronage of its citizens outside its borders.

ARTICLE 62

1. A citizen of the Russian Federation can hold citizenship of a foreign state (dual citizenship) as provided by federal law or an international treaty of the Russian Federation.

2. The fact that a citizen of the Russian Federation holds citizenship of a foreign state does not diminish his rights and freedoms or exempt him from obligations stemming from Russian citizenship, unless otherwise provided by federal law or an international treaty of the Russian Federation.

3. Foreign citizens and stateless persons in the Russian Federation enjoy equal rights and bear equal obligations with citizens of the Russian Federation, except when otherwise provided by federal law or an international treaty of the Russian Federation.

ARTICLE 63

1. The Russian Federation offers political asylum to foreign citizens and stateless persons in accordance with universally recognized norms of international law.

2. The Russian Federation does not permit the extradition to other states of persons persecuted for their political beliefs or for actions (or inaction) which are not considered a crime in the Russian Federation. The extradition of persons accused of having committed a crime, or the extradition of sentenced persons to serve their sentence in other states, is performed on the basis of federal law or an international treaty of the Russian Federation.

ARTICLE 67

1. The territory of the Russian Federation includes the territories of its components, internal bodies of water, and territorial sea, and the airspace over these.

2. The Russian Federation possesses sovereign rights and exercises jurisdiction over the continental shelf and within the exclusive economic zone of the Russian Federation in accordance with the procedure defined by federal law and the norms of international law.[16]

When ownership rights are so carefully enumerated as in the Russian Constitution perhaps a more direct accounting can be made of what property really belongs to whom and to what extent a people's ownership is represented by its government. It is too soon to say how well the Russian social contract will mirror the ideals expressed in its revolutionary constitution, but many of Russia's problems will be similar to those of dozens of other countries that have recently attempted to re-order their systems of ownership rules. Sovereign legitimacy (in the sense of the moral dimension of the term legitimacy) has become tied to the extent to which the system of rules leaves people as owners.[17] Government legitimacy is likewise being tied to the praxis of diffused ownership. Questions arise regarding the institutional management of force in support of the system of property rights. For instance, what is the mandate of a national military? If the armed forces are sworn to uphold a constitution expressly created to limit government incursion against individual ownership rights, what should be the limits of obedience of the military to that government? If the military swears to defend national sovereignty, when can the military be used to redress government errors or abuses in defining that sovereignty, and who decides? Overlapping callings to defend sovereignty create a puzzle of duties. Does a given armed force dedicate itself only to defeating trespasses against the nation's property by outsiders, or should it involve itself in the change or preservation of the system of ownership within the nation? Entrapment in this difficulty often seems to invite foreign interventions, especially into countries whose independence as nation-states is poorly secured.

INDEPENDENCE, DEPENDENCE, AND INTERDEPENDENCE

> For the past several centuries, international law and most international relations theory was based on the premise that what takes place within the boundaries of a state is nobody else's business, and that for one state to insert itself into the affairs of another is a hostile act ... Today's critique is that intervention, including military intervention by outsiders, is legitimate and even necessary when a government severely represses the human rights of its own people or when the erosion of central government authority creates conditions in which innocent people are made vulnerable. Typical is the position of the American Catholic Bishops in late 1993: '... the principles of sovereignty and nonintervention may be overridden by forceful means in exceptional circumstances ...'.[18] (Richard N. Haass, from *Intervention*)

Justifications for intervening in foreign countries for humanitarian reasons can be very compelling, but they can also be inconsistent, even arbitrary. On the other hand, a government's assertion regarding a supposed foreign infringement of national sovereignty may be at odds with the rights of the citizens of that nation. In other words, we might look under the surface of complaints about foreign violation of sovereignty. The complainers may be usurping their own citizens' sovereign rights. So when is an assertion of infringed sovereignty not in consonance with the exercise of citizen rights? Belize provides an illustrative and non-controversial starting point.

Belize is a sovereign nation, in a theoretical sense an equal partner with the United States in the community of nations – 180,000 Caribbeans stuck on the east coast of Central America. Belize is not Russia – the principal national industry is the simple fact of being a country. This condition allows for stamps, visas, airport taxes, and foreign aid from both the United States and Britain. A West Virginia county is better developed, and the source of Belizean ability to remain 'independent' is its complete dependence on other countries. Some might say the source of Belizean independence from neighboring Guatemala has been a combination of English pride and American enthusiasm for attractive theories – in this case, self-determination. Others would point to more *realpolitik* calculation of the dangers of leaving territories unprotected from potentially harmful uses, or of creating a bad precedent by failing to support international recognition of independence. Belizeans would prefer to be independent from Guatemala. They generally speak English rather than Spanish or Mayan Q'eqchi'. As Guatemalans, they could stand a chance of suffering a painful cultural invasion and a possible series of official and unofficial property forfeitures. As a practical matter it would make little economic or cultural sense for Belize to become part of Guatemala. Belizeans have a sense of nationhood that, whatever its strength, is identifiable as not Guatemalan. The protection of Belizean sovereignty is seated nevertheless in its complete inability to protect itself and even its inability to make a strong case as a self-supportable national entity. If the Belize–Guatemala border were completely open, Guatemalans would probably begin a peaceful (or at least war-free) migration of Spanish or Mayan dialect-speaking squatters into Belize. It would not be long before Guatemalans outnumbered the English-speaking Belizeans. A plebiscite of residents could then give a very changed message about self-determination and independence.[19]

Belize might be of some geostrategic interest to the United States because outlaws can use any unattended geography for nefarious purposes. However, in Belize, limitations on United States influence have included the interested presence of the British, for whom Belize retains an emotional value related to bygone imperial sovereignty. The British have identified sufficiently with the desires of their English-speaking former colonials to place British warplanes and troops in Belize as one guarantor of Belizean sovereignty from Guatemala. Besides some mild competition of interests between the United States and Great Britain, it is apparent that within the scale it deserves, both countries can define sovereign interests worth protecting in Belize. Within this context of shared and competing interests, to what extent should an assertion of sovereignty by a Belizean government command deference? What if the assertion is only an indignant diversionary tactic in support of an internal policy that violates human rights? A property analysis delineates specific rights and duties accruing to the citizens and weighs possible foreign infringement against each of them. Recalling that self-determination is an assertive legalistic form of the question 'Who owns this place, anyway?' it is perfectly reasonable to detail precisely the ownership environment to judge the legitimacy of nationalist-sounding claims.[20]

Belize is a land with a necessarily loud independence, that is entirely dependent, and where the commonalties of human rights, property rights and sovereignty are obvious. It is also a place where either or both of two foreign powers might justify interventions into the internal affairs of the state. Perhaps because of the perceived value of the Belizean property, or due to the Belizeans' care in legitimizing its system of ownership, it has not been the subject of any major interventions. A separate example from the Cold War offers a staple argument, based on the protection of an international system of ownership rules, for intervention. In late 1968, *Pravda* published the Soviet explanation of their invasion of Czechoslovakia earlier that year. The piece, which became known as the 'Brezhnev Doctrine', provides an appropriate demonstration of the reach of the property law analogy, and of parallel justifications for international interventions (but using class analysis). Part of the doctrine reads as follows:

> We cannot ignore the assertions, held in some places, that the actions of the five socialist countries ran counter to the Marxist–Leninist principle of sovereignty and the rights of nations to self-determination.
>
> The groundlessness of such reasoning consists primarily in that it is based on an abstract, non-class approach to the question of sovereignty and the rights of nations to self-determination.
>
> The peoples of the socialist countries and Communist parties certainly do have and should have freedom for determining the ways of advance of their respective countries.
>
> However, none of their decisions should damage either socialism in their country or the fundamental interests of other socialist countries, and the whole working class movement, which is working for socialism.
>
> This means that each Communist party is responsible not only to its own people, but also to all the socialist countries, to the entire Communist movement. Whoever forgets this, is stressing only the independence of the Communist party, becomes one sided. He deviates from his international duty ...
>
> The sovereignty of each socialist country cannot be opposed to the interests of the world of socialism, of the world revolutionary movement. Lenin demanded that all Communists fight against small nation narrow-mindedness, seclusion and isolation, consider the whole and the general, subordinate the particular to the general interest.

> Formally juridical reasoning must not overshadow a class approach to the matter. One who does it, thus losing the only correct class criterion in assessing legal norms, begins to measure events with a yardstick of bourgeois law.[21]

Conditions in Belize might seem an unlikely choice for comparison to decades old events in central Europe. The discussion about Belize is tied to that about Czechoslovakia by the similarity of the property assertions. The Brezhnev Doctrine asserted the owner interests of the international 'working class' and suggestively reminded of the security needs of ownership of Russia proper. Let us measure the Brezhnev Doctrine with our yardstick of bourgeois law. The Brezhnev Doctrine was produced to underline the lesson of the Czech invasion to wavering communist regimes. It was also needed as an explanation to the faithful – a thoughtful reconciliation of previous doctrinal columns, especially the right to the self-determination of peoples. A loss to capitalism of part of the property whole could threaten common ownership of all property by the working class.

By the time the Berlin Wall began its precipitous collapse after the withdrawal of East German guards on 9 November 1989, the relationship between ownership and tyranny was transparent. The Brezhnev Doctrine, for all its class analysis vision of proletariat ownership, was too easily seen as a front for protection of Russian property rights. The East German government, having lost the will to violently repress, and its illegitimacy bared, saw that the value of East German land might be raised for many citizens if they were given the choice to leave. Immediately, a wave of people visited the West, but returned to the East. With access to the West, the property value of East Germany did rise for many East Germans. A desire to remain in East Germany (with the hope of further increasing the value of their land) rose as well. Of course, the change of policies came too late to save the East German communist government. The process of reform entered an unwinnable sprint against the realization that the communist system of ownership rules could not survive.

It is all the more interesting that much of the argument in the Brezhnev Doctrine about narrow-minded nationalism seems to find some vindication in the national strife of former Russian domination. The Brezhnev Doctrine is not just superficial Marxist–Leninist sloganeering; it is a logical defense of intervention based on a broad theory of ownership rights and duties. Notably, the doctrine was extant for over three decades, but it was born of a doomed system of ownership rules and an obviously parochial set of national interests. The Western liberal democratic system of ownership rules may be more acceptable morally, and Western nation states may be less greedy and less paranoid. However, the justifications for intervention, the kind that might seem reasonable given the right circumstances, in a place like Belize, can be revealed as quite similar to the Brezhnev doctrine. They will almost certainly recall broad concepts of ownership rights and duties that supposedly transcend nation-state boundaries. Rewriting the Brezhnev doctrine, but replacing the references to class struggle and socialism with more acceptable abstractions could give us a fair-sounding draft of a justification for intervening in say, a Bosnia. It could start more or less as follows:

> We cannot ignore the assertions, held in some places, that the actions of the NATO countries ran counter to the democratic principle of sovereignty and the rights of nations to self-determination.
>
> The groundlessness of such reasoning consists primarily in that it is based on an abstract, undemocratic approach to the question of sovereignty and the rights of nations to self-determination.
>
> The peoples of the European democracies and societies around the world certainly do have and should have freedom for determining the ways of advance of their respective countries.
>
> However, none of their decisions should damage either human rights in their country or the fundamental interests of other democratic countries, and the whole movement toward democracy, which is working for human rights.
>
> This means that each free society is responsible not only to its own people, but also to all the democratic countries, to the entire cause of human rights. Whoever forgets this, is stressing only the independence of the one interest group, and becomes one-sided. ... etc.

The transformation above may be a bit rough stylistically, but the point is made. Whether called a Brezhnev Doctrine or a Monroe Doctrine, broadly held property interests become articulated in abstract terms. While such abstract terminology may be completely legitimate and its use sincere, the reasons for intervening are more transparent when brought back from abstractions to their basic elements. These elements can almost always be articulated as specific rights and duties associating identifiable peoples with nameable places. If these rights and duties are not articulated, it may be that strong national interests are absent, or that aggressive action is not warranted under the accepted system of rules of ownership. We might ask, for instance, in the Bosnia case, what and whose property rights do we want to enforce – and for how long? If we cannot answer such questions, it should be clear that we cannot apply the right type of physical enforcement. The words democracy, human rights, or pluralism are positive abstractions, but alone they do not communicate any specific rights that can be related to the physical control of people and places. If we cannot support our positive political abstractions with detailed description of the property at stake, we are vulnerable to the demoralizing application of negative abstractions, like 'interventionism'. 'Interventionism' and its kin, 'imperialism', have often been the foils of two other common characterizations of mass assertiveness – 'nationalism' and 'self-determination'.

Nationalism was, for the mainline Marxist–Leninist theorist, bad – while the right of 'self-determination of peoples' was good.[22] Nationalism was discredited in order to block changes in property relationships that threatened Soviet ownership in the lands of all the nationalities that made up the Soviet Union and its satellites. Self-determination was generally encouraged because it was more often associated with former colonies of Western powers. It threatened to change property relationships that supposedly favored the Soviet enemy. The Marxist distinction between the bad of nationalism and the good of self-determination was grounded in geopolitical, correlation-of-forces thinking. They are both absolutely the same quantities – categories of assertions of property ownership that are variously clothed for argumentation.

There should be no doubt about the existence of global movements intent on undermining the sanctity of sovereign membership in the post-Soviet era. A Global Cultural Diversity Conference was held in Sydney, Australia, sponsored by the Australian government and opened by Australian Prime Minister Paul Keating. It was held in celebration of the International Year for Tolerance, the first year of the Decade for the World's Indigenous People and the 50th anniversary of the United Nations. Delegates arrived from about 50 countries, including the Secretary-General of the United Nations and the Director-General of UNESCO. The overall direction of the conference, beyond applauding cultural diversity, was the diminution of sovereignty as the cornerstone of world order. Partly due to the absence of Soviet diplomacy, humanitarian intervention is now rapidly gaining ground against the principle of non-intervention. According to Prime Minister Keating, 'The nation-state ... is going through a period of profound transition, and the international community has to respond'. Keating suggested we rethink our definitions of what constitutes a state. 'One of the mantras of modern international relations – non-interference in the internal affairs of other countries – these days has a greatly modified and much reduced meaning.'[23]

NATIONALISM AND SELF-DETERMINATION

> Self-determination has come to mean independence from alien rule. It postulated that sovereignty rests with the people who are thus free to monitor the territorial limits within which they desire their sovereignty to be active. In order for a people to be free, they must be able to organize their future independently from others. Self-determination is therefore the process by which a people determine their own sovereign status ... But a belief in self-determination can have anarchical implications within the international system. It suggests an opportunity for a group of individuals to disregard all established political relationships in search for new ones. It further suggests that the aspirations of one group may often conflict with those of another. Thus a desire to be self-determining directly challenges the order within the international system.[24]

'Nation' is harder to define precisely than 'state'.[25] For most people it connotes something more than a tribe, the point when a given tribe is worthy of the term nation being a subjective judgement.[26] Nationalism, like tribalism, is often considered bad. For our purposes, nationalism, like tribalism, is a form of solidarity in ownership. It is neither the only nor even the most powerful ownership identity, and while nationalism may be on the rise, it also must compete increasingly with other owner identities, broad and narrow. As with spokespersons of other identities, the nationalist raises the rhetorical question (often aggressively, sometimes greedily), 'Who owns this place, anyway?' Nationalism, however, is a worrisome feature of the post-Soviet world, especially when combined with other powerful identities, such as religion or language. For instance, a direct result of the collapse of Soviet communism is the struggle for identity in spin-off proto-republics inside the former Soviet borders. At the inception of this writing, Russians were in the middle of a heated and transcendent debate over the fate of the Commonwealth of Independent States (CIS). The CIS was a poorly glued construction of former Soviet parts. Areas like Kazakhstan, Moldova, Azerbaijan, and Georgia sought independence and a fuller expression of sovereignty while simultaneously admitting and promoting favorable economic relationships with Russia. Many observers in Russia and abroad saw an irreconcilable dilemma – sovereignty and independence simply could not be attained in geographies that depended so much on Russia and on which Russia so much depended.

Debate about sovereignty versus dependence may understate the local nature of sovereignty-as-emotion, and of sovereignty as land ownership. Like the Wizard of Oz awarding a medal for bravery to the cowardly lion, sovereignty can sometimes be achieved merely by its announcement. A regional representative is no longer a member of Congress, but is instead an ambassador. This is too simplified, but symbolism is important and satisfies a great deal of the sovereign insistence. Many qualities of statehood, if divided out in detail in terms of ownership, can be drawn almost equally for a spiritually independent country as they can for a state of the United States or for an eighteenth-century English colony. The many amicable changes in sovereignty that occurred in many English colonies are evidence.

Rights and duties associated with the real estate of colonial regions of the Soviet empire are the post-Soviet relationships that must be re-ordered. What young men and women have to serve in what army? What kinds of tariffs and taxes can be levied? What rules can be asserted over church properties? Who can immigrate and emigrate? Who can vote, and who can invest in what? What military basing rights and leases will be allowed? What political links will pockets of ethnic minorities be allowed to maintain with their larger, contiguous 'nation'? These are the kinds of questions that the lands of the former Soviet Union are struggling with, and they are all property issues. The sovereign right to, say, place a tariff on imported goods, might be replaced by a free trade agreement that obviates the right. The right to form an independent army can be accepted then minimized by mutual training and service agreements.

Wrangling is almost unavoidable when there is a salient in one of the three elements of the property environment – the mix of property rights, the identities of competing owner groups, or the regimes of ownership rules. Problems of ownership are nearly intractable and almost require physical challenge and dominance if the salients cannot be reduced. These salients involve disparity in the value of adjoining properties, strongly cohesive emotional identity (especially where there is an emotion of resentment, vindictiveness and retribution toward another clearly identifiable owner group), or distinct sets of ownership rules..

Moldova is another example from the lands of the former USSR. The independent country that most Moldovans would own is a landlocked area between Romania and Ukraine.[27] Along the eastern edge of Moldova flows the Dniester River toward the Black Sea. Almost all of the industrially developed and economically viable portion of the former Soviet republic lies on a sliver of territory holding the east bank of the river. Unfortunately for the prospects of peace, most of Moldova's Russian ethnic minority lives in the Dniester region. The Russian minority, a majority in the Dniester enclave, claims its own independence from Moldova, but the property on which the Russians live is important to the prospects of Moldovan ethnic independence. The Russians, in no way willing to be absorbed by the ethnically distinct Ukraine, are understandably resistant to minority status in an independent Moldova where their privileged ownership could be severely reversed. Ethnic and linguistic competition, disparity in the perceived economic value of the land, and complex differences regarding the future system of ownership, are the ingredients of implacable disputes. Although a commonly acceptable set of national symbols might be produced – a Moldovan flag, sovereign relations with Moscow, unified sports teams – the salient property problems are less amenable to reconciliation.

Acceptable symbols of sovereignty quickly follow the problems rather than the agreements. There is little chance that stridency of ethnic identity can be ameliorated without a draconian demographic adjustment (such as departure of the Russian minority), something Moscow does not appear willing to allow. The disparity of property value between western Moldova and the east bank of the Dniester is not reversible within the foreseeable capacities of the Moldovans. Differences between systems' ownership rules are part of the conflict calculus the Moldovans have yet to resolve. Is there a way out without Muscovite arbitration and dominance or years of destructive conflict? Perhaps – if a property ownership strategy could be achieved by the Moldovans. The Moldovans would have to slowly buy ownership rights, provided the ownership system permitted it, in the industrial region of the Dniester until Russian ownership was small enough that it no longer threatened Moldovan cohesiveness.

It may be good to remember that for many human populations, hate and greed are as valid a pair of starting points for policy as any other. Sovereignty is still the same quantity. We are still left with the question about who owns the place. Denying ownership to a particular group can be just as emotionally persuasive as a positive assertion by a group of would-be owners. In many places no side wants or seeks the available peaceful compromises. The problems of former Yugoslavia jump to mind because of the pessimistic view regarding hate or greed as policy foundations. Fluid resolution of ownership problems faces obvious intransigence regarding basic property possession.

At two historic extremes, Slovenia leaves the former Yugoslavia and immediately embarks on a future of European integration while Serbia consolidates a narrow appraisal of national identity and determines to make the most enriching land grab it can. Interestingly, solutions proffered by American Secretary of State Warren Christopher included a complicated patchwork of properties in which specific ethnic identities were to be located – details to be worked out. The devil is in the details when it comes to competing property claims. The Europeans, who had been on the ground in a United Nations peacekeeping capacity much longer than the Americans, were circumspect and more willing than the Americans to let the competition of owner identities play out. Perhaps they were unable at the time to see a final arbitration of property rights that would satisfy the basic determinants of policy being pursued by parties to the conflict. West Europeans appeared less fearful that the Balkans would again be the spark to ignite the European powderkeg; at the end of the twentieth century, international commitment to the preservation of the ownership *status quo* was much less than it had been earlier in the century.

American negotiators intuitively applied a property analysis to the situation, since competitors in the conflict publicly defined 'national' goals in terms of boundaried real estate. A more detailed property appraisal, analyzing the three primary aspects of the ownership environment, might have led to a more saleable set of policy goals. More disturbing, a detailed property analysis might identify narrowly held property interests tied to policy lobbying and propaganda efforts.[28] As in most conflict areas, the market value of real estate, public services, or insurance can change dramatically in a short time. These changes present an irresistible opportunity for those with risk capital and inside contacts. Buying low, then promoting the stabilizing influence of American presence (often using moralist arguments attractive to American sensibilities) is hardly an innovative investment strategy. It is probably far more common than a gullible nation would care to consider.

Arguments for self-determination are the same as for nationalism to the extent that the rhetorical question 'Who owns this place, anyway?' is asked. The 1993 report from the Cuban propaganda newspaper *Granma,* included below, offers an example of the ways in which self-determination and sovereignty can be associated. The article's tone is a standard for the negative side of the ambivalence Latin Americans feel about the relationship of the United States to Latin America.

> Legislators from 17 countries assembled at the Latin American Parliament meeting in Mexico City once again stated their support for the validity of the principle of self-determination and condemned the extraterritorial aspects of national laws of one country which claim[s] jurisdiction over others ... The final declaration stated that the region must consolidate its sovereignty as the inalienable right to define the standards of coexistence within our countries and in order to define the policies we follow in our dealings with other nations.[29]

The parliament comments reported in the *Granma* article were made in the shadow of the 'Torriceli Act' that further tightened the US economic blockade against communist Cuba. The comments also allude to a US Supreme Court decision that upheld the right of the United States government to cause the apprehension and forcible delivery of a Mexican citizen to a United States court.[30] A predictable international stink frequented references to violated sovereignty. The court's decision generated a wave of angry response throughout the hemisphere. United States arrogance in violating sovereignty was supposedly transparent. The property rights involved can be reduced to, on one hand, the right of the apprehended Mexican to be secure in his property from government intrusion without due process. His 'property' was not only his private property, but also the common property he shared as a Mexican citizen. Mexicans, and for that matter, much of the hemispheric community, sensed the danger of precedence in the violation of these rights. Other ownership rights include those belonging to the citizens of the United States and again by extension to a larger international community. Foreigners in Mexico have a right to physical integrity and an expectation that the Mexican government will punish violations of physical integrity. Enrique Camarena, a Drug Enforcement Agency (DEA) agent working in Mexico with the knowledge and approval of the Mexican government, was a guest on Mexican property. Agent Camarena was captured and tortured by drug traffickers. Dr Alvarez-Machain was suspected of having used his medical knowledge to keep Camarena from falling unconscious from his torture immediately before his death so that his torturers could continue to try to extract information from him. Given that agent Camarena was in Mexico on behalf of the United States, it is reasonable that the US government act to ensure the case was swiftly investigated and prosecuted. The ownership rights of US citizens included redress for violation of basic physical integrity. In addition, the DEA felt a special sense of outrage at the heinous nature of a crime committed against one of its own.

Aggressive pursuit of the perpetrators was required to maintain morale within the community of US counterdrug agents, and it may have been an overly difficult act of faith to expect the Mexican authorities to pursue the case correctly. Ultimately, the court released Alvarez and returned him to Mexico. Prosecutors had failed to present sufficient evidence on which to proceed. The Mexican doctor enjoyed ownership rights in the United States, including due process. In this instance, the distance of identities (Mexican versus American) provided a heightened environment for conflict, but the most interesting aspect of the Alvarez-Machain case is found in reviewing the systems of ownership rules. The US Supreme Court ratified the observation that the President of the United States has constitutional authority to act contrary to customary international law. While there may be clear indications that the United States violated international law, the court held that the executive has the constitutional authority to do so. The regime of international law is not without its sway, but a US president is not always bound by it. Conflict exists between the regime of rules that protects Mexican property from incursions by US marshals and the regime of rules (US constitutional interpretation) that allows extraterritoriality.

Finally, we can see global drug trafficking as a transnational issue similar to environmental degradation. It is hard to show that a degradation of environmental quality in India constitutes a specific loss of property for a single distant Dutch claimant. A generalized property loss may nevertheless be recognizable. So it is with drug trafficking. Non-drug users in the United States suffer a degradation of property value because of the existence of an illegal drug trade, whatever the relative culpability of US consumers versus foreign suppliers. A logical argument is available that negligence, indifference or accessory behavior on the part of a foreign government deserves repudiation and perhaps justifies some disregard toward other aspects of their sovereignty. This attitude is an especially potent source of conflict between the United States and Mexico. Counterdrug strategies toward Mexico are limited precisely by United States diplomatic fears about appearing to offend Mexican sovereign independence. If nothing else, complaining too loudly about the Mexican illicit drug trade, or pushing the Mexican government too hard on the drug issue would be incongruous with State Department diplomatic culture. Other areas of common interest with a more quantifiable influence on the value of national property (NAFTA [North American Free Trade Association] highest among them) relegate US–Mexican counterdrug efforts to perpetual under-commitment and shared toleration.[31]

What does the Camarena episode have to do with the question of self-determination? First, it provides an example of the use of self-determination as an argument of national honor that involves comparable and balanceable rights and duties. In this propagandistic usage it becomes the same as nationalism. Second, the Camarena episode places the system of state sovereignty, exemplified by the authority of the president to ignore customary international law, against a broad philosophy of rights and duties that frustrates the state sovereignty system. Is self-determination a theory that a nation-state can apply? Is it something that an individual migrant or a group of migrants can apply? The answer is yes. Self-determination has no structured limits beyond the imaginative use that can be made of the term to claim property.[32]

THE OWNERS' CLUB

> Sovereignty defines a state as a member of the international community of states. It is like a membership card to an exclusive club. Sovereign states can sign treaties, swap ambassadors and join the United Nations.[33] (Peter Taylor, from *World Government*)

As suggested by the comments in Chapter 1 about Roman law, we can trace the idea of sovereignty in early Western tradition to the attempt to peacefully adjudicate competing ownership claims. Contested rights in ownership eventually conformed to a standard terminology within the early system of jurisprudence. This terminology evolved into the idea of property, even to include the separate association of 'property' with substantive things rather than merely a concert of rights. Dealing with modern sovereignty as property ownership appears quite logical if we accept this interpretation of semantic history. In turn, references to state sovereignty collapse easily into a property ownership description. Why might such an interpretation be unwelcome in an academic world claiming to seek new perspectives? For many, sovereignty is club membership (or union membership), and it is in the interest of those who feel an affinity to, or receive sustenance from, the club system that they protect the definitions that give membership its worth.

The idea of the modern state evolved almost hand-in-hand with the idea of sovereignty. In 1648 the Peace of Westphalia ended the Thirty Years War and consolidated a formal system of European state diplomacy. The event should be viewed in historical relation to achievements in political philosophy. Jean Bodin's advocacy of absolutism, his denial of a *Respublica Christiana* and his formulation for international dealings based on treaties contributed immensely to the intellectual paradigm within which the Peace of Westphalia was drawn.[34] Hugo Grotius published *On the Law of*

War and Peace, containing his prescription for a law of nations, in 1625. Thomas Hobbes' *Leviathan* was not published until three years after Westphalia, but his extension of Bodin's opinions was well known beforehand.[35] Inventions of the sixteenth-century Reformation in Europe changed theology, diminished the (transnational) property interests of the Catholic Church and changed the entire system of ownership rules. Without belaboring the obvious, inventions in political philosophy serve some property interests and assault others. Bodinesque or Hobbesian sovereignty was the centerpiece innovation that led to the modern state system, and theirs was not a philosophy dedicated to the cause of individual liberty (or ownership).[36]

Importantly, the founding fathers of the American constitutional system did not look to Bodin and Hobbes as their principal intellectual source. They chose John Locke, who, writing about 40 years after Hobbes, refrained from even using the words state or sovereignty.[37] Framers of the Constitution faced a property problem they could not solve with a system in which each of the various former colonies would be independent externally and exercise supreme authority internally. Hobbes' philosophy, calling for individual submission to an all-powerful central state, could not appeal to many delegates of the former colonies. The United States was to be a federal system in which the various states maintained limited sovereignty, and in which power was divided and balanced. The states would retain the power to determine certain ownership rules.[38] Delegates to the Philadelphia convention in 1787 struck a deal in which powers and obligations pertaining to either the central government or to the individual states were enumerated. Constitutional scholars may speak of the fiction of sovereignty of the states because the federal government can change the rules of ownership. This may overstate reality, or at least restate arguments of those who opposed the constitution out of fear of central government power. At any rate, the US Constitution provided a system of ownership rules that did not find its inspiration in the same philosophical determinants that produced the Peace of Westphalia.[39]

The new United States needed to deal in the community of nations that by the end of the eighteenth century had conducted diplomatic relations under the state system for well over a century. Partly because of great power competition in Europe, the United

States gained international recognition and entrance into the club of sovereign states virtually before it existed as a single nation. Benjamin Franklin and Thomas Jefferson, both opposed to Hobbesian philosophy, were also the first American diplomats in Europe.[40] One of the immediate goals reached by the new constitution was to unify power in the central government to deal with foreign nations. Still, the constitutional history of the United States serves as an example of conflict analysis and resolution using a property-based vision of political relationships. We are reminded that the framers of the American Constitution were able to look beyond an entrenched and supposedly imperative idea regarding the nature of governments. They dealt pragmatically within the state system as it existed and yet were able to critically examine the philosophical determinants of that system.

What criteria are required for gaining membership to the club of sovereign states today?[41] A tongue-in-cheek article in *The Economist* penetrates the problem nicely.[42] The article asks what the rules are for becoming an independent state. It points out that Antarctica issues postage stamps, has a lot of territory, and even has an assigned international country code. It does not have any people. Palestine has plenty of people and recognized diplomats, but no land. The article goes on to mention many ironies and inconsistencies of statehood. The article muses over the plight of a place called Sealand that has stamps, a constitution, a flag, currency, passports, and leaders. It is an old World War II antiaircraft tower sitting outside British territorial waters. Its would-be head of state cannot achieve international recognition for his land – that is, he cannot get in the club.

Sealand's problem is a cute anecdote that points out an important, well-known, and too often overlooked aspect of global politics. The state system is a mishmash of authorities. There is no single organization that deems sovereignty and confers statehood. The International Postal Union, GATT (General Agreement on Tariffs and Trade), the World Bank, Telecom, or the International Standards Organization all have benefits to offer recognized entities. Sealand's effort to peddle itself as an independent sovereignty could win privileges and recognition incrementally. Sealand's petitions will continue to be ignored as frivolous, but more serious petitions constantly threaten the reputations and well-being of the institutions. The world's geography, save for curiosities like Sealand and Antarctica, is already distributed into parcels recognized by most of the status-grantors. Rebellious entities may have far more credible arguments than Sealand, but they threaten to cut ownership away from an existing member of the club. Status-granting organizations are naturally reluctant to extend recognition. This is because the health of many status-granting organizations depends on its members as much as vice versa. If important existing members pull out, if they cease to recognize the authority of the status-granting organization, that organization weakens. Inertia in the world system of ownership nearly ignores objective arguments about government legitimacy. We see that for membership in the sovereign's club, what a candidate lacks is more important than what it has. If no larger ownership entity exerts an enforceable claim over the candidate's territory, membership is possible even for relatively insignificant polities. The Maldives is a member of the UN; Taiwan is not.

Incredulity about the moral objectivity and *status quo* politics of independent sovereigns is an old emotion. Consider St Augustine's observations from the early fifth century:

> In the absence of justice, what is sovereignty but organized brigandage? For, what are the bands of brigands but petty kingdoms? They also are groups of men, under the rule of a leader, bound together by a common agreement, dividing their booty according to a settled principle. If this band of criminals, by recruiting more criminals, acquires enough power to occupy regions, to capture cities, and to subdue whole populations, then it can with fuller right assume the title of kingdom, which in the public estimation is conferred upon it, not by the renunciation of greed, but by the increase of impunity. The answer which a captured pirate gave to Alexander the Great was perfectly accurate and correct. When that king asked the man what he meant by infesting the sea, he boldly replied: 'What you mean by warring on the whole world. I do my fighting on a tiny ship, and they call me a pirate; you do yours with a large fleet, and they call you a Commander'.[43]

St Augustine's viewpoint might be taken to represent some reasonableness to be found in the shared ownership philosophies of the Middle Ages – like *Republica Christiana*.

Whatever moral weaknesses are to be found in the state system, it is not about to disappear overnight. Professor Ivo Duchacek may be correct that:

> A very long process ... of an intertwining of territorial parochialism and globalism (or regionalism) is to be expected. The process clearly will lack dramatic qualitative changes that could exhilarate a globalist and depress a parochialist – and vice versa. Instead of daring we should anticipate, to paraphrase Max Weber, a slow boring into the brittle walls of territorial sovereignty. The speed with which territorial communities have so far adapted themselves to challenges presented by both external and internal environments suggests the pace of geological changes rather than the velocity of contemporary missiles.[44]

Given the accelerating spread of new information technologies, the weakening of sovereignty as an owner status may be quicker than Duchacek predicts. However, accepting that the claim of sovereignty is but an argument for preferential ownership, we should anticipate the mutation of the legalistic meaning of the term and of the qualifications and privileges of membership in the official club. These trends will speed the deterioration of the state sovereignty system as we know it now, but allow it to survive in a changed form.

ENVIRONMENTALISM

> The environment is not a new security concept, but in the past it has primarily been seen as a victim rather than a cause of conflict. Today, its role as a primary variable in regional stability is unquestioned.[45] (Kent Butts, from *Environmental Security*)

The term 'environmentalism' is serendipitous for use in this book since it and 'geopolitics' or 'geographic determinism' were virtual synonyms in decades past. Now the connotations of environmental protection outweigh any connection to national strategy the term used to carry. Here, sovereignty and human rights are bound together in a property ownership explanation of human conflict. Environmental protection is related directly to the value of sovereignty, that is to say, the value of land in which a nation claims ownership rights. Some people see protection of the physical environment as a luxury afforded by those who have already attained economic security and the free time with which to enjoy the appealing balance of God's creation. The blessings of a post-industrial society accrue to environmental activists able to afford titanium backpacks. At least this is a common Third World argument – that affluent enthusiasm for rules regulating industry is selfishness. To the extent they are correct we must remember that Adam Smith's invisible hand is also guided by self-interest. It is a self-interest that has proven beneficial for general well-being when regulated, and it is not a selfishness of which the United States should be ashamed. We need, however, to understand what the reach of this self-interest means in property terms. Domestically, plaintiffs bring environmental protection suits under theories that balance the free use and enjoyment of private land (or private easements on public land) with the free use and enjoyment of public lands (or of neighboring private lands).

We are not far from seeing these same plaintiffs' theories applied successfully in international forums. Brazilians allow a liberal economic exploitation of their Amazon rain forest. Numerous scientists have alleged that irreparable damage is being caused under a nationalist flag of self-interest that under-accounts for the cost that exploitative land use policies have to sovereign value. So far, arguments for a patrimonial stewardship honoring the global value of Brazil's jungle property have not yet overcome arguments about the industrializing needs of Brazil's economy. The result may be eventual destruction of what some popularly refer to as the 'global lung'. Without attempting to measure the role of the forest in global atmospherics (political and physical), it is possible to see how the loss of the Amazon jungle could be perceived as a loss of valuable rights in land by non-Brazilians who have little chance of setting foot in Brazil. These people are today able to engage various forms of strategic power to confront decisions that ignore their complaints. Property analysis can provide answers about the specifics of this strategic power and about the nature of the property rights involved. The rest of the world, as a community or as individual countries, exercises some right to insist on more conservationist Brazilian policies toward the Amazon based on a theory of property waste. The Brazilians, as neighbors, supposedly have a duty not to destroy property if such destruction means the lowering of the value of other properties. Brazilians may attempt to defeat international pressures to protect the Amazon by claiming infringement of sovereignty, but the Brazilian argument will be taken as incongruous. If sovereignty is a concert of property rights, then the destruction of Brazilian sovereignty is logically tied to the destruction of other sovereignties. A better Brazilian argument points to the lack of will on the part of other countries to keep their own entrepreneurs from participating in the destruction of the Amazon. Can other governments make a credible claim against Brazil for wasting a world patrimony if they participate as accessories in exploitative practices of their own countrymen?

The United States cannot expect always to be the plaintiff in environmental cases. Acid rain is perhaps the best-known international issue involving the United States as an accused violator. What blows onto Canada is a US problem. Because of the international effects of acid rain, the United States could at least suffer diplomatic assaults that undermine international solidarity and US credibility in other environmental cases. In a more exaggerated situation, offending factories in the United States might conceivably be subject to outlaw attack. One optional response to this possibility is to increase domestic spending, public and private, on security systems for the offending industries and on law enforcement capacity against ecological guerrillas. Cleaning up is probably cheaper. The right in land that leads to the operation of our industries brings a correlative duty to operate industry in a way that does not damage foreign property. Fortunately, the problem of acid rain is being addressed without recourse to violence or our having to suffer arguments justifying violence. Although it will not be resolved to the complete satisfaction of some radical ecologists, it is being resolved at a speed that will most likely prevent any successful leap into the world of ecoguerrillas. Modern international conflict, however, extends beyond the state. Individuals and small voluntary associations can cover vast geographies and obtain sophisticated *matériel* with which to manifest radicalism and even lunacy.

Ecoguerrilla movements are not so bizarre that we do not have current examples. Radical environmentalists seeking to protect California redwood stands have used dangerous sabotage (spiking trees to ruin power saw blades) to bring home their message. Madly inconsistent policies taken in relation to the maquilla factories along the Rio Grande River provide a more distressing example. After evolving environmental protection laws to regulate United States industry, the United States promulgated treaties with Mexico, allowing fabrication industries to operate on the Mexican side of the border. There they would employ cheaper Mexican labor. Costs to the companies were low not only because United States labor standards did not have to be met, but because environmental protection laws would not be enforced. It does not take much of a property analysis to see how ruinous was the disrespect for the existing environmental laws. Both sides of the border are fouled. If that insult were not enough, any argument that the maquillas would help lessen the flow of illegal aliens into the United States has been proven absurd. The mass of border factories attracted millions of Mexican families to the northern border from where the next step to international migration was a matter of yards. The potential exists that violent expressions in favor of the environment may accompany more traditional labor arguments. These could be delivered in the company of national, factional, and ideological identities. Foreign counterguerrilla experience teaches that when the firepower and organizational sophistication of radical groups exceed the ability of police organizations to apply the law, either government military forces are required, or the police must take on new capacities. The United States military establishment has been called upon already to provide support to counterdrug operations within the United States because the problems tax the ability of civilian law enforcement agencies. The United States is not immune from the effects of environmental abuses allowed just over the border, or from violent groups who would signal these abuses as part of a package of grievances.

Earlier discussion of city parks shows its relevance at this point. The real estate analogy remains consistent respecting the nature of modern sovereignty. Dispute over common property is the joining thread. A look at ocean fishing rights serves as the next appropriate example. According to many ecologists, the reach of international fishing fleets and fishing technology spelled the destruction of traditional fishing banks around the world. The local value of adjacent seas became clearer to the countries most directly affected. Rather than have the Japanese and others fish out the banks, many countries claimed economic exclusionary zones. The ancient ideal of total common property of the seas gave way to a system closer to private ownership. The effect appears to be better stewardship of renewable, but destructible resources.

Animal rights is a fascinating crosscurrent that supports a new expression of common property rights. Activist groups translate what may have until very recently seemed a crank issue of minor physical power into a significant property value claim with international implications. They interpret the right to enjoyment of the land (sea) to include aesthetic pleasure and moral satisfaction derived from the preservation of species. One organization, Greenpeace, attempts to redefine who owns whales. The Greenpeace claim does not imply any sub-unit of humanity as privileged owners, or does it limit the geographical reach of full possession, the fee. It at least claims that international ownership rules must preserve a generalized right to enjoyment of the presence of certain species. The arguments at times go further to suggest that a non-human species be itself the ownership group in question. These animal rights propositions are difficult to incorporate into a system dependent on legal theories of human rights. In spite of any spiritual difficulty they might cause, they are easily contained by property analysis.

Also more easily contained by analyses that begin with property rights rather than with human rights are the menacing results of global environmental degradation. Journalist Robert Kaplan's 1994 *Atlantic Monthly* article entitled 'The Coming Anarchy' is a good example of apocalyptic (and plausible) visions regarding the pressures that an increasingly abused natural environment will put on human politics.[46] Kaplan's main negative example (he provides positive ones as well) is the West Coast of Africa, a region seemingly in the grip of environmental revenge. Kaplan's theme is reasonable. Degradation in the environment causes new political stress, especially where caused and exacerbated by increased population pressures. Political friction can be sparked, however, by more mundane changes than those boded by writers like Robert Kaplan. As an example, consider a luxury beach hotel that has become the economic linchpin of the surrounding community. When tides threaten to take away the beachfront sand, either because of other human engineering interventions along the same coast or because of disfavorable oceanic trends, the hotel's future becomes threatened. Technological answers that promise to allow the hotel to survive economically in the near to mid-term become very attractive. The political problems are at least two-fold. The most obvious may be the effect of any new breakwaters on the hotel's neighbors, but subtler is the certain attempt by the hotel owner to involve the whole community in paying for the project. Environmental changes, whether man-made or nature's own, change the value of property and create arguments as to who will pay. The beach resort problem typically involves several hundred yards of coastline, but the example is transferable to the scale of international politics.

GEOPOLITICS

> Do not be narrow-minded, but think in large terms of great spaces. In continents and oceans, and thereby direct your course with that of our Fuhrer. (Karl Haushofer, from J.T. Lowe, *Geopolitics and War*)

For many readers, 'geopolitics' conjures up a worldview at odds with human rights – one that still carries unpopular connotations as a vindicating pseudo-science for national arrogance. As a school of strategic thought it is, as its name implies, a cross of geography and politics, but its dominant scholastic parent is geography rather than political science. Geopolitics is a twentieth-century instruction, geography itself being fairly young as institutionalized academic disciplines go. The first English and American university geography departments and textbooks date back only to the latter half of the nineteenth century.[47] Geopolitics was one of geography's early progenies. Because it was born in an epoch of high imperialist pretensions, and given its undeniable German ancestry, geopolitics was destined for dishonor by entanglement with Nazi racism. The term has survived because it intimates the connection between geography on the macro level with grand strategy and international diplomacy. Its pre-World War II abusers are little remembered and, in some circles, excused. Geopolitics, ugly still for some, is the correct term to describe the theoretical parameter within which most military strategy resides. This is as true for United States military strategists in the late twentieth century as it was at the beginning of the century. While many military planners may be unaware of the intellectual and historical baggage that geopolitics lugs with it, they are generally content that the term represents a more worthy engine for national decision-making than does human rights.

Geopolitical theory has had a transcendent effect on US foreign and military policy, beginning with the influences not of a German, but of a British geographer/politician. Halford Mackinder, building on Friedrich Ratzel's notion of continental power, attributed preeminence to the Eurasian landmass in what became his Heartland Theory. The theory was published in 1919 in a study titled 'Democratic Ideals and Reality', and is summarized by his famous phrase: 'Who rules East Europe commands the Heartland: Who rules the Heartland commands the World Island: Who rules the World Island commands the World.'[48]

Geopolitics would obviously merit the attention of anyone looking to define the world in property terms, except that geopolitical perspectives begin from characteristics of the land, not ownership rights. However, digging at the substrata of geopolitics, one can uncover fascinating evidence of the universality of man's attitudes toward land. German geographer Friedrich Ratzel (1844–1904) is acclaimed as the father of human, or political, geography. A Swede, Rudolf Kjellen, is known as the propounder of geopolitics, while Karl Haushofer can be credited for warping geopolitics to the advantage of Nazi dogma.[49] Ratzel presented his theories of political organization in terms of 'laws' related to space and location. Ratzel formed a concept of the 'state' which treated the state as a type of biological organism with spiritual and moral character derived from the ties which men shared due to common presence on a definable piece of ground. The spiritual dimension of the relationship between man and land reflects the antecedent and ever nationalist writings of philosophers such as Immanuel Kant and Georg Hegel. These German expressions are not shared universally, but they are not as far removed as we might think from other people's conclusions regarding their political and spiritual relationship to land. Consider the importance of land to the Native American Indians in face of the privations imposed upon them by the White man.

> Land, moreover, has many meanings for the Indian. The relationship of a tribe to its land defines that tribe: its identity, its culture, its way of life, its fundamental rights, its methods of adaptation, its pattern of survival. Land also defines the Indians' enemies – those who covet the land and desire to expropriate it for their own use. Because Indian land is, or may be, of value, it has been, and remains, the source of almost every major conflict and every ongoing controversy between the Indian and the white man. Indian land is synonymous with Indian existence. A tribe's title to land often proves to be its death warrant.[50]

With changes only in the group identities, this expression could have been safely attributed to German geopoliticians. At the level of rights associated with land, differences in belief systems are not so great as is often claimed. Geopolitics responds to atavistic ties between man and place. However, especially in its most abrasive forms, geopolitics does not deal well with multiple dimensions of ownership.[51] Emphasis on space and location is the Ratzelian heritage of geopolitics. Intuition about domestic real estate tells us that space and location are indeed the principal determinants of land value in fiscal terms, but the body of rights associated with a piece of land also has a close relationship to its value. Geopolitical analyses are poorly conformable to multiple, occasionally shared, changeable rights in land held by overlapping owner groups that only sometimes can be delineated according to nationality. The more distant a problem gets from competition by nation-states over the fee simple of demarcated land, the less useful geopolitics becomes.

Another, and perhaps the most significant, weakness of geopolitics involves its relation to technological change. Geopolitical interpretations of national interest can be seen as lagging reflections of technological history. Most US national strategies, geopolitics-based, have been built around control of mineral resources, like oil.[52] This is an indirect response to technologies. Strategic minerals and oil are geologically visible because of the technologies that lend them value. Geopoliticians, observing the demand for these natural resources, imbue with a correlated value the places where the resources can be found. The weakness is obvious. Many technologies that are not well defined geologically nevertheless create changes in the value of places. Widespread use of the automobile, or the development of the jet engine were ultimately reflected in geopolitical analysis, as was the passing from history of the wooden warship. Use of the Internet, electronic banking, or DNA labeling, however, are less likely to be incorporated into geopolitical viewpoints because the varying changes that they make to the value of places is not geologically visible. This again is because geopolitics does not begin from an integral theory about what makes a place valuable. We would suppose that any theory capable of explaining the value of places must incorporate technological change.

NOTES

1. J.L. Brierly, *The Law of Nations: An Introduction to the International Law of Peace*, 6th edn, edited by Sir Humphrey Waldock (Oxford: Oxford University Press, 1963), p. 13.
2. 'As a man is said to have a right to his property, he may be equally said to have a property in his rights', James Madison, 'Property', *National Gazette*, 19 March 1792; 'In fact, a fundamental interdependence exists between the personal right of liberty and the personal right in property', Potter Stewart, majority opinion, *Lynch v. Household Finance Corp.*, p. 552, 1972.
3. Hans Morgenthau, *Politics Among Nations: The Struggle for Power and Peace*, 5th edn (New York: Alfred A. Knopf, 1973), p. 307.
4. Ibid., p. 320.
5. J.L. Brierly, *The Law of Nations*, p. 13.
6. Reinold Noyes, *The Institution of Property* (New York: Longmans, Green, 1936), p. 182. *Res* means thing, *res corporales* refers to corporeal or tangible property. *Jus* means right, justice, or law.
7. J.L. Brierly, *The Law of Nations*, p. 9.
8. Brierly argues, however, that Bodin did not intend his sovereign to be an irresponsible supra-legal power. Brierly notes that Bodin discusses, for instance, certain laws of government that the sovereign does not make and cannot abrogate. These laws of government include the laws that determine in whom the sovereign power is to be vested and the limits within which it is to be exercised. Brierly suggests these are what we would today refer to as the laws of a constitution. J.L. Brierly, *The Law of Nations*, ibid.
9. Ibid, p. 8.
10. Brierly points out that Bodin was seeking legal resolution to what he observed as the political disorder of his time. According to Brierly, Bodin in no way announced sovereignty as a supposedly eternal principle concerning the nature of states as such. Ibid.
11. 'At the head of each household, there was a patriarch, a *paterfamilias*, whose absolute authority, limited only by custom and opinion, extended equally over everything connected with the household, both human beings and things. He alone also represented the household to the outside world ... He was sole proprietor, not only of the products of the labour of his slaves, his wife, and his children, but strictly of everything, including his wife and his children, whom he could sell as he could his cattle and his slaves', Reinold Noyes, *The Institution of Property*, p. 44.
12. Ibid., p. 48.
13. Ibid., p. 51.
14. Harold K. Jacobson, *Networks of Interdependence: International Organizations and the Global Political System* (New York: Alfred A. Knopf, 1979), p. 395.
15. Many modern national constitutions incorporate mention of sovereignty in their texts. For instance, the Colombian constitution states, 'Sovereignty resides exclusively in the people, from whom public power issues. The people exercise that sovereignty directly or through their representatives as provided in the Constitution.' Title I – Fundamental Principles, Article 3, *1991 Political Constitution of Colombia,* as translated in FBIS-LAT-91-170-S, 8 July 1991, pp. 1–25.
16. William O'Malley, 'New Russian Constitution', World Radio Transcription Service, 12 April 94 08:27:22 PDT.
17. See 'Struggle For Property Intensifies', *Moscow News*, 5–11 May 1995, p. 9. 'Recently, an increasing number of conflicts has been arising in the real estate market, particularly in the sphere of tenants' rights and ownership of uninhabitable premises.' Ibid.
18. Richard N. Haass, *Intervention* (Washington, DC: Carnegie Endowment, 1994),

pp. 12, 13.
19. In early 1994, the Guatemalan and Belizean governments were squabbling over a group of 18 Guatemalan families who had taken up residence in the disputed border area. Meanwhile, Guatemala was working in the United Nations to clarify Guatemalan and Belizean rights regarding territorial waters, the economic exclusionary zone and the continental shelf. The Guatemalan human rights ombudsman weighed in, calling on the Guatemalan Army to ensure the protection of the rights of Guatemalan citizens against abuses by the Belizean government. In this one argument we see the leverage relationships of internal and external politics, and the pressures that can conceivably be applied by one form of property assertion to gain advantage in respect to another.
20. 'The United States embraced the presumptively anti-colonial idea of self-determination in our own fit of absent-mindedness. There were wartime uses. But after a point, self-determination no longer seemed such a good idea. So many of the new states promptly turned Marxist or, as in the case of India, proclaimed themselves socialist with a Marxist bent. What kind of gratitude was that? The puzzlement was painfully in evidence at the United Nations. The United States had fashioned the new world order as much as possible in an American image.' Daniel Patrick Moynihan, *Pandaemonium: Ethnicity in International Politics* (New York: Oxford University Press, 1993), p. 158.
21. The Judge Advocate General's School, 'The Brezhnev Doctrine', in *Source Documents on International Law for Military Lawyers, Volume II, Security Arrangements* (Charlottesville, VA, The Judge Advocate General's School, US Army, 1969), pp. 44–9.
22. For standard Soviet arguments against nationalism see V.Y. Chertikhin *et al.*, *The Revolutionary Movement of Our Time and Nationalism*, trans. by Vic Schneierson (Moscow: Progress Publishers, 1975).
23. C.T. Ryan (9 May 1995), Cultural Diversity Conference [online], available:<NATIVE-L@TAMVM1.TAMU.EDU>Message-Id: <199505090555. AAA09775@info.tamu.edu>. This a consolidation of two articles in *The Guardian* (issues of 3 and 10 May), published by the Socialist Party of Australia.
24. Harold S. Johnson and Bajit Singh, 'Self-determination and World Order', in Yonah Alexander and Robert A. Friedlander, eds, *Self-Determination: National, Regional, and Global Dimensions* (Boulder, CO: Westview Press, 1980), p. 349.
25. For a basic primer on nationalism, see Boyd C. Shafer, *Faces of Nationalism* (New York: Harcourt Brace Jovanovich, 1972) or Hugh Seton-Watson, *Nations and States* (Boulder, CO: Westview Press, 1977). 'I am driven to the conclusion that no "scientific" definition of a nation can be devised; yet the phenomenon has existed and exists', ibid., p. 5.
26. 'Those that use the word "tribe" of others are usually convinced that they themselves belong to a higher culture and are looking at persons of a lower culture', Hugh Seton-Watson, *Nations and States*, ibid.
27. See Neil V. Lamont, 'Territorial Dimensions of Ethnic Conflict: The Moldovan Case, 1991–March 1993', *The Journal of Slavic Military Studies* (formerly *The Journal of Soviet Military Studies*), 6, 4 (December 1993), p. 576.
28. In Sarajevo and its environs, for example, well-connected outsiders have exploited the wartime situation to acquire real property cheaply. Simultaneously, they have been ingratiating themselves with the Muslim government to acquire reconstruction projects when the fighting subsides. The most visible effect of these speculative investments has been current propagandizing and influence peddling for the Muslim cause.
29. 'Latin American Parliament: Exercising Sovereignty', *Granma International*, 14 February 1993, p. 15. *Granma* is the best known of the communist Cuban international propaganda organs.
30. The court did not comment on whether or not, as a matter of diplomacy, the action

of the US government was a good idea. The court only decided that there was nothing in the Constitution of the United States that prohibited the administration from doing what it did. See Robert Bork, 'The Reach of American Law', *The National Interest*, 29 (Fall 1992), p. 3. As Judge Bork points out, the same extraterritoriality seems more just and expedient in the context of international terrorism, drug trafficking, or antitrust issues.
31. See Jorge Chabat, 'El narcotráfico en la relación Mexico–Estados Unidos: lo que se ve es lo que hay' (Narcotrafficking in US–Mexican relations: what you see is what you get), *Estados Unidos*, 3, 3 (Autumn 1993), p. 5.
32. By following the argumentative limits of 'self-determination', we get an idea regarding the perception of rights and duties around the world. The surprise comes when we realize that self-determination carries little weight in some contexts that would otherwise appear appropriate. Migration to the United States is one of them. When Californians voted for Proposition 187, limiting illegal alien access to social services, the Mexican government, usually keen to avoid interventionist comments about laws in other lands, was quick to criticize.
33. Peter J. Taylor, ed., *World Government* (New York: Oxford University Press, 1990), p. 10.
34. *Republica Christiana* refers to early fourth-century theory binding political authority with spiritual authority in the Pope of Rome. If 1648 was the birthyear of the modern state system, 1517 was the beginning of the end for what preceded it. That is when Martin Luther tacked his famous Ninety-five Theses to the door of the castle church in Wittenburg. In property terms, Luther was disgusted with Church taxation, especially in the form of indulgences. He attacked the system of ownership rules and engaged a series of property conflicts that would last for two centuries.
35. Brierly notes that Hobbes' definition of sovereignty would today be called pure and simple totalitarianism. Hobbes felt that the state of nature in which men lived was nasty, brutish and short, and that the individual had to relinquish his freedom to an all-powerful sovereign for the purpose of survival. Hobbes, like Bodin, wrote his pessimistic philosophy having experienced the violent disorder of a civil war.
36. Bernard Bailyn, *The Ideological Origins of the American Revolution* (Cambridge, MA: Harvard University Press, 1967), p. 198. '[O]f all the intellectual problems the colonists faced, one was absolutely crucial: in the last analysis it was over this issue that the Revolution was fought. On the pivotal question of sovereignty, which is the question of the nature and location of the ultimate power in the state, American thinkers attempted to depart sharply from one of the most firmly fixed points in eighteenth-century thought; and though they failed to gain acceptance for their strange and awkward views, they succeeded nevertheless in opening this fundamental issue to critical discussion, preparing the way for a new departure in the organization of power', ibid., p. 198.
37. John Locke's *Two Treatises of Government* was published in 1690, well after the state system had taken hold in Europe; see John Locke, *Two Treatises of Government*, 2nd edn, Peter Laslett, ed. (Cambridge: Cambridge University Press, 1967). Locke attacked Hobbes' negative view of the state of nature, and argued that sovereignty did not reside in the state but in the people. Locke returned to the belief that certain rights owed to man's nature and God's grace, among these being life, liberty and property. Like Hobbes, he considered government a necessity for the preservation of order, but he believed that the government derived its authority from the consent of the governed and that, rather than have a government with unified power, government power should be limited and controlled by checks and balances. Locke saw government as the protector of individual property, but he was not completely consistent or clear regarding the conditions in which that property was to be enjoyed, and happiness pursued. The American constitutional debate about property relationships was somewhat confused as a result. See Forrest McDonald, *Novus Ordo Seclorum: The Intellectual Origins of the Constitution*

(Lawrence: University of Kansas Press, 1985), pp. 60–6.
38. McDonald, ibid., p. 276.
39. 'And if the word property today carries sinister philosophical overtones, to the Convention of 1787 it had an altogether different connotation: property was not a privilege of the higher orders but a right which a man would fight to defend. Men had indeed died to defend it in the war with England.' Catherine Drinker Bowen, *Miracle at Philadelphia: The Story of the Constitutional Convention May to September 1787* (Boston, MA: Little, Brown, 1986), p. 70.
40. Thomas Jefferson followed Benjamin Franklin as minister to France. He witnessed the coming of the French Revolution in 1789. Interestingly, he suggested that the French adopt a parliamentary monarchy like that of the English. Apparently, he did not think American style democracy was for everyone. It is also notable that these two, Jefferson and Franklin, were influenced by the writings of eighteenth century French physiocrats, who believed that all wealth was derived from land.
41. *Ballentine's Law Dictionary* defines the *sovereign state* as 'A people permanently occupying a fixed territory, bound together by common laws, habits, and customs into one body politic, exercising through the medium of an organized government, independent sovereignty and control over all persons and things within its boundaries, capable of making war and peace, and of entering into international relations with other communities.' James Ballentine, *Ballentine's Law Dictionary*, 3rd edn (San Francisco, CA: Bancroft-Whitney, 1969), p. 1196. Even this authoritative definition, summarized, holds the standard tautology – that a sovereign state is a people exercising sovereignty.
42. 'My land, your land and Sealand', *The Economist*, 2–8 October 1993, p. 48.
43. Saint Augustine, *The City of God* (edited by Vernon J. Bourke and translated by Gerald G. Walsh, Demetrius B. Zema, Grace Monahan, and Daniel J. Honan) (Garden City, NY: Doubleday, 1958), p. 88. St Thomas Aquinas admitted the right to private property, being an addition to natural law devised by human reason. He nevertheless expressed concern and distaste for commerce and profit. See Edward Allen Kent, ed., *Law and Philosophy: Readings in Legal Philosophy* (New York: Meridith, 1970), pp. 503–5.
44. Ivo D. Duchacek, *The Territorial Dimension of Politics Within, Among, and Across Nations* (Boulder, CO: Westview Press, 1986), p. 297.
45. Kent Hughs Butts, ed., *Environmental Security* (Carlisle Barracks, PA: US Army War College, 1994), p. 3.
46. Robert Kaplan, 'The Coming Anarchy', *The Atlantic Monthly*, February 1994, pp. 44–76.
47. German geography was established as a separate academic discipline about a half century earlier. See Arild Holt-Jensen, *Geography: History and Concepts* (Totowa, NJ: Barnes & Noble Books, 1988), p. 3.
48. Halford J. Mackinder, *Democratic Ideals and Reality* (New York: W.W. Norton, 1962), p. 150. There is some debate about when exactly the term Heartland was coined. Mackinder had delivered an influential lecture in 1904 titled 'The Geographical Pivot of History' in which the term appears and in which the essence of his theory is propounded. See James Trapier Lowe, *Geopolitics and War: Mackinder's Philosophy of Power* (Washington, DC: University Press of America, 1981), p. 5.
49. Arild Holt-Jensen, ibid., p. 32. Note the following from a post-World War II textbook on political geography: 'Before and during World War II, German geopolitics (Geopolitik) was used to blueprint world conquest, and the Nazi creed incorporated those portions of political geography that served to justify German expansion. The natural result has been an attempt by some scholars to divorce the discipline of political geography from geopolitics. In the words of Karl Haushofer, "Political Geography views the state from the standpoint of space, while Geopolitics views space from the standpoint of the state". In the final analysis the difference is

one of emphasis'. N. Marbury Efimenco, ed., *World Political Geography: Second Edition* (New York: Thomas Y. Crowell, 1957), p. 5.
50. Edgar S. Cahn and David W. Hearne, eds, *Our Brother's Keeper: The Indian in White America* (New York: New American Library, 1970), p. 68.
51. An indigenous, or 'Fourth World', movement is afoot that seeks to build solidarity among indigenous peoples of the world in order to promote similar if not common interests. One might suppose that this movement would find common cause with environmental protectionists. This is often the case. Greenpeace, for instance, has played a sympathetic observer role in the context of Mexico's Zapatista uprising, which has a significant indigenous claims dimension. Still, activists for indigenous rights just as often find their agendas at odds with the goals of environmental protection activists, especially when the bottom line is land use and ownership. See, for example, Aboriginal Peoples: news & information (23 April 1995), 'Treaty/land rights "vs" deep e 1/2' [online], available: <NATIVE-L@TAMVM1.TAMU.EDU>, message-id: <199504241449.JAA01949@info.tamu.edu>.
52. See, generally, Ronnie D. Lipschutz, *When Nations Clash*.

3

Technology and the Modernity of Conflict

> If the works of the great poets teach anything, it is to hold mere invention somewhat cheap. It is not finding of a thing, but the making something out of it after it is found, that is of consequence. (James Russell Lowell, from 'Chauser', 1871)

Washing machines, automobiles, contraceptives, credit cards and uncountable other inventions have shaped twentieth-century ideas about freedom. Not only has Western society set the rules for individual liberty, but also its inventiveness has continually expanded it. Some innovations have had only a superficial consequence more related to convenience than to basic liberty, but others have had a transcendental effect on the relation of the individual to government. Often, as James Burke's television video series *Connections* has eloquently portrayed, inventions can have unexpected and distant influence on the nature of our political lives.[1] We can easily lose sight of the relationship invention has to our liberties, and to whatever strategies we apply in liberty's service. It is therefore important to show that a property-based interpretation of political struggles can digest the phenomenon of human technology. To that end, geoproperty divides the relationship of technology to property into three parts. They are the influence of inventions on the value of property, the phenomenon of inventions as property, and the influence of innovation on our ability to protect and gain property. These three do not form a comprehensive explanation of the influence of technology on man's existence. They only highlight a few of the less-discussed relationships between invention, national interests and national strategy. Following this three-part reduction, discussion turns in another direction. An integrated process, urbanization, is the theme used to present the relationship of technological change to the property nature of conflicts.

TECHNOLOGY AND THE VALUE OF PROPERTY

> The car is a superb piece of uniform, standardized mechanism that is a piece with the Gutenberg technology and literacy which created the first classless society in the world. (Marshall McLuhan, from *The Medium is the Message*)

Drafters of the United States Constitution showed the remarkable quality of understanding the relationship of technology to liberty. The political power of printing presses and firearms were explicitly recognized. The drafters could hardly foresee the effects of later technologies on individual liberties, but their recognition of technology as a dynamic factor in human relationships helped create a political environment in which new technologies were more likely to have a positive than a negative effect. Depending on the body of rules regulating the relationship of the individual to government, the computer can be a repressive tool or it can be a servant to liberty. In other words, not only can an invention affect political freedom, the political environment influences the properties of an invention. It is easy to attribute the failure of Russian communism to a lack of freedom, but that failure can be specified further as the inability of a culture to adopt technologies that require freedom. We can see that the designers of the American political revolution were more pragmatic and more insightful about inventions than were the intellectual authors of the Soviet communist revolution.

As for invention, how was the dialectic march of history unfolding for the Russians by the early 1980s? The American president's 1983 'Star Wars' speech must have had an impact, threatening as it did an unwinnable new arms race.[2] His description of the Soviet Union as an evil empire probably also hit a chord of self-doubt that further lowered Soviet morale.[3] It was, however, the tinkering of Stephen Wozniak and Steve Job that heralded Russia's technological doom.[4] Their garage-built Apple® computer was a special nail in the Soviet coffin. The Russians could steal the design, copy it, make some poor quality production runs, even decide to distribute thousands of them, but they could not have the technology. The technology of the microcomputer, of the personal computer, could not be had by Soviet Russia, and no amount of technical expertise or espionage could get it. The personal computer, an instrument that races ideas around from one inventive head to another, is that which can only be in a free society. In a society where no one is trusted talking on the telephone, desktop publishing cannot be – the personal computer cannot be. At the dawn of the Internet, the Soviet locomotive was off history's tracks.

The computer's value and its properties depend on the rest of the concert of rights that constitutes land ownership. In other words, where individuals decide the use and enjoyment of land as owners, the computer assumes its full character as an accelerator of ideas. Consequently, the value of land is enhanced still more. The individual's right to use a computer as an empowering tool exists indivisibly from other rights. This fact makes land in a free society more valuable. Because the personal computer could not exist in Russia, Western land (Western sovereignty) became radically and obviously more valuable than Soviet land. When Ronald Reagan labeled the Soviet Union 'the evil empire', exposure of their moral reality may have stung the Russians. But observant Russians began to sense that the logarithmic rate of technological progress would only accrue to a free society. Strategic reality became a weightier argument for political change than moral critique, though the two had the same roots. In Soviet communist failure we see the link between the manifestation of political philosophy, the exercise of human rights, the value of property, and technology.

Another feature of innovation history is how the timing or sequence of innovations (when one invention is introduced in relation to the next) influences the political *status quo*. Americans were well accustomed to owning a car long before they saw a plastic credit card, for instance. In uninventive and poor countries, changes arrive in a far different order than in the technological states. For some, vaccinations come before potable water systems, fax machines before washing machines, television before publishing. All this out-of-order introduction of technologies must impinge on the relationship inventions have with the development of individual liberties. Consequentially, introduction of a given technology in one society today may not have the same significance in respect to liberty that the technology had in another society in the past. The drafters of the United States Constitution were aware of the political significance of physical inventions, having explicitly recognized both the printing press and the firearm. We can see the importance of the timing of technological introduction by comparing the impact of these two technologies in the context of two distinct cultural histories.

We can cogently argue that individual possession of firearms in the United States has been an influential political right. Can we export the same influence to other lands? A widespread increase in firearm ownership might not affect individual liberties in most countries today as it has in America. This observation may seem a divergence from the train of thought tying property ownership to international human rights and sovereignty, but the connection lies in the historical ability of populations to relate basic human rights to their personal status as owners, rather than as parts of the property. This is true for private and public ownership rights alike. The firearm example is instructive. Today in the United States, the scope of the right to bear firearms is widely debated and continually eroded. When the Bill of Rights was written and for more than a century after that, there was no debate at the federal level.[5] Now, light automatic weapons, fast transportation and personal wealth give great range of expression to outlaw and lunatic individuals. This fact lies at the heart of widespread discomfort about the idea that every individual might arm himself as he or she pleases.

In the late eighteenth century, though, America's founding fathers understood the importance of existing technologies in the relationship between not only man and his neighbor, but between the individual and the government. Americans, gun owners or not, came to understand a relationship with the state that included no exclusive control of firepower by the latter. The United States Constitution's Second Amendment underpinned the strength of its Fourth Amendment concerning searches and seizures. The Second Amendment was a substantial warning to government authorities who would violate the Fourth.

Of course, gun ownership is only a sliver of the story of the psychology of land ownership in America. Americans have long been aware they have the right to deny access to officials and to demand a warrant for a search or an arrest. They have also been empowered to enforce these rights on their own. Two basic civil rights – habeas corpus and search and seizure (and the right of physical integrity that follows closely behind these rights) – are inseparably bound to the individual's ability to uphold rights in land. This relationship between rights and individual empowerment is absent in the history of, say, Peru or Russia. The Russians and the Peruvians cannot replace their history, and it is difficult to bridge existing psychological differences regarding the relationship between 'human rights', rights in land, and personal empowerment. As for many societies, it would require a dangerous leap of faith to test widespread increase in firearm possession as a means to invigorate the protection of individual rights. In the United States, the opposite question reigns. Might not a widespread decrease in firearm possession threaten the protection of individual rights?

Colombia has one of the most violent societies in the hemisphere, if not the world.[6] During the nineteenth century, debate in the United States about the right to possess firearms was limited. In Colombia, meanwhile, personal gun ownership was a salient issue in an ideological struggle that continued well into the present century. Liberal and Conservative ideologues planted flags around Colombian interpretations of the North American and French revolutionary debates. That interpretation stripped away gray scales and polarized a society that was at its heart very distinct from the colonies of North America. One Liberal insistence was personal ownership of the firearm, and the ultimate reason for this insistence was the same as in North America. To avoid a government monopoly on the application of the technology, individual ownership of the firearm had to be guaranteed. The Conservative ideal was exactly the opposite – to preserve the government monopoly on firearms as a necessary condition for the state to secure a common peace. Gun ownership was hardly the only polarizing issue, and personal ownership of firearms eventually disappeared from the Liberal platform of ideals.

The average, law abiding Colombian is not likely to interpret his political heritage to include a right that he or she possesses a firearm. To this extent, the Conservative current won. On the other hand, decades of Liberal argument left a competing understanding that firearms correlated to political sovereignty. Gun possession is widespread in Colombia today, but it is in the main an illegal ownership by persons with relatively great wealth, or by outlaws. The principal, and powerful, armed guerrilla opposition group in Colombia calls itself the Colombian Revolutionary Armed Forces, or FARC. For over a decade the FARC has enjoyed a condition of semi-legality for the carrying of weapons; the FARC and the government reached cease-fire agreements that did not include a demand that the FARC lay down its weapons. Colombian drug trafficking organizations and other Mafia have also armed themselves immensely well and now appear beyond the threat of being disarmed by the government. In Colombia, individual control of firearm technology did not triumph politically, but government monopoly of firearms did not result.

Before the early nineteenth century revolutionary period began, the Colombian peasantry did not possess firearms. Political leaders provided them with firearms for partisan purposes. This gave the firearm a different definition than in the United States, where the firearm was an individual's technology. What would the condition of social violence be today had Liberal views prevailed and gun ownership been widespread early in Colombia's history? This author suspects that Colombians would have adopted a more assertive sense of individual rights and duties that may very well have precluded many abuses of property rights by governments, guerrillas, and Mafia.[7] The suspicion is gratuitous. This one thread cannot be torn from the rest of the cultural fabric. Historical hypotheticals are logic monsters, but at least the Colombian example helps demonstrate how the timing of the introduction of technologies is a factor in their impact on ownership competitions.

The other technology relates to the First Amendment to the US Constitution. In the late eighteenth century, there were two printing presses in the Viceroyalty of Nueva Granada (what are now Colombia, Venezuela, Panama, and Ecuador). One of these presses operated in the coastal city of Cartagena de Indias and the other was in the mountain capital, Santa Fe de Bogota. The Viceroy ordered the Cartagena press brought to Bogota to assure that only approved religious and governmental information be printed. Control of 'the press' was actually control of the two presses. At about the same time, in the colonies that became the United States, there were hundreds of presses and even hundreds of regular publications. The North American colonists understood the political reach of this technology in the context of its energetic and widespread use. Freedom of the press was imitated as a principle in other lands in the nineteenth century, including Colombia. In many places, however, popular illiteracy left control of ideas in almost the same hands that had previously restricted the presses. The press in America was an instrument to assure ownership for the individual against possible tyrannies. In lands where the technology was not really part of the culture, the press often became another tool of ownership for small elites. Had popular literacy been an established condition earlier in Colombian history, the printing press would have had a different impact on the revolutionary and constitutional debates. By the time the printing press had become a truly available invention (and public literacy had expanded) in Colombia, the radio and then the television had taken over as the primary instruments of mass dissemination of information. It is facile to speculate on what might have happened had the timing of the introduction of the press been different, but the point stands. Comparing the technological history of Colombia to that of the United States reasserts that technology is not the thing. It is only what it is in the context of cultural conditions.

TECHNOLOGY AS SOVEREIGNTY

> What are they doing with our oil under their sand?
> (anonymous)

Concentration on ownership causes a more sweeping observation about inventions and the international environment. Technology affects the existence of ownable property. When something important is invented, it not only creates new wealth in the form of fungible power (money), but new property. That is to say, a new idea creates a new concert of rights and duties. This new ownership is cause and effect of new relationships, and a principal cause of new frictions. A small assortment of examples shows how technology creates new ownership relationships that constitute new sovereignty and new conflict:

1. Discoveries leading to the control of yellow fever are significantly responsible for the realization of the strategic value of the Isthmus of Panama.[8] Construction of the canal created a new concert of property rights and duties related to that land. We could dissect this concert of rights and duties in a sterile fashion by considering treaty conditions or canal passage rules and the like, but they can also be viewed in terms of real estate. Digging the canal created a new world patrimony and military key terrain. Passage through the canal delivered a distinct trading advantage and so created a worldwide expectation that access to the canal would be

granted impartially. The United States may have 'taken' Panama and has considered the canal a piece of American sovereignty, but the fact of its great value made it the property of all nations.

Although the United States acceded to this globally perceived right, it did not relinquish the whole bundle of rights associated with the canal. The status of the United States has been more than that of a mere steward for the world community. Even temporary exclusive use of the canal extends a strategic military advantage. Therefore, the US has considered physical possession necessary to ensure that the use of the canal would remain to the United States and not to its enemies in an emergency. Still, outside the context of war, denial of common use of the canal would fall out of bounds of the rules of ownership understood by the United States and the rest of the world.

The Panama Canal presents an example of a special bundle of rights in a particular piece of geography. The world community holds some rights (with their correlative duties) at large while the United States has retained other rights. A set of inventions, highlighted by discoveries about yellow fever, presented the world with new property – a new bundle of ownership rights. The invention presented an ownership advantage to the inventing nation, and has since been the cause of international friction and the object of United States military strategic concern. The argument has been about sovereignty. Who claims to own the place has ever since been a central question.

The Republic of Panama is itself essentially a property invention. The Spanish recognized and exploited its value, first using it as a staging area for Francisco Pizarro's conquest of Peru. Then, for over 200 years, Panama was a principal shipping corridor for treasure en route to Spain. Panama enjoyed brief episodes of independence during the nineteenth century and often expressed rebelliousness against Colombian rule. Colombia claimed inheritance of the Isthmus, since Spain had designated Panama as part of the Viceroyalty of Nueva Granada in the early eighteenth century. Curious and ironic, the United States gained transportation rights across the Panama in 1846 in return for recognizing Colombian sovereignty there. One of the factors leading to Panamanian independence in 1903 was the lack of movement on the part of Colombia in negotiations with the United States over the digging of the canal.

Theodore Roosevelt wanted to shift the sharing of the bundle of rights associated with Panamanian geography in a way that would enable realization of the special advantage inherent in a transoceanic canal. With Panamanian independence, Colombia was the loser, but Colombia did not lose a canal. It lost the possibility of negotiating the financial value of the potential of a canal. Colombia also lost a measure of national honor. Colombia recouped part of the value by way of a cash payment in a later reconciliation treaty. The loss of national honor is still a sour memory, though it seems to serve Colombians well as a reminder to pay attention to their sovereignty. What sovereignty Colombia did lose was more intangible than tangible. The strategic importance of the geography has since changed, as has the identity (and cohesiveness of identity) of would-be owners. The canal is not as important an element of physical security of the United States as it once was. Meanwhile, many Panamanians have promoted a cohesive national identity around the idea that the canal is theirs. When the two countries complete the transferal of property rights as the 1979 Carter–Torrijos treaties prescribe, the Panamanians will be left with less than they figured to get. This will not be because of any perfidy or cheapness by the United States. It is because the value of the special property is still wrapped inseparably in a sharing of rights that involves the application of organizational as well as physical technologies. Panama, due to the nature of its society, probably cannot maintain the canal. Therefore, Panama cannot have a canal. Panama may be incapable of canal owning almost in the same way that Soviet society could not own the personal computer. Panamanians can claim sovereignty, but when the whole bundle of rights in the land is supposedly again theirs, they will have to look for another exchange relationship to preserve any of the special value of that sovereignty. They will have to rent, mortgage or contract away part of the bundle of rights.

As for the Colombians, the loss of the canal will continue to be a symbol of sovereignty lost to an ambitious and imperialistic United States, but they do not want Panama back. Interestingly, Colombian society is now capable of owning and running a transoceanic canal; Colombians have been investigating the possibility of installing one in northern Colombia. If they ever do so, they will have succeeded in retaking Panama (that is, in the economic sense of the original special value of that land). Colombians might then see Panama as having received the comeuppance for its rebellion.

2. The invention of the advanced communications satellite created special value in places called geostatic orbital spaces. The United States places satellites in these orbits to serve the communications needs of many countries. The satellites reside over a number of countries, mostly equatorial. At least one alert, nationalistic Colombian made note of imperialist arrogation by the United States of yet another chunk of Colombian sovereignty.[9] The suite of inventions and discoveries that allowed the placing of a satellite in geostatic orbit created new property, and by reference to existing international rules, it was natural to identify the property as Colombian. Colombia may be capable of running a transoceanic canal, but Colombia could not yet have produced original value in geostatic space. The Colombian government has not petitioned the United States about the offense, so it is not very consequential in terms of real world bilateral relations. In this case, Colombia did not lose much to US imperialism, but space property will cause frictions between other polities. Many world leaders predicted these competitions when space exploration became commonplace. In 1967, the United Nations succeeded in sponsoring the Outer Space Exploration Treaty, which theoretically turns space into global common property.

3. People around the world enjoy the Coca-Cola® formula. Coca-Cola®, including the whole array of inventions that accompany it, e.g. bottles and cans and caps and bubbles, have seemingly created ownership rights for Americans everywhere. These ownership relationships are recognized as so worth protecting that free trade and economic development are primary and explicit parts of every broad statement of American foreign policy. The rights involved are property. That is to say, they are rights associated with land. Coca-Cola®, as a company, exercises the right to come and go, to sell, to advertise, to contract, to enjoy the profits of its enterprise – in far off places. This is, in essence, the exercise of a slice of sovereignty. In order for Coca-Cola® to be allowed to operate in a foreign land, that land must have waived a right to deny access. Coke® must have been extended an invitation to share ownership – the right to exclusive use of the brand in China, or the right to sell at a profit in Thailand. Popular products have given Americans rights … and duties. Companies accept responsibility for a faulty product in other lands, disburse part of

the profits, and share in social programs. They have given Americans property in other lands. It is American, even if the only little slice really seen or enjoyed by an American citizen was a profit share on corporate stock. Nevertheless, that American stockholder owns a tiny piece of many foreign lands. This would not have been so if not for the invention of a good drink, or a computer chip or a potato chip. The foreign lands gain, too. They get to enjoy the product. The value of their sovereignty increases as much as America's.[10] It is no wonder that the Coca-Cola® corporation likes to advertise its role as a fluid for international cooperation and understanding. It is also no wonder that the Coca-Cola® sign is for many in the world a symbol of imperialism and a challenge to national sovereignty.

Foreign products irritate the nationalist, but such thinking is not good macroeconomics. It is tied to the emotion of sovereignty rather than to the reality. If someone really owns land, he can sell, sell part, contract out, rent, or offer to guests. In so doing, the value usually goes up. Conversely, if land cannot be shared or divested, it was not owned fully to begin with.

4. The internal combustion engine gave crude oil its worth. Without the constellation of inventions that made crude oil a resource, there would be little sovereignty in the Middle East to fight over. The English would not have encouraged any Arab nationalism, and Bedouins would still be poor Bedouins. A set of inventions created a new concert of rights in land for Westerners in the Middle East. While the most frequent occupiers of land may be accorded primary ownership rights, subsurface rights can be so important to the value of other sovereignties that an overly exclusive restriction in their exploitation is not going to be allowed. This is the case with major oil discoveries. The surface sovereign is welcome to grab what price the market will bear, but views about ownership that threaten to restrict the flow of oil will naturally invite challenges. In the Middle East, since the value of oil is based on the nature of the worldwide industrial economy, the global community will sense a right to it, barring application of purely dog-in-the-manger ownership theory. Some rights owe to the residents. However, it would have been very costly for the United States to insist that only US ships, or ships bound for the United States, could pass through the Panama Canal. It would be an even less supportable assertion of sovereignty for an oil-rich country to

place draconian restrictions on the exploitation of oil.

Debate about the necessity or morality of the 1991 Persian Gulf War included the question of Western and especially US motives. The United States government invoked the importance of recovering and defending Kuwaiti sovereignty as a lesson and precedent for world order – sovereignty of a small nation had to be protected in principle. The United States government admitted the importance of oil, but downplayed it in the justification for taking military action. Pundits smelled some inconsistency and moral hollowness. According to them, if Kuwait had had no oil, the United States would not have been so concerned about the principle of sovereignty. Looking at sovereignty in property terms puts another light on the question. Support of Kuwaiti sovereignty was not that far distant from fighting for oil. Protecting the property rights of the Kuwaitis meant protecting the sovereignty of many countries. Kuwaiti acceptance of international ownership relationships is more amenable to global property rights than would be the case under Saddam Hussein. Protecting the principle of sovereignty was significant, since protection of Kuwaiti sovereignty was tantamount to protection of the property rights of other countries. Property value made the difference. Would the international coalition have formed to defend the Kuwaitis' land if there was nothing much of worth there? Doubtful, but the value of Kuwaiti land is the value of technologies that describe Western culture. Without the historical course of Western inventions, Kuwait would not have been defended – or needed it, since it would not have been worth invading. Furthermore, since the nature of Western liberties and social values is so tied to the nature of our technologies, and since the functioning of those technologies is dependent in the short term on the flow of crude oil, there exists a logical nexus between the exercise of our liberties and access to oil. In other words, in a property sense, the short-term value of Western national sovereignty is closely related to access to other property – oil. Sovereignty is property ownership, and ownership is human rights. The United States need not have been so coy about fighting for oil. The United States government played unconstructively to the idealist vision of legitimacy, feeling it had to camouflage realist motives. When we recognize property and sovereignty as concerts of rights, however, realism and moral idealism are completely reconcilable. It becomes more obvious in this case, as in others, that

America's realist objectives deserved no shame.

The paragraphs above presented a single idea using four examples: control of yellow fever, the communications satellite, Coca-Cola®, and the internal combustion engine. A consequence of technological progress is the creation of new property, new concerts of rights and duties that can be associated with geography. In effect, invention creates new sovereignty and new fights along with it. Without incorporating the new property relationships caused by technologies, we could not discuss cogently the dynamic of geopolitics. The list of examples could go on and on. Treaties and other agreements on electromagnetic wavelengths and jamming are debated in relation to the broadcast of *T. V. Marti* to Cuba. Titanium in jet engines gives importance to the sovereignty of select African countries. Brazil and China dispute intellectual property rights. All involve rights and duties associated with invented property and all attract arguments of sovereignty. This is because sovereignty is ownership and ownership is what some inventions create across national boundaries – often in ways that national governments cannot anticipate or control. Technological change constantly presents us with something new to fight about.

TECHNOLOGY AND THE ABILITY TO PROTECT AND GAIN PROPERTY

> As science goes forward it distributes its uses both to those who destroy and to those who preserve.[11]   (Vannevar Bush, from *Modern Arms and Free Men*)

Innovations can decide the outcome of international struggles and greatly alter prospects in internal ones. In Chapter 5 the significant role of weaponry is considered, but here broader technological phenomena that threaten the state are mentioned. Indeed, there are a number of technologies available to the service of preserving the *status quo* of international sovereignty. More powerful, however, are trends working against current governments. Of these trends, two are paramount. One is the spread of communications technology that radically improves the chances that small groups can successfully aspire to statehood. The other is the growing global differential in innovativeness. Unevenness in the proclivity of peoples to invent spells long-term competitive failure for some states. Internal conflict is an urgent concern throughout the world. The feasibility of independent status is now apparent to countless micro-nations, and the requirements for international club membership are not especially odious. Meanwhile, an increasingly persuasive regime of international humanitarian law makes demands for self-determined autonomy harder not to accommodate. Political appeals can be broadcast discreetly, cheaply, immediately and worldwide. Separatism, insurgency, ethnic conflict, tribalism, environmentalism – whatever the label – the Internet and fax continue to amplify their voices.

As for those violent competitions that might yet occur between the established states of the existing international system, the acceleration of technological change seems to weigh insurmountable disadvantages against countries whose cultures are uninventive. The United States patent office has kept careful by-country records of all utility patents over many decades. These statistics, published by the Commerce Department, constitute a virtual registry of the world's new wealth and an indicator of global technological activity.[12] Organizational inventions and discoveries of natural resource deposits constitute new wealth not recorded by the Commerce Department for patent purposes, and the registry of patents doesn't weigh inventions according to their relative worth to mankind.[13] Nevertheless, taken together, these statistics are a powerful geographic description of the contribution to new material wealth in the world. A minority of countries led by the United States has registered the vast majority of patents in the last 30 years. Recent year statistics show improvements for some countries, notably Japan, but registrations from less developed countries are diminishing in number. Per capita patent earnings statistics heavily disfavor most of the world. Interestingly, the Swiss, rather than the Japanese, vie for top honors with the United States for per capita patent earnings. Russia has produced only a moderate number of patents, but could be expected to contribute more heavily in the future. Some country data clusters in a way that suggests a cultural dimension to the data results. For instance, many Latin American countries have similar patents per capita rankings in the midrange of patent-earning countries.

These statistics may support assessments beyond the intention of this book, but here the patent statistics offer a relative measure of the technological capacity of a country. The statistics provide insight into potential military power, and they can be correlated to military expenditures per military member to derive a comparison of the distance between technological capacity and the level of capitalization of an armed force. We would expect a country with no history of patent earnings to be underdeveloped technologically and to have little capability of maintaining or fully applying modern weapons without outside help from a technologically more advanced partner. If that country has a high index of military spending per soldier, it may indicate that it is providing its military with weaponry beyond the reach of its own technological capability, beyond the level of its civilian technological status. Oil-rich microstates, like Kuwait, have little domestic technological capacity, but they have armed their military with advanced weapons. These represent an extreme type.

Some governments, given the size of a country's economic and population base, may successfully fund a research and development sector capable of producing high-technology instruments. This ability resonates in the US Patent Office. But, even given an impressive ability to produce weapons, a society may not be advanced enough technologically to support broad weapons systems. In other words, a country might be able to fund research on an advanced jet design, but not be able to produce large numbers of qualified maintenance personnel. A suggestion of this disparity is evident if one looks at the amount spent on defense, per member of the military, in relation to per capita patent earnings. Australia, high in both capitalization of its force and in inventiveness, has armed its military force in line with its technological culture. We would expect countries like India to display great distance between capitalization of their armed forces and per capita patent earnings. This is indeed the case.[14]

In the sections above, selected innovations were artificially isolated to discuss their impact on the ownership environment and therefore on the nature of conflicts. Rather than as individual technologies, however, it is the combined, interrelated and interdependent march of innovation-driven change that most influences the form of conflict. Urbanization refers to perhaps the most widely recognized dynamic of technological change, one that creates new landscapes, new property, new owner groups and new quarrels. It is surprising and worrisome that analysis of urban armed conflict has been avoided by military strategists and international security specialists. With this in mind, the following sections address urbanization from a property bias.

URBANIZATION

> Walls and ditches were quite incapable of helping governments, which, after a decade or more of peace, allowed a coolness to grow between themselves and their peoples, and entrusted their strongholds to feeble governors.   (Christopher Duffy)[15]

Having stated that technology makes new sovereignty and changes owner relationships, it is natural that we turn our attention to the most obvious technological phenomenon – urbanization. Distinctive features of the largest or so-called 'world cities' include marked economic and social polarization and intense spatial segregation.[16] We also find what is probably an effect of these conditions: the complementary agendas and overlapping identities of a large array of anti-state actors. Anarchists, criminals, the dispossessed, foreign meddlers, cynical opportunists, lunatics, revolutionaries, labor leaders, ethnic nationals, and other activists can all form alliances of convenience. They can also commit acts of violence and handle ideas that provoke others. These ideas may be as specific as resisting a rise in bus fares, as immediate as an opportunity for looting following a mass celebration, or as broad as ethnic identity. Analyses that focus on a single strand of the fabric of violence – that isolate on ethnic rivalry, or Mafia, or revolutionary cadre as state threats – underestimate the disruptive power that those phenomena gain when they coincide. Troubles will not come as single soldiers; they will come in battalions. Our future promises complex competitions between agencies of the state and shifting combinations of challengers, especially in urban areas. The coming center of gravity of armed political struggles may be indigenous populations, youth gangs, drug cartels, foreign expatriates, or insurgents. But if we could identify a single focal point for urban violence, it would probably be an advanced form of organized crime. Patterns emerge in the nature of this organized crime that betray themselves under analyses of basic urban property.

Unique morphologic and demographic factors have a cause and effect relationship to urban-specific sociological phenomena. We can trace urbanized landscape forms and population shifts, as well as urban legal and psychological conditions, back to elements of technological processes. Any theory used to address human competitions in urban space – where physical description of the land is itself a complicated task – must incorporate the dynamics of technological change. Not only does the immediate physical condition of the space constrain human activities, but ongoing change in the conditions of the physical space constrains future activities. As such, it makes sense to look at the disciplines of architecture, engineering and city planning (as much as to criminology, law, or military studies) to discover the variables that will influence human conflict in urban areas. All these various disciplines can be subsumed under an urban geopolitic.

We can consider the specter of urban violence geopolitically – that is, as an interaction of terrain, demographic and political factors. Urban geographers visualize urban relationships in terms of space, territoriality, and distance.[17] Geopolitics for urban strife, however, needs to be downscaled from the continental reach of a Mackinderesque Heartland Theory. To help reconcile traditional geopolitics to urban morphology, we can apply lessons from the study of architecture and a legal understanding of property ownership. In shorthand, 'real estate' becomes the didactic key for resizing geopolitics to the urban scale. The changes of greatest importance to an interpretation of urban conflict are those that involve architectural change and change in real estate ownership. As urban geographer Paul Knox puts it, 'There is ... a constant restlessness to the built environment, as both simultaneous and sequential processes of investment, disinvestment, and reinvestment take place.'[18]

Ownership relationships reflect technological change and vice versa. For instance, if we accept barbed wire as a classic example of a simple invention that changed rural land use (closing the open range and sparking range wars), then the elevator provides an archetype for city growth – contributing as it did to the acceptance of tall buildings. Tall buildings allow higher population densities that engender other technologies that allow and encourage population density. Migrations to and coagulation within cities of groups with cohesive ethnic identities also contribute to territorial competition. Along with these changes in landscape, architecture and demographics comes an evolution of tenancy relationships, changed requirements for population control, and conflict.

Therefore, the geopolitics of urban strife must include investigation of the way in which property is owned and protected, as much as who owns it, or what the land looks like. Urban property analysis must consider the whole scope of ownership. It must consider the cohesiveness of owner identities and leadership. It must account for the property itself in broader than two-dimensional terms. Chapter 2 described the multitude of separable slices of rights that can be identified in a piece of urban land – rights that may be recorded and agreed upon in a variety of ways, both formal and informal. A typical area of urban soil may be the subject of water and sewage easements, occupier rights in condominium space, zoning ordinances limiting building height, unwritten drug marketing limits between street gangs, and corporate ownership of mortgages. We must see the property of urban geopolitics, therefore, as more than the surface area falling between latitudinal and longitudinal limits. It is ownership rights. These property rights and their values are reflected in broadly discernible, and mapable, land use and architectural types. Furthermore, conflicts that arise from property competitions may also be reflected by what urban geographers call the 'built environment'.

Population expansion and urbanization continue throughout the world.[19] Urban scenes have long been the focalpoint of organized political violence, of revolutionary theory, and of scholarly consideration of the same.[20] Recent indicators suggest that city venues for anti-state use of organized force may become still more commonplace. Nicaraguan revolutionary Tomas Borge, interviewed at the Mexico City airport on his way to Brazil for the second meeting of the Permanent Conference of Latin American Political Parties, said that armed struggle was no longer the way to seize power in the region.[21] At the same time, however, he noted that 'If the Latin American political leaders do not defend the interests of the people, the emergence of rebel groups in urban areas – as recently happened in Venezuela – cannot be prevented.'[22] We might take Borge's comment as a matter-of-fact observation about political realities in Latin American cities. We might also take it as a warning note implying a strategic analysis by the violent left that while rural Marxist guerrilla strategies may be obsolescent, there is great potential for translating urban misery into violent political action.

Isolating on any particular type of spatial setting has its limitations. We cannot theoretically wrench the city away from surrounding countryside and leave any conclusions logically complete. Indeed, rural-based revolutionary movements are not obsolete, as Mexican Zapatistas or Burmese Karen separatists will attest. In some cities, Bogota and Lima being clear examples, established leftist guerrilla groups with rural bases of support have mounted high profile challenge to the state.[23] Nevertheless, this book does not posit resurgence of the violent left as the centerpiece of future national security threats.[24] The violent political left will be but another, albeit formidable, actor in a full firmament of armed interests. We should also treat 'Insurgency' with caution. 'Insurgency' has grown doctrinaire barnacles. It would be incorrect to presume that an organized, armed group is a less dangerous entity because it does not have as its goal the overthrow of the state, or because it fails to assert a radical ideology. We should look at armed organizations without predicating that any realistic, strategic political goal or identifiable ideology be a prerequisite for serious consideration of that organization as a threat to the state.

Besides the characterization of violent actors, another of the difficulties in forming a geopolitical view of urban conflict is the gaseous definition of urbaness.[25] 'City' is a status awarded intuitively.[26] There are no clear numerical breakpoints between what constitutes a city and what does not, but the continuum of urban attributes is marked by various identifiable salients that change the nature of potential armed conflict. These include such obvious physical phenomena as subway systems, large public stadiums, or bypass highways. All of these have an effect on urban violence. Whatever the physical attributes of a populated area, it need not reach the status of 'world city' to be home to many of the same ingredients of violence. In addition to these directly observable attributes of urban size are several tangible qualities of the mind that affect the nature of organized conflict. For instance, the urban environment offers individual anonymity, a factor that can be of great use to the anarchist, but can also be of great use to government intelligence. In this regard, urban terrain, like any other, does not necessarily give advantage to any side in a political contest. It may present an advantage to the contestant that understands, adjusts, or adapts to it.[27]

URBAN CLAIMANTS

> Thieves respect property. They merely wish the property to become their property so that they may more perfectly respect it. (attributed to G.K. Chesterton)

In a huge city it is possible to unite and organize a club of identical triplets – or of psychopathic anarchists. Not only can individual members of a rare identity meet and communicate, they can find ways to communicate their solidarity discreetly. It is also possible, because of the nature of modern information media, for these rarities to project an image of commonness or great numbers. The public can interpret a high density of what would otherwise be statistical oddities into an influential sector. With an impression of strength, even a minuscule group can reach out to tap whatever marginal sympathies might exist in the larger population. The percentage of a population that involves itself in organized outlaw behavior need not be very great to present a dangerous threat to stability. Even while insurgent and counter-insurgent theories have hailed the need for public or mass support, many revolutionary organizations have survived year after year with the active support of very small fractions of the citizenry. On the other hand, an identity claiming support of only one-tenth of 1 per cent of 20 million persons still enjoys a base 20,000 strong.

Individuals are now empowered to service fractional, fleeting, even capricious parts of their own sympathies. People of every economic status can gain intelligence about rare identities and can translate support in perfectly discreet increments through the electronic transfer of funds, the writing of supportive letters, and so on. People who would never lend themselves fully to any given movement will, given the private opportunity, manifest a little support. This bit of support may run contrary to more dominant opinions and attitudes within the same head, but once all the little bits of uncertain or briefly impassioned support are collected and aggregated, they can lend surprising power to strange identities. This is the effect of the particularization of power and diffusion of ownership described previously.

Neither urban violence nor its leadership is limited to society's fringes. It can draw on the entire, broad range of urban dwellers. Participants, victims and audiences are likely to include all economic categories, all ages and both sexes. Some groupings of people merit special attention. Dispossessed, desperate masses may be the most obvious human dimension in the urban property struggle. In the Third World, these marginalized populations are growing in cities of all sizes, and apparently fastest in the largest cities.[28] Not only has the size of these masses been alarming, the rate of growth is a variable contributing to social strain. While there may be some correlation between economic growth and urbanization, there seems to be no demonstrable correlation between migration to the cities and improved economic well-being of the migrants in under-developed countries. 'This pessimistic picture poses the question of why urban population growth should be so high in countries that offer so little in their cities. The reason is, of course, that prospects are even worse in the countryside and it is the perceived advantages of the city that draw migrants to it.'[29]

Curiously, the political radical's presumption that all of these masses would be ripe for revolutionary behavior has not so far proven to be completely correct.[30] Still, while sweeping generalities about potential armies of dispossessed may be inaccurate, huge populations of poor and aspiring people are a factor in the potential for organized violence. Of particular importance is the geographic result of immense, under-serviced slums and shantytowns. The existence of a huge slum sanctuary apparently favors criminal organizations more than revolutionary ones. It is in the shantytown that, even without active support, a criminal organization can disappear behind the effects of intimidation and disaffection.

The linkage between organized criminals and insurgents has been a controversial topic. In the words of Carlos Marighella,

> The Urban Guerrilla ... differs radically from the outlaw. The outlaw benefits from the action, and attacks indiscriminately without distinguishing between the exploited and the exploiters, which is why there are so many ordinary men and women among his victims. The urban guerrilla follows a political goal and only attacks the government, the big capitalists, and the foreign imperialists, particularly North Americans.[31]

There may be some truth to Marighella's distinction, but it is an insignificant truth compared to the extensive involvement of supposedly principled revolutionaries in gangstering. The Colombian example is most convincing.[32] There, debate over the existence of a 'narcoguerrilla' is dead. Colombian guerrilla groups have long been engaged in a variety of common criminal endeavors including the drug trade. Drug cartels, meanwhile, have inserted themselves into the political environment. In either case, lack of a stable or well-articulated ideological azimuth by an armed group should not be cause for a depreciated status as a threat to governance. There may exist a presumption that organized criminal groups do not present as extensive a threat to a local or national government as does an insurgent force, but as French student of urban warfare Roger Trinquier warned, 'Even a band of gangsters, lacking any political ideology at all, but without scruples and determined to employ the same methods, could constitute a grave danger.'[33]

Perhaps more than the armed leftist movements of the past, large criminal organizations count on international connections, and have both the liquid financial resources and ruthlessness to directly corrupt government institutions.[34] Moreover, they are often guided by ethnic factors that lend another element of political friction to their growth.[35] In Latin America, and perhaps elsewhere, the post-Cold War generation of gangster leadership benefits from another coincidence – the jailing of Marxist revolutionaries during the 1960s and 1970s. Many members of the current generation of organized criminal leaders learned from co-incarceration with Marighella's lieutenants, jailed Tupamaros or captured Senderistas. Prison stays became a seminar for the criminal, given by the revolutionary, in proven anti-state tactics including kidnapping, bank robbing, clandestine organization, recruiting, and, of course, mob behavior and control.

Latin American cities are seeing a resurgence in the mobilization or manipulation of students in support of political demands. Novel, perhaps, in this resurgence is a greater emphasis on organizing high school as opposed to university age students. This is probably due to a more politically moderate character of many university student bodies, and to the traditionally leftist political leanings of teacher unions and state ministries of education. The urban violence in Venezuela, to which Tomas Borge alluded, seems to have its focus in the public high schools.[36] Street violence caused by high school students in Guatemala City was a catalyst for the events that led immediately to the closure of Congress and attempted *auto-golpe* (self-coup) of President Jorge Serrano in 1993.[37]

More than just a shift from college-age to younger teen-age mass support, there is a remarkable involvement of children in several dimensions of urban violence. Street gangs in all parts of the world have been known for their Faginesque hierarchies. In the United States, notorious street gangs, such as the Los Angeles Crips, involve children from 10 or 11 years old who serve as couriers and lookouts.[38] In Latin America, organized use of children by criminal groups is not something unique to the city, but the city does provide criminal and revolutionary leaders an exploitable quantity of un- or under-parented youth. In Brazil, for instance, investigators claim there are millions of orphaned children.[39] In Rio de Janeiro, drug gangs provide employment and protection for many street youths.[40] Children represent the ultimately dispossessed. A gang leader can provide an abandoned or under-parented child not only with protection they are denied, but also with a hope for material success, personal fulfillment and social respect – all without having to go to school. Often, a child's entire enculturation may occur within the parameters of criminal society. Thus, battle lines are drawn that have generational, territorial, and anti-state dimensions.

Another major participant in potential urban disorder is the trade union.[41] Unions in Latin America are maturing in their international reach and benefiting from changes in human rights and political participation advances in most countries. The relationship that some labor organizations have to popular political movements has many current examples across the hemisphere. Ecuador's labor tribulations may be instructive. There, the Confederation of Ecuadorean Indigenous Nationalities (Confederación de Nacionalidades Indígenas del Ecuador, 'Conaie') mounted a virtual Indian uprising to resist changes in rural land ownership brought on by a new agricultural development law (these changes are similar to those opposed by the Chiapas-based Zapatistas in Mexico). The major Ecuadorean labor affiliation, United Workers Front (Frente Unitario de Trabajadores, FUT) threatened a general strike and mounted stoppages in support of Indian demands, and as a timing strategy to make wage demands. Environmental protection groups have come down on the side of the Indians, and the Church has participated as mediator while showing a clear preference for the Indians.[42] Some mobilization of the Ecuadorean military was necessary to open a few urban areas, though a more widespread confrontation between the military and labor organizations did not occur. In summary, labor organizations, whose demands are generally related to higher wages, call on support of many dwellers of the same neighborhoods where organized crime takes hold. Trade unions are vulnerable to influence and control by organized crime, and their actions obey correlations of forces that include seemingly unrelated organizations and movements – but that all carefully monitor the minute-to-minute vulnerability of the state.

URBAN TERRAIN

> To speak of innovation and growth is obviously to suggest that cities change through time. Yet there is a sense in which they are also imprisoned in their own past. For they cannot be built anew to adopt the technology and suit the needs of each new era. (James Heilbrun, from *Urban Economics and Public Policy*)

We could refer to urban geopolitics as the architecture of ownership, since architecture and city planning have grown so close. Architect and political activist Mike Davis offers an intriguing appraisal of the future of urban struggles.[43] Davis examines the determinants and consequences of the Los Angeles riots and the status of American urban life from an architect's viewpoint. He draws on the work of Ernest Burgess of the University of Chicago School of Sociology who in the 1930s drew a spatial model of the modern city. The model is formed of concentric rings in which are located types of community or function. The dartboard-like model displays Burgess's generalized interpretation of Chicago life.[44] These generalizations regarding relationships between urban location and human activity became an influential theory, one that today would be very understandable to the geopolitician. For Davis the architect, it served to guide his observations about violence in Los Angeles.

Davis dedicates a significant portion of his observations to the architecture of control. He points out that fear of a repeat of the 1965 Watts Riots counseled planners of Los Angeles' new downtown business core. He writes:

> Key to the success of the entire strategy (celebrated as Downtown L.A.'s 'renaissance') was the physical segregation of the new core and its land values behind a rampart of regraded palisades, concrete

pillars and freeway walls. Traditional pedestrian connections between Bunker Hill and the old core were removed, and foot traffic in the new financial district was elevated above the street on pedways whose access was controlled by the security systems of individual skyscrapers. This radical privatization of Downtown public space – with its ominous racial undertones – occurred without significant public debate or protest.[45]

Whatever else one might say about the social or financial determinants of the Los Angeles business core architecture, it worked to secure the district from the 1992 riots.

> By flicking a few switches on their command consoles, the security staffs of the great bank towers were able to cut off all access to their expensive real estate. Bullet-proof steel doors rolled down over street-level entrances, escalators instantly stopped and electronic locks sealed off pedestrian passageways. As the *Los Angeles Business Journal* recently pointed out in a special report, the riot-tested success of corporate Downtown's defenses has only stimulated demand for new and higher levels of physical security.[46]

The architecture of security (or control) has many more common and less ambitious manifestations than the core of downtown Los Angeles. Gated neighborhoods are an example that is familiar to Latin Americanists and one that has come comparatively late to communities in the United States. It is an extrapolation of the walled residence, which is a cultural standard in Latin America and a depressing prediction for the United States. This trend has been labeled the 'landscape of fear' and 'can become something of a self-fulfilling prophecy, in which the belief that places are unsafe both deters the deterrent presence of the law-abiding and attracts potential lawbreakers'.[47] Paradoxically, 'The more security is sought by physical protection against the city outside, the less powerful are the social controls upon that city, and thus more unsafe it becomes.'[48] Students of Latin America require no proof that these observations about US cities can be applied elsewhere.

Monied interests in the Third World continue to isolate, physically and socially, the sprawling poor communities. These communities then become independent of mainstream state control as criminal organizations secure loyalties, impose law and order, provide justice, and offer economic opportunities within identifiable physical borders. The shantytowns become separately governed areas. They mark the physical dimensions of what in some ways are autonomous nations within nations. At some point, a government will view their leadership as a national security threat rather than merely a public security threat. Therein lies their geopolitical importance.

URBAN OWNERSHIP RULES

> It should be borne in mind that zoning regulations arise from the political process and are not the work of omniscient planners. (Werner Z. Hirsch, from *Urban Economics*)

As Davis points out, the walled community has its parallel expressions in legal contraptions.[49] In Los Angeles, zoning has advanced to include abatement zones that extend police powers to control nuisances, such as graffiti or prostitution; enhancement zones near schools and other institutions (where criminal penalties are increased for crimes such as drug dealing); containment districts created to control pests (like the Mediterranean fruit fly); and exclusion zones.[50] The latter exclude selected groups like campers or gang members from park or business areas. Davis calls these examples of 'status criminalization' where group membership, even in the absence of a specific criminal act, has been outlawed. Of course, we might call the criminal act 'trespass', and that is precisely the property question – what kinds of preferential ownership can be maintained? The constitutional strength and therefore the practical application of many control devises in US cities may be questionable, but their growth can be a guide to urban futures everywhere. Most of the new exclusion zone types are designed against two categories of persons – street gangs and the homeless (that is, the potential squatter). In most cities around the world, territorial (organized criminal or gang) control of urban neighborhoods, and invasion of open plots by would-be homesteaders are constant realities.

In addition to the formal rules of urban ownership, only a few of which have been mentioned, we must add urban criminal boundaries, which establish the geographic applicability of select rights for and against outlaw groups. These gang boundaries have counterparts in more traditional business practices. Sales territories, paper routes, or trademark limits differ from street gang borders in their written formality and management of violence, but they do similar things. They define access to precise areas for certain activities.

Money questions, like legalities, cannot be separated from the physical and social aspects of urban terrain, and are intimately tied to conditions for urban conflict. Paul Knox states:

> Another important dimension of the emergent geography of American cities is the way in which the different combinations of money capital and cultural capital associated with class fractions give rise to preferences for architectural style, residential milieu and work environments.[51]

In the same anthology, in a chapter titled 'Cycles and Trends in the Globalization of Real Estate', John Logan stresses the importance of understanding the 'securitization' of real estate.[52] The term is not a reference to physical security. He notes that, like stocks and bonds, mortgages can be traded through semi-public agencies which buy home mortgages in bulk then sell bonds based on the value of the mortgages. Securitization is just that process – converting an asset (homes or other real estate) into a financial obligation that has identifiable characteristics and can be rated as to its investment risk in capital markets. This phenomenon is one key to operationalizing a 'geoproperty' approach to modern urban conflict. The market value of real property becomes increasingly well-defined on the map. It shows neighborhood property value significant to an owner group far larger than the set of dwellers in that neighborhood.

Therefore, sophisticated extortionists can aim the threat to diminish real estate value at absentee owner audiences – even international audiences. The constituency interested in the physical security and control of real estate includes investors whose financial well-being follows insurance, interest and bond rates that are in turn affected by threats and violent actions against or even near their properties. This larger owner reality will guide both intuitive and explicit conflict planning. Astute criminal or outlaw-political leaders conduct strategic extortion against these larger owner targets. Mortgage interests matter even on a modest geographical scale. A simple wall around a gated community – that is, the fortress architecture, finds its funding beyond the collaboration of neighbors. The wall has become an initial funding requirement by corporate insurers of the mortgages. As such, a violent group can wield leverage against a consensus-led set of private, semi-private, or government entities interested in preserving market values of real property.

We noted how differences in priorities for land use affect its perceived value. Environmentalists will be at odds with the coal miners, hermits at odds with restaurateurs, over the priority of values to be assigned specialized rights in a piece of land. For some groups of owners, especially those seeking profitability, giving away rights in land can often raise value. The owner of a restaurant accrues the full worth of his property only if he is willing to give up his right to deny access. Related to these points is the often observed but neglected aspect of modern war just mentioned. Outlaws take action against the value of property, against the value of the ownership rights as prioritized by their enemy owner. Guerrillas may blow up a high-tension tower or a telephone exchange box to reduce the indices of value of property. This war against sovereign value is obviously more effective where the process of urbanization, the application of capital-intense technologies, or the sharing of rights to accrue greater profitability, are greatest.

FORMS OF URBAN VIOLENCE

> You may buy land now as cheap as stinking mackerel.
> (Shakespeare's Falstaff on the consequences of internal war, *Henry IV*, Part 1)

The foregoing paragraphs painted a mixture of potential participant identities in anti-state violence. The built environment, as well as legal and financial regimes, contribute to the nature of urban violence. Property determinants will be causes for violence, objects of violence, and delimiters of violence. They will also guide violent strategies. Many city-suitable, violent approaches for achieving political leverage exist. Some are associated almost exclusively with cities while others are more broadly applied. The standard terrorist approach has been labeled the 'strategy of recognition' and defined as the rational use of violence to convey a message.[53] 'The strategy requires a continuous cycle of three sequential events: an outrageous act staged in a way that carries a message, a subsequent international news story about the act that conveys the message, and consideration of the message by an international audience.'⁵⁴ Perhaps an international audience is not required, but achievement of international attention is definitely one measure of the success of a recognition strategy.

A related strategy is to provoke overreaction by the government security forces, thereby causing public and international outrage.⁵⁵ This technique is familiar in smaller, isolated urban areas. Masses of (usually) unarmed people confront small military or police outposts and demand their withdrawal or the surrender of their weapons. This mob provocation technique is harder to use in larger urban areas where police and military reinforcements are quickly available. Next is the use of kidnapping and bank robbing to support other aspects of an armed movement. The most direct use of terror is to eliminate local leaders. This technique has the dual benefits of physically eliminating unsupportive opinion leaders in the community and terrorizing any would-be replacements into either leading in the preferred direction or abandoning the idea of leadership altogether. These techniques are well known and proven. Less understood is the use of the mob. Mobs, even when none exists, provide leverage to leaders able to credibly claim the potential to incite, mollify, direct, disperse, or abort a mass gathering of people. As E.J. Hobsbawm pointed out three decades ago, mob leadership is not only worthy of respect, mob control may constitute a precursor to more formal and ideologically directed movements.⁵⁶ Fear of the mob, more than fear of individual acts of terrorism, may be what drives the physical 'landscape of fear' mentioned earlier.

> The reaction of the authorities to riot, or in the longer term to the fear of the possibility of riot, has throughout much of urban history been either to fortify refuges within the city (the 'citadel solution') or to remove themselves from the city, or from parts of it where the actions of the mob were most prevalent (the 'Versailles solution'). The former option was adopted by the Norman conquerors of eleventh-century England, where the castle on its motte was designed to protect the new government from the existing citizens and to cow the city into submission rather than protect it from external attack. Such a use of the castle was as much the rule as the exception through much of the Middle Ages. London's Tower, Paris's Bastille, Utrecht's Vredenburg, and many other such citadels, sheltered the urban government against enraged citizens whose lawlessness was allowed to burn itself out in the town outside.⁵⁷

Criminal organizations can make a credible claim to mob control. As Davis mentions in reference to the Los Angeles gangs, 'Yet if the riot had a broad social base, it was the participation of the gangs – or rather their cooperation – that gave it [the L.A. riots] constant momentum and direction'.[58]

The reaction to rioting is to try, when prevention fails, to isolate the mob, keep it away from key areas, or to disperse it. As noted by Ashworth, it is here that the morphology of the city is especially influential. For instance, if police can push or scatter a mob (with water cannon or gas, for instance) from an open area such as a plaza, the street pattern leading from the plaza often causes the mob to break up. In Latin America, while the symbolic 'taking' of a central plaza is still a common mass event in some countries, mob behavior in many cities reflects thoughtful strategic leadership. Large demonstrations temporarily close targets, such as vehicle arteries passing nearby a shantytown sanctuary, causing public displeasure and a palpable economic cost. By the time security forces arrive, the mob has dispersed and disappeared into the santuary. The act ably demonstrates power in the hands of strategic extortionists against the government.

Government mob control is best mounted before the mob exists, and government blundering can be as important to the existence of a mob as any supposed mob leadership. The 1993 Los Angeles riots provide another excellent example.[59]

> People were initially shocked by the violence, then mesmerized by the televised images of biracial crowds in South Central L.A. helping themselves to mountains of desirable goods without interference from the police. The next day, Thursday, April 30, the authorities blundered twice: first by suspending school and releasing kids into the streets; second by announcing that the National Guard was on the way to help enforce a dusk-to-dawn curfew.
>
> Thousands immediately interpreted this as a last call to participate in the general redistribution of wealth in progress.[60]

THE URBAN GUERRILLA

Men are not made for safe havens.[61] (Robert F. Kennedy)

The garrisoning, provisioning, and equipping of high towers is sometimes but pandering to pride. And it sometimes happens that even when men build high towers and great fortresses, at much cost and with untold labor, when they are completed they are not worth a straw, unless they be defended by true friends, who are both old and wise. And understand well that the greatest and strongest garrison a powerful man may have, as well to defend his person as his property, is the love of his vassals and his neighbors. For Tullius says that there is a kind of garrison which no man can vanquish or disperse, and that is the love of a lord's own citizens and people. (Prudence, in Geoffrey Chaucer's *Tale of Melibeus*)

In the taxonomy of urban violence, 'urban guerrilla' seems to enjoy the highest status, though there is some debate about whether or not there even is such a thing.[62] Ignoring that debate, we can find lessons on the tactical consequences of correctly interpreting urban property factors from events in recent urban guerrilla history. Below are a few examples, the first taken from the period of urban guerrilla war experienced in Guatemala in the latter half of 1981 and the early months of 1982.[63]

With a boost from information provided by a neighbor's domestic employee, the Guatemalan Army intelligence service assaulted and destroyed an important guerrilla safehouse in an exclusive residential zone of the capital. From information gained in that assault, the army quickly took another house, then another. In quick succession, based mostly on interrogations, the army took more than 15 safe houses in a period of one month, and approximately 20 more houses were shut down during the ensuing four months. Intelligence came mostly from informants, though some technical intelligence was also used. For instance, it is said that extraordinary electric power usage late at night (used to run propaganda presses) in selected residential areas was a tip-off in more than one case. However, bad security on the part of the guerrillas, due to overconfidence born from several years of invisibility, was the most important contributor to the virtual end of guerrilla presence in the Guatemalan capital. As Abraham Guillen writes in 'Urban Guerrilla Strategy' in critiquing the Uruguayan Tupamaros:

> When urban guerrillas lack widespread support because of revolutionary impatience or because their actions do not directly represent popular demands, they have to provide their own clandestine infrastructure by renting houses and apartments. By tying themselves to a fixed terrain in this way, the Tupamaros have lost both mobility and security: two prerequisites of guerrilla strategy. In order to avoid encirclement and annihilation through house-to-house searches, the guerrillas can best survive not by establishing fixed urban bases, but by living apart and fighting together.[64]

In Guatemala, the urban guerrillas apparently made exactly the mistake that Guillen alludes to. It was a mistake with disastrous strategic consequences for the revolutionary enterprise.[65] Had the Guatemalan guerrillas been able to sustain themselves within an expansive and impenetrable slum like those found in the larger capitals of Latin America, the results of the Guatemalan insurgency might have been different.

A 1985 attack by the M-19 guerrilla group on the Colombian Palace of Justice (supreme court building) provides another example of the relation that the urban geopolitical factors ultimately have on the course of violent crises once they occur. It appears that immediacies of a guerrilla–drug relationship, combined with an impatient revolutionary timetable, were behind the M-19 decision to attack. After the guerrillas took the court building located at the geographical heart of Bogota (and, for that matter, the political heart of Colombia), Colombian military intelligence identified a threat of mass demonstrations along the approaches to the city center.[66] According to Colombian military officers, a plan was in place to support the guerrilla takeover with a mob presence. In this light, military commanders sought the most rapid movement of troops to the scene possible, and an immediate resolution of the crisis. Such a resolution was achieved. Consequences included the death of almost the entire membership of the Colombian Supreme Court and destruction of a large part of the M-19 leadership. Had the coincidences of timing been different, had a mob formed before the deployment of troops to the palace, and had then President Belisario Betancour attempted to negotiate a settlement with the guerrillas, there might have been a military coup. As it occurred, a new convergence of interests of drug dealer and guerrilla seems to have had one of its first major effects. As well, the morphology of Bogota's urban center determined timing decisions because of the associated mob threat. Distance along principal roadways between the guerrilla occupation site and military garrisons, the location and availability of mass public transportation, and the existence of open space near the city plaza invited a decision for immediate, violent action.

In 1991, San Salvador suffered a major guerrilla offensive by the Marxist FMLN. From this battle came an inside look at the FMLN urban guerrilla tactical doctrine.[67] As would be expected, the FMLN had observed special architectural characteristics in residential areas where they expected to enjoy the greatest support. Their written doctrine called for tunneling from building to building through adjacent walls in low rent housing areas to provide covered internal lines. It also showed a sophisticated block defense arrangement and defense in depth of residential neighborhoods. Urban doctrine or not, the offensive was a failure, at least in the immediate military sense, but some phenomena of the battle support the points raised earlier. For instance, the FMLN made widespread use of young (8–13-year-old) children for a variety of combat support and at times combat chores. In addition, many front groups working in San Salvador, misled by hopeful thinking that the offensive would lead to a general, mass uprising, abandoned their civilian cover to instead take armed positions behind guerrilla barricades. The San Salvador example unites the importance of building design, supportive neighborhoods, and participation of diverse groups of people, especially children.

Examples above show a relationship between geopolitical factors at a metropolitan scale – urban landscape, demographics, and political challenges. Revolutionary guerrillas in Guatemala could not tap the advantages of a shantytown urban sanctuary. In Colombia, guerrilla timing failed to secure mob support for a terrorist occupation. In San Salvador, the guerrilla more successfully identified the psychological advantages of the poor neighborhoods, studied architectural specifics for military application, and involved children. While the examples are of revolutionary groups acting in the context of the Cold War, the mix of lessons still applies to the future of urban violence dominated by criminal organizations rather than by leftist revolutionaries. Criminal organizations have shown a greater intuitive understanding of the security inherent in the development of virtual liberated zones in slum neighborhoods. They have also been able to lure children into the criminal culture, and to master the strategic management of mobs. Most of all, freer from ideological abstractions, the criminal organization is closer to the bottom-line – who owns what and where the boundaries are.

This chapter described technology as property and as an influence on property – in the manner of individual inventions, groups of inventions or as a complex evolutionary processes. One message is that our inventiveness will continue to create some property conflicts as fast as it helps us resolve others. How we understand power, then, depends on a grasp of the relationship of ownership and technology.

NOTES

1. James Burke, *Connections: An Alternative View of Change*, BBC TV and Time-Life Media.
2. Ronald Reagan, 'Address to the Nation', 23 March 1983, *Weekly Compilation of Presidential Documents*, 28 March 1983, 19, 12 (1983), p. 442. This major address by the president, which became known as the 'Star Wars' speech, radically altered the strategic defense debate by rejecting mutually assured deterrence and self-imposed nuclear vulnerability. President Reagan committed American strategic vision, in theory at least, to technological defense.
3. Ronald Reagan, 'Speech to the National Association of Evangelicals', Annual Convention, Orlando, Florida, 8 March 1983, *Weekly Compilation of Presidential Documents*, 14 March 1983, 19, 12, p. 364. Given only two weeks before his 'Star Wars' address, President Reagan's speech before the Evangelicals Association renewed and accentuated debate on the nature of the US – USSR ideological competition. 'I urge you beware the temptation of pride – the temptation of blithely declaring yourselves above it all and label both sides equally at fault, to ignore the facts of history and the aggressive impulses of an evil empire, to simply call the arms race a giant misunderstanding and thereby remove yourself from the struggle between right and wrong and good and evil.'
4. Henry Fords of the computer generation, Stephen Wozniak and Steve Job built their Apple I® computer in 1975, then in 1977 introduced the Apple II®, which would finally bring computing to the masses.
5. 'That the Second Amendment recognized an individual right to keep and bear arms was not an issue for partisan politics, and the courts consistently so held. The only exception to the rule appeared in the context of slavery. Specifically, in order to disarm slaves as well as black freemen, certain courts originated the view that the guarantee was limited to citizens rather than to all of the people and that the Second Amendment did not apply to the states. The exceptions were aberrations intended to prevent black liberation.' Stephen P. Halbrook, *That Every Man Be Armed: The Evolution of a Constitutional Right* (San Francisco, CA: Liberty Tree Press, 1984), p. 89.
6. Colombian police reported that in 1992 there were 28,237 murders including 102 massacres where more than four were killed. That is 77 murders per day or 86 murders per 100,000 population. The Ministry of Health used a lower figure of 21,560 violent deaths. According to the report, the Latin American average is 17

murders per 100,000. 'Murders Increasing at over 4% a Year', *Latin American Weekly Report*, 6 May 1993, p. 203. The *Latin American Weekly Report* article also claims that only 15 per cent of the murders in Colombia are associated with the guerrilla war there. Also from the article – 1,320 abductions in 1992, mostly for ransom; see also Douglas Farah, 'Colombia's Violence, Before and After Escobar: Narco-Terrorism is just the Latest Chapter in the Country's Long History of Violence', *The Washington Post National Weekly Edition*, 13–19 December 1993, p. 15; Interestingly, even in Colombia, more people still die of vehicle accidents than of any other un-natural cause. 'Morir sobre ruedas' (Dying on Wheels), *Semana*, 20 July 1993, p. 44.
7. There is one major study that describes foreign gun cultures (Japan, Great Britain, Canada, Australia, New Zealand, Jamaica, Switzerland) and analyzes aspects of America's gun history to compare the American experience to that of other nations. It is David B. Kopel, *The Samurai, the Mountie, and the Cowboy: Should America Adopt the Gun Controls of Other Democracies?* (Buffalo, NY: Prometheus Books, 1992). Kopel's discussion of foreign experiences with gun control suggests important answers about the relationship of gun control measures to overall social control and to internal violence. Responsible gun ownership is probably a more important ingredient than restriction of gun ownership in achieving social peace or the promotion of liberty.
8. Some mention of the Panama Canal is mandatory for a book that pretends to discuss international politics in terms of property. 'Apart from wars, it represented the largest, most costly single effort ever before mounted anywhere on earth. It held the world's attention over a span of 40 years. It affected the lives of tens of thousands of people at every level of society and of virtually every race and nationality. Great reputations were made and destroyed. For numbers of men and women it was the adventure of a lifetime. Because of it, one nation, France, was rocked to its foundation. Another, Colombia, lost its most prized possession, the Isthmus of Panama. Nicaragua, on the verge of becoming a world crossroads, was left to wait for some future chance. The Republic of Panama was born. The United States was embarked on a role of global involvement.' David McCullough, *The Path Between the Seas: The Creation of the Panama Canal* (New York: Simon & Schuster, 1977), p. 11; see also Darrell Hevenor Smith, *The Panama Canal: Its History, Activities and Organization* (Baltimore, MD: Johns Hopkins University Press, Institute for Government Research, Service Monographs of the United States Government, No. 44, 1927).
9. Jose Roberto Ibañez Sánchez, *Teoría del Estado, Geopolítica y Geoestrategia* (Bogotá: Imprenta y Publicaciones de las Fuerzas Militares, 1985), p. 185.
10. On this matter see the movie *One Two Three*, starring James Cagney and Horst Buchholz, directed by Billy Wilder, MGM United Artists release 1961.
11. Vannevar Bush, *Modern Arms and Free Men* (New York: Simon & Schuster, 1949), p. 263. 'The course of history is determined by the faith that men are guided by. If they misread the lessons of expanding knowledge and in their brazen egoism believe that all things are known or knowable, then they will see nothing but an endlessly repeating pattern of sordid strife, the ascendancy of ruthlessness and cunning, a little time on an earth where there is nothing higher than to seize and kill and dominate. If they see beyond this they will see by faith, and not by reading instruments or combining numbers.' Ibid.
12. US Patent and Trademark Office, *All Technologies Report, January 1963–June 1992*, 1992; *Patent Counts By Country/State and Year, Utility Patents, January 1993–June 1992*, Office of Information Systems – OEIPS/TAF Program, 1992.
13. Comments from the program brochure of the Patent and Trademark Office's Technology Assessment and Forecast program provide a summary of the potential power and the doubt regarding patent office statistics. 'This apparent relationship between technological and patent activity gave rise to the basic premise of the

Technology Assessment and Forecast program – that patent activity is an indicator of technological activity, both domestic and foreign ... As a new tool, the parameters of appropriate use of patent data, the limitations and strong points, have not been well established and are themselves the subject of discussion and study ... It may be, as some allege, that patenting trends are more indicative of the health of the patent system than of the health of technology.' Patent and Trademark Office, *Technology Assessment and Forecast Program Brochure* (Washington, DC: US Department of Commerce, 1992).
14. Geoffrey Demarest, 'Patent Earnings and Military Power', *Arms Control*, 14/3 (December 1993), p. 440. Patent earning statistics may be an overrated gauge of military power, but they are compelling. 'The nature of modern technological war has placed military size in deference to questions of technological capacity. It may be illuminating that a single data source, in this case US patent statistics, may gauge a country's dependence on foreign military technology and its ability to conduct modern war. Insight into which countries will or will not be competitive militarily in the foreseeable future is perhaps found in the patents earnings tables. A few countries have entered the group of patent producing countries in the past two decades, but the trend is against the great majority of nations.' Ibid.
15. Christopher Duffy, *Siege Warfare: The Fortress in the Early Modern World 1494–1660* (London: Routledge, 1996), p. 247.
16. Paul L. Knox, *Urbanization: An Introduction to Urban Geography* (Englewood Cliffs, NJ: Center for Urban & Regional Studies, Virginia Polytechnic Institute and State University, Prentice-Hall, 1994). This social and economic polarization and spacial segregation involves 'a growing international elite, dominated by a transnational producer-service class (in law, banking, insurance, business services, accounting, engineering, advertising, and so on; pronounced inner-city gentrification and development for luxury use; a large informal economy; and a large and growing class of multiply disadvantaged people', p. 62.
17. Ibid., p. v.
18. Ibid., p. 177.
19. John H. Kasarda, *Third World Cities: Problems, Policies and Prospects* (Newbury Park, CA: Sage Publications, 1993). 'Contemporary and projected aggregate increments of urban population in developing regions are nothing short of breathtaking. In 1950, only 285 million people, or 16 per cent of the developing world's population, resided in urban places. By 1990 this number had multiplied five-fold to 1.5 billion urban residents, making up 37 per cent of the total population in developing countries. The United Nations (UNDIESA 1991) projects that during the next 35 years the urban population of the developing countries will triple again, reaching 4.4 billion in 2025. At that time, four of every five urban dwellers in the world will be in countries currently classified as developing, and within these countries, about two in three people (61 per cent) will be urban.' Ibid., p. ix.
20. For observations on urban guerrilla war by South American revolutionary Abraham Guillen, see *Philosophy of the Urban Guerrilla: the Revolutionary Writings of Abraham Guillen* (New York: Morrow, 1973); 'Urban Guerrilla Strategy', in Gerard Chaliand, ed., *Guerrilla Strategies: An Historical Anthology from the Long March to Afghanistan* (Berkeley: University of California Press, 1982); and in Walter Laqueur, *The Guerrilla Reader: A Historical Anthology* (Philadelphia, PA: Temple University Press, 1977), p. 230; see also Mario Orsolini, *Montoneros: Sus Proyectos y Sus Planes* (Buenos Aires: Círculo Militar, 1989); James Kohl and John Litt, *Urban Guerrilla Warfare in Latin America* (Cambridge, MA: The MIT Press, 1974); Brian Michael Jenkins, *An Urban Strategy for Guerrillas and Governments* (Santa Monica, CA: The Rand Corporation, 1972). For an example of a practical manual in English on urban violence, see Urbano, *Fighting in the Streets: A Manual of Urban Guerrilla Warfare* (Fort Lee, NJ: Barricade Books, 1991).

21. The Permanent Conference of Latin American Political Parties is a post-Cold War open forum of leftist parties, many with historic roots in violent political expression.
22. 'FSLN's Borge Sees Passing of Armed Struggles in Region', PA0811192993 Mexico City NOTIMEX in Spanish, 1819 GMT, 6 November 1993, as translated in FBIS-LAT-93-215, 9 November 1993.
23. 'Guerrilla: Del monte a la ciudad' (Guerrillas: From the Mountain to the City), *Semana*, 12 October 1993, p. 44; Wilson Ring, 'Guatemalan Guerrillas Take Fight Close to Cities', *Washington Post*, 17 April, 1990, p. A-18; Sally Bowen, 'Peru's "Shining Path" Presses War in Capital As Public Doubts Grow', *Christian Science Monitor*, 31 July 1992, pp. 1, 4; '"Red Path" Seeks To Gain "Strategic Balance"', Lima, *Expreso*, in Spanish, 4 May 1994 as translated in FBIS-LAT-94-093, 13 May 1994. According to this report, remnant Shining Path ('Sendero Luminoso') dissidents were organizing in a number of Lima's outskirt shantytowns. Their aim was to recover the strategic balance lost after Sendero Luminoso leader Abimael Guzman fell.
24. See, however, Jorge G. Castaneda, *Utopia Unarmed: The Latin American Left After the Cold War* (New York: Alfred Knopf, 1993) for a vision regarding the future energies of leftist politics in the Hemisphere; see 'Renace la izquierda?' (Rebirth of the Left?) Bogotá, *Semana*, 9 November 1993, p. 88, for a broad critique of Castaneda's prediction of a potent non-violent influence for the far left.
25. See David Drakakis Smith, *The Third World City* (New York: Routledge, 1990), p. 2. 'It must be admitted at the outset that there is little homogeneity in the nature of urban growth in the Third World, and this is perhaps not surprising in view of the large number and varied nature of the countries involved ... This diversity also extends to definitions of what is "urban" or what constitutes a "city". In an effort to overcome such variations the United Nations has standardized its data to recognize settlements of over 20,000 people as "urban", of more than 100,000 as "cities" and of more than 5 million as "big cities"'; see also Martin T. Cadwaller, *Urban Geography* (Englewood Cliffs, NJ: Prentice-Hall, 1985), p. 19. 'The subject matter of this book is not easily defined, as it is sometimes difficult to distinguish between urban and rural settlements. This difficulty is reflected by the wide variation in population sizes used by different countries in order to categorize urban as opposed to rural settlements. In Sweden and Denmark, for example, settlements of only 200 people are counted as urban, whereas in Japan settlements have to contain at least 30,000 people before they are designated as urban. These different definitions make it difficult to compare levels of urbanization across countries.' Ibid. It is not even to be presumed that the first societies were agricultural/rural and that follow-on societies were urban. Convincing arguments have been put forward that the first societies may have been urban/craft and that early agriculture developed in cities. See Powelson, *The Story of Land*, p. 3.
26. See Gerald Michael Greenfield, ed., *Latin American Urbanization* (Westport, CT: Greenwood Publishing Group, 1994) for an up-to-date, encyclopedic treatment of major Latin American urban areas. For a penetration into the cultural bases of Latin American urban tragedy and survival, see Alma Guillermoprieto, *The Heart That Bleeds* (New York: Alfred Knopf, 1994); for a graphic presentation of the development of urban areas in Latin America see CEHOPU (Centro de Estudios Históricos de Obras Públicas y Urbanismo) (Historical Study Center of Public Works and Urbanism), *La Ciudad Hispanoamericana: El Sueño de un Orden* (The Hispanoamerican City: The Dream of Order) (Madrid: Ministerio de Obras Públicas y Urbanismo, 1989).
27. Most of the arguments and examples made herein are taken from analyses of United States cities. The implication that they apply to cities in Latin America must be somewhat discounted, since Latin American cities are in ways distinct from cities in the United States. For instance, Los Angeles is mentioned often, and while some would argue that Latin America begins somewhere north of Orange County, Los

Angeles is the quintessential automobile city. In Latin America, the vast majority of city dwellers depend on public transportation. As will be argued again later, this fact has considerable geopolitical consequence. Also, in addition to the differences between North American and Latin American cities, there are differences in character among Latin American cities themselves.
28. Drakakis Smith, *The Third World City*, p. 5.
29. Ibid., p. 8.
30. Radical activists find more barriers to their message than they expect. 'Many of the early investigations of the urban poor in the late 1960s and 1970s analyzed their voting patterns and concluded that they voted more conservatively than the middle classes ... Such conservatism is not an innate quality of the poor, although many do have aspirations for themselves and their children and prefer not to jeopardize their future. However, most poor communities are influenced by conservative leaders. Many of these are religious leaders.' Ibid., p. 50.
31. Carlos Marighella, *Minimanual of the Urban Guerrilla*, 1969, p. 2.
32. See Merril Collett, 'An International Story: the Myth of the "Narcoguerrillas"', *Nation*, 13 August 1988, Dialog File 647, 07886253. Collett claims that United States Ambassador to Colombia Lewis Tambs invented the narcoguerrilla, that he had 'conjured up a phantom'. But Collett makes his arguments in a contradictory apology for the violent left. Earlier he states, 'The notion of a "narcoguerrilla" unites what can't be united: Top traffickers are hugely successful capitalists bent on boosting their earnings and their social status. Marxist rebels want to overthrow capitalism altogether.' Later in the same piece he affirms, 'The guerrillas, who now have at least a third of their forces in coca-growing regions, fix prices for day-laborers on coca plantations, agitate to keep paste prices up and prevent abuses by cartel gunmen. "It's a contract arrived at under the threat of force", says historian Alvaro Delgado, a member of the communist party's central committee.' Collett, enamored by the union image of a revolutionary organization standing up for the rights of workers, amazingly overlooked the obvious marriage of interests between the drug dealers and the guerrillas. Ambassador Tambs 'narcoguerrilla' referred from the outset more to a phenomenon of cooperation and intermixed conduct than to a one-in-the-same guerrilla-narcotics trafficker. Now even the latter's existence is hardly in doubt. In August 1993, the Colombian press reported the capture of the chief of the 43rd Front of the FARC. According to the report, Eladio de Jesus Gracian Higuita, alias 'Marlon Montealegre', had also been chief of security for Carlos Lehder Rivas, one of the most powerful and notorious of the drug Mafia dons. The press report, citing information provided by the military, noted that Gracian had been involved in arms trafficking, was closely tied to drug trafficking networks, and had been commander of the 15th and 16th FARC Fronts as well as the 43rd. See 'Capturado el jefe del 43 frente de la FARC', *El Tiempo*, 1 August 1993, p. 11D. If one is inclined to believe the Colombian military reports, Mr Gracian constitutes the definitive *narcoguerrillero*. The motivations bringing the guerrilla into the drug business are well described historically in 'The Big Guerrilla Business', *Semana*, 7–14 July 1992, pp. 26–32; see also Geoffrey Demarest, 'Narcotics Trafficking and the Colombian Military', in *Global Dimensions of High Intensity Crime, Low Intensity Conflict*, Graham H. Turbiville and Richard H. Ward, eds (Chicago, IL: Office of International Criminal Justice, University of Illinois at Chicago, 1995).
33. Roger Trinquier, *Modern Warfare: A French View of Counterinsurgency* (New York: Praeger Publishers, 1964), p. 24. Trinquier's comment should be challenged to the extent that he suggests that criminal gangs have no ideology. Today's gangster rap bands like 'Ice Cube' provide at least the precursors of an expressed ideology. Gangs also have scruples, even if non-standard. In this regard see Elijah Anderson, 'The Code of the Streets', *The Atlantic Monthly* (May 1994) for an essay about how the inner-city environment fosters a need for respect and a self-image based on violence.

34. Graham H. Turbiville Jr, 'Operations Other Than War: Organized Crime Dimension', *Military Review* (January 1994), p. 35; 'The Chechen Ethno-Religious Conflict, Terrorism and Crime', *Military Review* (March 1994), p. 19.
35. See Graham H. Turbiville, 'The Chechen Ethno-Religious Conflict, Terrorism and Crime', *Military Review* (March 1994), p. 19.
36. 'Nation's Most Important Cities Militarized', and 'Witnesses Say Police Shot 3 Students at Protest', *Caracas Union Radio Network in Spanish*, 1200 GMT, 12 May 1994, as translated in FBIS-LAT-94-093, 13 May 1994.
37. 'Government Closes 3 Schools', Mexico City NOTIMEX in Spanish, 2259 GMT, 12 May 1993, as translated in FBIS-LAT-93-091, 13 May 1993, p. 8; 'Losses in May Disturbances in Capital Amount to 1 Million Quetzales', Guatemala *El Gráfico* in Spanish, 13 May 1993, p. 5, as translated in FBIS-LAT-93-093, 17 May 1993, p. 16
38. Michael D. Lyman, *Gangland: Drug Trafficking By Organized Criminals* (Springfield, IL: Charles C. Thomas, 1989), p. 99.
39. Maguel, Bayon, 'La masacre de niños en Brasil es un espejo para el mundo' (The Massacre of Children in Brazil Is A Mirror for the World)(interview with Gilberto Dimenstein), Brazil *Pais*, 24 May 1994, p. 27. Brazil is not unique in Latin America in this regard, see David Aponte, 'Vive 62% de la población de AL (America Latina) y el Caribe en "pobreza crítica"' (62% of the Population of LA [Latin America] and the Caribbean Lives in 'Extreme Poverty'), Mexico *Jornada*, 16 February 1994, p. 12. Aponte cites Organization of American States statistics which also claim that almost 280 million Latin Americans live in extreme poverty; see, however, Don Podesta, 'Rio de Janiero: Carnage at Its Ugliest', *The Washington Post National Weekly Edition*, 15–21 November 1993, p. 6. Podesta also notes that the number of killings per capita is still lower than in Washington, DC.
40. Katherine Ellison, 'Kids Are Casualties of Rio Drug War', *Miami Herald*, 10 April 1994, pp. 1A, 14A. Ellison reports that the gangs, most of whose members are youths or children, are dominated by a guerrilla-seeming organization called the Red Command. The suggestion is again apparent – Marxism–Leninism is no longer trumpeted – avoiding the consolidation of a frightened anti-communism. Instead, the equal of communist radical philosophy may thrive and grow under the cover of less politically affronting outlaw forms. As long as an organization appears to be a public security problem and not a national security problem, it may remain safe from effective physical reaction by the state.
41. See James L. Payne, 'Democracy by Violence', in *Labor and Politics in Peru: The System of Political Bargaining* (New Haven, CT: Yale University Press, 1965), p. 269. Payne described the use of the threat of violence on the part of labor organizations to leverage political concessions from Peruvian presidents. He suggested that the model was applicable throughout Latin America.
42. 'Unions Call Off General Strike', *Latin American Weekly Report*, 7 July 1994, p. 290; 'Duran Ballen Backs Away from Conflict', *Latin American Weekly Report*, 14 July 1994, p. 309.
43. Mike Davis, *Urban Control: The Ecology of Fear* (Westfield, NJ: The Open Magazine Pamphlet Series, 1994).
44. Burgess's Concentric Zone theory has also drawn criticism and has been followed by several alternatives including the Sector theory and the Multiple Nuclei theory, either being more appropriate for the growth histories of some cities. See J. Ross Eshleman and Barbara G. Cashion, *Sociology, An Introduction* (Boston, MA: Little, Brown, 1983), p. 510.
45. Ibid., p. 4.
46. Ibid.
47. G.J. Ashworth, *War and the City* (New York: Routledge, 1991), p. 92. Ashworth cites Yi-Fu Tuan, *Landscapes of Fear* (Oxford: Blackwell, 1979).
48. Ashworth, ibid., p. 93, citing R.N. Davidson, *Crime and Environment* (London: Croom Helm, 1981).

49. Davis, *Urban Control*, p. 9.
50. These exclusion zones evoke what Davis refers to more generally as 'the city of the excluded', see Paul L. Knox, *The Restless Urban Landscape*, p. 27. He notes, 'The exclusion and segregation of the poor is of course a well-worn theme in urban geography', p. 28, and, 'Most striking among the landscapes of the excluded are "impact ghettos" ... spatially isolated concentrations of the very poor ... often drained of community leaders and containing very high proportions of single-parent families struggling to survive in downgraded environments that also serve as refuges for the criminal segment of the informal economy', p. 29.
51. Knox, ibid., p. 27.
52. Ibid., p. 37.
53. Rod Paschall, *LIC 2000: Special Operations & Unconventional Warfare in the Next Century* (Washington, DC: Brassey's (US), 1990), p. 107.
54. Ibid.
55. Copies of a guerrilla manual titled 'Instructions for Urban Combat' were captured by government forces during the FMLN attack on San Salvador in November 1991. An analysis of that manual concludes that 'The FMLN doctrine was designed to try to put the armed forces and government of El Salvador in a no-win situation. The longer they took to drive the guerrillas out, the greater the political victory would be for the insurgents, and the stronger the national and international press would perceive them to be. On the other hand, if the government forces used their heavy weapons-artillery, aviation, and armor – they would quickly drive the guerrillas out, but at such a high civilian cost that it could provoke a general uprising.' David E. Spencer, 'Urban Combat Doctrine of the Salvadoran FMLN', *Infantry* (November–December 1990), p. 19.
56. E.J. Hobsbawm, *Primitive Rebels: Studies of Archaic Forms of Social Movement in the 19th and 20th Centuries* (New York: W.W. Norton, 1959).
57. Ashworth, *War and the City*, p. 96.
58. Mike Davis, *L.A. Was Just the Beginning – Urban Revolt in the United States: A Thousand Points of Light* (Westfield, NJ: The Open Magazine Pamphlet Series, 1992), p. 5; see also Martin Oppenheimer, *The Urban Guerrilla* (Chicago, IL: Quadrangle Books, 1969), p. 37, quoting Tom Hayden. 'Men are now appearing in the ghettos who might turn the energy of the riot in a more organized and continuous revolutionary direction ... During a riot, for instance, a conscious guerrilla can participate in pulling police away from the path of people engaged in attacking stores.' Ibid.
59. The Los Angeles riots of 1993 can be used to argue a number of points about urban violence only tangentially related to revolutionary theory, relative social deprivation, or property. See, for example, 'A Potent Brew: Booze and Crime', *US News & World Report*, 31 May 1993, pp. 57–8. 'It was no coincidence that when the riot did erupt, both looters and arsonists made liquor stores a prime target. ... South Central [L.A.] had a staggering 728 licensed liquor outlets – 13 per square mile.' Ibid.
60. Ibid., p. 2.
61. Appologies to Martin Oppenheimer, *The Urban Guerrilla*. Oppenheimer uses this quote, said to have been made only a few days before Robert Kennedy's assassination, before the book title. It is appropriate here given the lesson on the unsuccessful use of safe houses mentioned later in this section.
62. Ashworth, *War and the City*, p. 104: '[A] number of commentators would doubt the logical possibility of the existence of urban guerrilla warfare [Ashworth cites V. Ney, 'Guerrilla War and Modern Strategy', *Orbis*, 2, 1 (1958), pp. 66–82]. Blanqui's handbook on urban insurgency technique was, for example condemned by Lenin for failing to distinguish between insurrection and revolution. In part this is also a reaction to the pretensions of many urban terrorist groups that they are a guerrilla army when in reality they are no more than "half-baked criminals perpetuating acts

of violence" [Ashworth cites J. Ellis, *Armies in Revolution* (London: Croom Helm, 1975].'

63. Information on the Guatemalan urban guerrillas is based on author interviews of Guatemalan military and other government principals.

64. Abraham Guillen, 'Urban Guerrilla Strategy', in Laqueur, *The Guerrilla Reader*, ibid., p. 231.

65. At about the same time, in the fall of 1981, the Guatemalan government mounted a rural military offensive that caught the guerrillas in the highlands west and north of the city. The guerrillas were marshalling for a major offensive toward Guatemala City at the time. As a result of the urban defeat, however, the weight of the guerrillas' logistic trains shifted 180 degrees. Instead of 80 per cent of the matériel, financial and personnel support originating or being routed through the capital of Guatemala and 20 per cent from elsewhere, it was now the reverse. When the rural guerrilla units were beaten tactically by the Guatemalan Army, strategic recovery would prove impossible.

66. Information about the 1985 attack on the Colombian Palace of Justice is taken in part from author interviews with knowledgeable Colombian military officers. For another viewpoint on these events see Ana Carrigan, *The Palace of Justice: A Colombian Tragedy* (New York: Four Walls, Eight Windows, 1993).

67. David E. Spencer, 'Urban Combat Doctrine of the FMLN', p. 17; Charles Armstrong, 'Urban Combat: The FMLN's "Final Offensive" of 1989', *Marine Corps Gazette* (November 1990), p. 52.

4

Power and Proprietors

> We have said that by power we mean the power of man over the minds and actions of other men, a phenomenon to be found whenever human beings live in social contact with one another.[1] (Hans J. Morgenthau and Kenneth W. Thompson, from *Politics Among Nations: the Struggle for Power and Peace*)

Defense policy specialist Colin Gray defines the essence of power to be simply influence over behavior. 'From a strategic viewpoint, military, economic, or cultural power can all be reduced to the common currency of greater or lesser control over behavior.'[2] These two definitions are standard and usable. As a complementary definition, following a property analysis, power means the ability to gain or protect ownership rights. Strategic power for a country means the ability to protect or gain ownership rights inside and outside its borders.[3] If a nation can take possession of a piece of distant territory and hold on to it indefinitely against opposition, it seems to have great strategic power. The British showed as much in 1982 when they acted to repossess the Falkland/Malvinas Islands from Argentina and hold on to them. That event offers all the ingredients for a concise, property definition of strategic military power. Consider the distance, the amount of geography disputed, the time it takes to gain physical control of the geography, and the amount of time the ownership can be upheld after taking possession. Within six weeks of losing the islands, the British moved an attack force 8,000 miles, repossessed 12,170 square kilometers of territory within four more weeks and maintained possession indefinitely against a hostile claim. The British demonstrated power relative to an adversary. They displayed strategic power greater than that of the Argentines, since the British traveled farther, repossessed, and then retained possession indefinitely. Does this type of strategic power have to be measured in relative terms? Does the measure of strategic military power always require competition? According to Hans Morganthau, apparently so:

> When we refer to the power of a nation by saying that this nation is very powerful and that that nation is weak, we always imply a comparison. In other words, the concept of power is always a relative one. When we say that the United States is at the present one of the two most powerful nations on earth, what we are actually saying is that if we compare the power of the United States with the power of all other nations, as they exist at present, we find that the United States is more powerful than all others save one.[4]

The relativity of national power is patent in many situations, but insistence on the relativity of power can produce a false logic for at least two reasons. The first reason concerns the diminishing marginal utility of many kinds of power. Personal acquisitiveness provides a parallel example. Trade allows for cooperative attainment of wealth. While we can always measure one person or firm to be wealthier or poorer than another in financial terms, there comes a practical point where additional personal wealth cannot provide much greater comfort, safety or fulfillment. In other words, as people come to realize, stating wealth in relative terms can perpetuate false logic regarding the possible application of wealth. One can have a cat as good as the king's. Likewise, a nation can achieve liberty, security and economic progress without aggregating power for the purpose of controlling other lands. Nations often gain wealth without relative reference to the power of other nations and can claim great national power – great because it is sufficient to achieve security and prosperity. More than one people can maximize their power without the imperative that they have great or even relative ability to influence the behavior of others. In fact, accumulation of the instruments that seem able to change the relative balance of power often add little to the practical well-being of a nation. While the power to resist the aggressive behavior of other nations may indeed be necessary, it is generally far less power than needed to project physical control outside the nation. We need not suspend our disbelief regarding the goodness of the species. The point is not a denial of the competitive and dominance-seeking nature of man. It regards only the parameters of logic about military and diplomatic power used internationally. Unfortunately, when power is defined in terms of the relative ability to influence others, there follows (by intuition if not by logical imperative) a corollary that well-being depends on the ability to control other nations. False though this reasoning is in many international relationships, it has motivated most strategic thinking.

The second reason insistence on the relativity of national power is a false logic has to do with the less tangible ingredients of power. Perceived power is often as important as real power, and national will – the quantity we have portrayed earlier as national morale translated by leadership into resolve – is often as important as all other factors combined. It is no surprise that in many contests, nations around the world are emboldened to challenge the United States. This is often because of the widespread knowledge that although the United States has tremendous potential national power, both real and perceived, it is power only equal to the measure of national will applicable to a given situation. Early in 1994, it made perfect sense for Colonel Raul Cedras and the other military leaders of Haiti to defy the military might of the United States. Chances of success were far greater than they would have been against any number of less capable, but more ruthless, antagonists. Their defiance at least gained them a buy-out negotiated through ex-president Jimmy Carter. So how is national power to be reasonably measured in relative terms away from the context of a specified competition? The answer is that it cannot. The clearest theoretic measures of power are presented within the confines of an artificial test – that of imagined all-out, winner-take-all war. In such a context, the United States wins against any single foe and against most combinations as well. So what?

Adding things up in a different way, we can see that the United States is the most powerful country not because it might or might not prevail in an unconstrained war, or because it has relatively more power than any other individual country. What it has is more visible property claims in more places and against more claimants than any other country. The possibilities of getting mixed up in a property dispute are greater for the United States because its citizens claim more rights and more duties in more places than anybody else. These ownership claims don't exist because of unilateral presumptions on the part of US citizens, though this is hardly unheard of. Most of the time they are the result of evolved mutual or common understandings of rights and duties. In cases that may seem strange to some and simple to others – like the feeding of starving Rwandans – many peoples expect the United States and a handful of Western allies to do something, as though the pitiable results of every failed system of ownership created a responsibility. Such expectations resonate because so many persons in the United States and other Western countries admit a responsibility. How then are psychological components of national will such as this group conscience to be factored into national power? They cannot be correlated with access to strategic minerals, or control of ocean choke points. They can, however, be understood in a property context given, as we have asserted, that property entails shared identities, rights and duties.

THE ELEMENTS OF POWER

> You cannot divorce property from power. You can only make them change hands. (John Randolph Roanoke speech to the US Senate, 1926)

As mentioned in Chapter 2, German geographer Freidrich Ratzel is the father of modern political geography. Ratzel presented his creative theories of political organization in terms of 'laws' related to space and location. Ratzel stressed space as of extreme importance to national power, and concentrated much of his study on the United States, which he felt would become a twentieth-century world leader. Halford Mackinder, a Britisher, built on Ratzel's notion of continental power, and attributed preeminence to the Eurasian continent in what became his Heartland Theory. Mackinder is considered a determinist in that he stressed basic geography as the controlling (determining) influence over the fate of a country.[5] In this vein he intimated that if the Germans or the Russians were to control East Europe and Russia (the Eurasian heartland), they would be in a natural position to control the world. His, however, was a limited determinism in that he always left a hint that human initiative was available to change the basic geographical space. Given the orientation of his theory on the world-controlling importance of Central Europe (i.e. Germany, Poland, Russia), speculation turned toward the effect physical control of these areas might have on possibilities for world domination. In a submission to the march of history, Mackinder changed the measure of his theory, saying toward the end his life in 1943 that the human influence was a more important element in the future of a nation than was territorial endowment.

How is it that Mackinder's geopolitics enjoyed such longevity on the back of a theory that originally claimed that whoever held the heartland of Europe would control the world? Americans were unwittingly co-opted, or perhaps even conned, to internalize the protection of Western Europe as essential to United States national security. Therein lay one attraction to British statesmen, if not British geographers (Mackinder was a member of the British Parliament), of theories holding that nobody should be allowed to get hold of the biggest chunk of Europe. (Ratzel's stress of the importance of space must be digested against the background of German claustrophobia.) Halford Mackinder's Heartland Theory is less and more than it appears. More than scientific observation, it was also an intellectual device managed in the service of great power politics. It was for Britain an exportable fear and a simultaneously popular hope for Germans. Mackinder's was a theory promoted in part, even if only intuitively, to aid in involving the United States in the event of European continental war. The British applied political geography to a specific end, as did the Nazis. After all, at the turn of the century, US wealth and security had depended immeasurably more on how it controlled its own land than on what nation controlled the heartland of Europe. In retrospect, it is clear that at the turn of the nineteenth and twentieth centuries it hardly mattered one iota who controlled the heartland of Europe as far as American security was concerned. Geopolitics is almost oblivious to how land is owned, or to any ownership below that of the collective nation. The Heartland Theory presented a nexus between control of central Europe and the security of the United States, but there was far less science to the theory than its tone purported. More important that it made an inferential, subliminal appeal to American identity. That identity included solidarity both with Europe as a whole and with the English-speaking British in particular. The theory may have proposed that specific territorial space was the principal determinant of world domination, but the political message was that 'they' (Russians or Germans) were in an important property competition against 'us' (British and Americans).[6] The Heartland Theory continued to be cited throughout the Cold War, but ultimately it was the range of nuclear missiles launched from central Eurasia that made the Soviet Union a direct threat – not control of the heartland. If the Soviets were ever to have possessed all of Germany, they would have gained about five per cent more land and about 15 per cent more ungovernable people. Without ICBMs, rule of the Eurasian heartland would have meant rule of the Eurasian heartland, and little more. Likewise, he who controls Kansas ... controls Kansas. The Heartland optic can be taken as a self-centered European a priori, although the continental control generalization and the Eurasian conclusion were billed as one-in-the-same.

Even dismissing the Heartland Theory, Mackinder and other geopoliticians must be taken seriously because of their assertions about the essential relationship of nations and territorial space. The Ratzelian vision of national identity and power as a relationship of a people to geography has intrigued strategists since the middle of the nineteenth century. Many military thinkers gravitate to geopolitics since it emphasizes, on a grand scale, spatial relationships and the relative military value of terrain. It is large-scale map analysis for competitive thinkers – geography with an attitude. It has also had some notorious practitioners, so the term and the host of analyses that accompany it are unwelcome in some political science and international studies circles. The use of geopolitics as a starting gate for analysis of international conflict is very much alive, however.[7] Geopolitical thinking also sports some aggressive roots in the United States, and it remains a central intellectual column for mainline US military strategists. Geopolitics has also influenced the methodology of measuring US national power in relative terms.

For instance, in 1975, intelligence and national security expert Ray Cline wrote an analysis in which he explained why the balance of world power seemed for many to be slipping toward the totalitarian countries.[8] The book was published at a moment when United States power was perceived to be unfocused and the nation confused after the debacle of Vietnam. Dr Cline's analysis featured a United States in apparent strategic decline faced by a 'clear and present danger' of totalitarian assertiveness. Sir Halford Mackinder is admired in the book's introduction for his prescience in portraying the Eurasian heartland as key to command of the world's resources and peoples. While Dr Cline was careful to reject adoption of the term 'geopolitics', he sets a geographical foundation for his strategic analysis and uses the then novel theory of the movement of tectonic plates to propose a substitute term, 'politectonics'. The tectonic plate idea was evocative of the continental scale of bipolar competition – intercontinental missiles and so forth – but the methodology was not an offspring of plate theory. Cline derived calculations of perceived power using a combination of mathematical formulae and subjective weightings of several power factors. His formula looked as follows:

$$PP = (C+E+M) \times (S+W)$$

PP = Perceived Power
C = Critical Mass = Population + Territory
E = Economic Capability
M = Military Capability
S = Strategic Purpose
W = Will to Pursue National Strategy

Without accusing Dr Cline of perpetrating a statistical fraud, we may say that his mathematics are in great measure a Trojan horse to make a larger point about the importance of national will and coherent national strategy. The weights of the various factors are such that national strategy and will are the notably weak components in the United States' rating for perceived power. The math seems to deliver a conclusion that Dr Cline planned into the formula. Nevertheless, the particulars of the methodology deserve a separate consideration. The property analysis promoted in the present work is only partly at odds with the sort of geopolitical calculating exemplified by Cline's assessment. This is because property analysis can also apply a geophysical starting point. However, Cline's measurements of power did not incorporate consideration of the value of different pieces of geography as seen by different potential owners. They did not incorporate the essential question of how land is owned. His assessment of power also does not satisfy the basic question about the use of power. For the geopolitician, or great power theorist, power is the power to exert will over others. This definition, accepting it as true, still begs a question. While there is some pure pleasure in having control over others, the next question has to be asked – power to get others to do what? What do people want when they gain control over other people? The answer is that they want property rights. Unlike geopolitics, property analysis considers human conflict in terms of the subjective value of distinguishable rights associated with land and assesses power according to the ability to gain or protect these rights. Geopolitical analysis encourages consideration of pieces of geography taken whole, that is, taken with all the bundle of rights together (what we referred to as the fee).

In *Games Nations Play*, author John Spanier overviews the same kind of analysis about national power suggested by Dr Cline.[9] In a chapter entitled 'The Ability to Play: Calculating Power', Spanier lists the components of national power as geography, population, natural resources, economic capacity, military strength, political systems and leadership, and national morale. Spanier also notes that power may exist only in the mind and so the perception of power must be measured as well. The type of reduction of national power exemplified by Spanier's list is an ever-recurring axiomatic foundation in American military writings on strategy. It is not exactly wrong, but it is not so right that it deserves such pervasive acceptance. To begin with, the components could be organized into a variety of different taxonomies. 'Geography' could subsume 'population' and 'natural resources', if not the other terms. Economic power, which some theorists might say is of ultimate importance, depends on the other factors, so economic power could be the lead term and the others subordinate. Only temporary national power is separately measured by men and *matériel* in an organized armed force – so military power could be the apex term and the others could be its determining subordinates.

As normally portrayed, the relationship of the elements of national power is an unstable and unessential condition. But there is another, more important, problem. The elements mislead when we take them as aggregate statistics whose influence is greater when their size is greater, instead of taking them as mere introductions to human dynamics. It is obvious that great population or extensive territory might lend potential power, so there is a tendency to presuppose that incremental increases in population or territory, or minor advantages of these factors, correlate to power advantages. When we look at the world's nation-states, we see many countries with great populations, Bangladesh perhaps, with insignificant power. Adding a new increment to Bangladesh's population does not make it more powerful; it probably makes it less so. The fact that the United States is a superpower is based in part on large territorial size and large population. So what? An increase in population or territory (isolated from accompanying factors) will not make the United States more powerful. National will is important, but, being completely situation dependent, is a different type of quantity than population and territory. While the national population can be counted and reported at any given time regardless of other things, national will has to be measured in relation to a competitive issue of some kind. Not only is national will an intangible, it can't exist apart from some other intangible. Economic power is important, but only if it can be corralled by national leadership and backed by national will. Because of the long gamut of reasonable and unreasonable patterns of interaction, formulae of basic elements of national power cause confusion.

Notwithstanding, writings on strategy continually revisit the supposed elements of national power because strategists seek perspectives of relative strengths and weakness to predict outcomes in interstate competition. To articulate a property-based strategy vision, on the other hand, a property-focused idea regarding the elements of power is a prerequisite.

What components might be included in the calculation of national power, or any power, that will fit a property-based analysis of international competitions? The answer includes the following: cohesiveness of owner identity, system of ownership rules, leadership, wealth and technology.[10] The first component, and the starting point for calculating national power in a given international circumstance, is cohesiveness of owner identity. When the United States citizenry is powerfully committed as citizens of the United States to gain or protect property, the power of the government of the United States concerning that property is great. This is the national morale listed by Spanier and it is the upshot of Ray Cline's politectonic essay. Resolve is the start point for application of any wealth that might be brought to bear on a problem, and cohesiveness of owner identity is the source of community resolve.[11]

Next on the component list is the system of ownership rules. If the rules of ownership, the ideology, that guides the national will in a given circumstance are legitimate (acceptable), such legitimacy lends great power. The United States enters most international competitions from a position of advantage because its basic values regarding humans as owners are broadly acceptable. However, the government of the United States can distance itself from the sources of national power in two ways. First, even if Americans begin with great national cohesiveness regarding an international issue, cohesiveness and resolve will diminish if the United States government appears to promote ownership rules that are not clear or not fair. In other words, resolve will collapse to the extent that the ownership environment produced (or to be produced) by the government's objective does not satisfy Americans' beliefs. Second, the United States government must appear to act within the system of American ownership rules. The government must appear to act according to the laws of the United States, international law, and according to the customs and mores of the nation. In other words, one way the government can undermine national power is related to its objectives, the other is related to the manner in which it proceeds.

The Vietnam War is a useful example. Large-scale American involvement in Vietnam began in front of the force of great national will. The Tonkin Gulf Resolution evidenced national resolve, but the resolution was achieved by dissemblance on the part of President Lyndon Johnson as to the details of the Tonkin Gulf incident.[12] At any rate, national cohesiveness began to dissolve in two broad ways. Policy objectives (the ownership environment that was to be gained or preserved) were not sufficiently legitimate according to the perceptions of a growing number of Americans. The authoritarian regime of South Vietnam did not appear sufficiently noble to deserve American sacrifice, and the importance of Vietnam to other aspects of American ownership was seemingly insubstantial. In addition, the manner in which the United States prosecuted the war was increasingly portrayed as in violation of American moral standards. The My Lai massacre became emblematic of the perceived military behavior that determined this portrayal. In retrospect, the quantity of public resolve to wage the Vietnam War was great considering the limited direct US property interests. Geopolitical arguments were laid that loss of control of Vietnam would lead to Soviet control of Southeast Asia, threaten the United States' ASEAN allies and finally result in loss of open passage through the Straits of Molucca, a key ocean choke point. Oil resources of Indonesia and throughout the region would also be lost to communist exploitation. Another communist victory would embolden communist radicals in other parts of the world, and would embolden the Soviets to support them. But these arguments, to the extent they were credible, lost importance to the American public. The United States fought for over a decade expending more than 54,000 lives. Attempted strategies did not produce a favorable conclusion within the time made available by the existing quantity of American resolve. The North Vietnamese strategies did.

A third component of power, already outlined together with ideology, is leadership. Whatever the identity of a group of owners, whatever the cohesiveness of their identity, and however compelling the system of ownership rules, leadership initiative and vision must be present in order for power to have any active meaning. Effective leadership builds cohesiveness, translates cohesiveness into resolve, and preserves resolve by ensuring that goals and actions are in consonance with the accepted system of ownership. Adolf Hitler was an effective leader in this sense – he identified the keys to building German cohesiveness and to turning it into aggressive resolve. His property enterprise was not subtle or complex. Aryans were rightful owners, others were not, and some, like the Jews, were not fit even as property. Germans, according to Nazi vision, had a right to more land, and had a right to own other peoples as part of it. Hitler worked to maintain cohesiveness, constructed a system of ownership rules that fed on and satisfied the German mindset, and translated German resolve into specific territorial goals. His system of ownership rules was fueled by an arrogance that misjudged the resolve of the rest of the world. Hitler's leadership might have been sustainable if Nazi pretensions regarding ownership had not been so exaggerated. In the Ukraine, for instance, German domination might have been accepted as a favorable alternative to the enslaving Soviet rule. The Germans seized a lot of geography, but they could not incorporate enough demography into the shared ownership identity. They increased the amount of land but not the number of owners. They therefore could not increase the amount of potential resolve favoring the national project. German failure to understand the dynamics of ownership doomed the Third Reich.

Wealth is obviously a component of power. National wealth is determined to an extent by geography, which is to say, basic factors such as territorial space, location, minerals, water, or population. As discussed in the first chapters, some properties are worth more than others. Few except the Mongolians would disagree that the Middle East oil fields are worth more than Mongolia. Even so, the Mongols enjoyed a long historical period of dominant continental ownership due to national cohesiveness, leadership, military technology, and a system of ownership rules that was not out of place considering the standards of the age. Wealth is power only when it is applied to some project. The United States enjoys so much national wealth that it can be led into endeavors even when the national will is limited and divided. With great national wealth, average leaders can successfully undertake a project that does not enjoy a high degree of national cohesiveness. Great leadership, on the other hand, can make up for a lack of basic geographic wealth. Genghis Khan, with limited geographical resources, decided to conquer all of Asia. An American president, with the greatest geographic wealth in the history of man, can be turned back, at least temporarily, by a dozen Haitians with clubs. A country's poverty can force its leaders to be more patient in their interpretation of national will, thereby gaining power advantages. Wealth alone is not power, but it is property. Wealth is the element of power that is both means and end.

Technological capacity is well recognized as a primary element in a society's ability to compete strategically. The author lists it separately as a component of power because it translates basic geographic factors into wealth, but does not fit well as basic geography. Technology is an aspect of culture that, in property competitions between societies, invites comparisons of relative advancement or primitiveness. A society with a changing technology tends to be dominant, other factors of power being more or less equal. 'Technology' could be absorbed, in another reduction of the components of national power, into economic or military capacity or into wealth. But, as noted in Chapter 3, inventions not only impinge on the value of property, and on the ability to gain or protect property, they also at times create or constitute property. An important invention creates not just new, fungible wealth, it creates new property. A new concert of rights may be created by the new idea, or existing owner relationships changed. Weapons are a very specialized technology that help physically coerce, capture or kill people, and they are used to gain and protect property. Weapons technologies will be considered separately below because they are centrally important to the development of military strategies. Technology of all kinds paces the relative competition of modern states and yet, aside from weaponry, little scholarly work has been done on the effects or meaning of uneven technological progress as it relates to international conflict.

The military is only an instrument (as opposed to a basic element or component) of national power.[13] The military instrument is a product of wealth, technology and leadership, and is a manifestation of resolve on the part of the nation to defend or arrogate property. The demographic strength of the United States could comfortably sustain a larger number of military personnel, but it is the level of technological capitalization, rather than numbers, that currently makes the US military a superior force. This advanced equipping and organizing depends on the inventive character of American culture, and must be reinforced by study and investment.

Military technology is more than weaponry or intelligence and communication hardware. It includes organizational and doctrinal innovation. Organizational change seems often to lag behind significant changes in weapons technology and behind the environment of threats. An often cited historical example is the World War I mismatch between the lethality of the machine gun and nineteenth century set piece infantry formations. At times, new weapons that by themselves radically changed military organizational structure and doctrine faced greatest institutional resistance. Examples are legion, two in the twentieth century being the tank and the aircraft carrier. Today, admission of this delayed acceptance invigorates the search for military doctrine that will be adequate for the post-Cold War world.

The above restatement of the elements of national power was a necessary exercise. As author Geoffrey Blainey, in his study, *The Causes of War*, states, '[I]t is the problem of accurately measuring the relative power of nations which goes far to explain why wars occur.'[14] Blainey cites sociologist Georg Simmel, who, in 1904 argued that the most effective way of preventing war was to possess exact knowledge of the comparative strength of the two opponents. Such knowledge, however, was generally attainable only by fighting the war. Blainey takes aim at theorists who have debated the importance of national power within the axiom that an imbalance of power promoted war and that a balance of power was an explanation for peace. According to Blainey, the balance of power theory of peace is not borne out by the history of conflicts. Whether there have been seven major powers, or two, or one, the number and intensity of wars would vary according to other factors. A balance of power among major nations may, according to Blainey, be a formula for maintaining independence, but not necessarily peace. On the other hand, when power is understood, the relations between nations are less likely to lead to war than if the potential parties are mistaken as to their relative strengths and weaknesses.[15] Generalizing about war aims, Blainey states that 'the aims are simply varieties of power. The vanity of nationalism, the will to spread an ideology, the protection of kinsmen in an adjacent land, the desire for more territory or commerce, the avenging of a defeat or insult, the craving for greater national strength or independence, the wish to cement or impress allies – all these represent power in different wrappings.'[16] Blainey correctly confuses power with property. Again, when asking what power is for, the logical answer is to gain and enforce preferential rights. (Interestingly, Blainey's list has a lot in common with current United States government foreign policy objectives.) The measurement of power is greatly complicated by the changing distribution of power, which is the important substantive feature of the post-Cold War world. Changing distribution of power influences strategic policy and military doctrinal innovations.

PARTICULARIZATION OF POWER

> It is increasingly difficult to keep one's citizens out of the global conversation. As Tolkien would say, 'The road goes ever on and on'. But on this road one travels at the speed of light down a million pulsating pathways, and the trolls are just not clever enough to catch you. (Walter Wriston, from *The Twilight of Sovereignty*)

Diffusion of property and particularization of power are closely related, but they acquire distinct connotations. Diffusion of property refers to the constant re-division and redistribution of rights and duties, while particularization of power refers to the greater and greater number of individuals and entities that can assert and enforce rights and duties. Particularization of power refers to the multiple concentrations of ownership cohesiveness and the appearance of leadership initiatives to translate that cohesiveness into resolve. This particularization reaches to the level of the single individual. Today, an individual American can effect his own foreign policy, visit countries pretty much as he chooses, write to a congressman to ask that aid be restricted to a particular country, send money to a special interest group supporting a variety of causes overseas, use his fax machine to send political propaganda around the world, invest or withdraw money from a company doing business in a given country, publish opinions and recommendations about foreign governments, sue in international courts, respond to foreign claims against him, even become the defense minister of a foreign country, all with little regard to the opinions or preferences of the United States government. If he carries an emotionally powerful owner identity, perhaps as an Armenian refugee, or a Chilean leftist, and if he has attained some degree of material wealth, he can exert a great deal of international influence.

In addition to the individual there are uncountable kinds of owner identities that manifest global policies, some in close coordination with nation-state governments, some oblivious to governments, and some in diametric opposition. Organizations that deal with finances or information have especially powerful foreign policies and these in turn attract the participation of individuals and other organizations. In each case some person is benefiting from a right to access, use and enjoyment, expectation of safety, or profit. The government of the United States is not unified within itself in its foreign policy, thus the individual company or citizen picks and chooses which government foreign policy to support – that of a congressional committee staff member, that of the National Security Council, or maybe the foreign policy of a federal court. Not only is there no hope of a unified voice or a *summa potestas* in American foreign dealings, there is more and more a marketplace for foreign policy in which the government of the United States is only a major player. If an item of foreign policy interest has a central place on the current administration's foreign policy agenda, the government will be a very important player. There is, however, a finite amount of attention that can be given by varsity leaders, and when this is occupied, matters fall to the second and then third string. With each lowering of the bureaucratic level that the executive system can give to a problem, other parts of the government, and influences outside the government, gain a greater share of power.

The particularization of power is not limited to non-violent or legal expression. Within a country, property claims may be mounted via labor sectarianism, banditry and gangsterism, religious sectarianism or cultism, mob manipulation, and armed insurgency. Some of these are what E.J. Hobsbawm called primitive or 'archaic' forms of organized political action.[17] Writing in the late 1950s, Hobsbawm looked at the political motivations and aspirations in what today might be referred to as gray area phenomena or 'ungovernability'. In 1959, the kinds of movement about which Hobsbawm wrote were to remain a secondary academic concern while three more decades of Cold War unfolded. If written in 1997, Hobsbawm's examples might perhaps have included environmental, racist, homosexual, animal rights or anti-abortion activists. Technological advancement has lent the possibility of sophistication and renown to an ever-increasing number of the types of archaic movements that drew Hobsbawm's attention 30 years ago. The intermingling of the legal and non-legal, violent and non-violent becomes more and more complex as technology empowers a greater number and variety of participants. The mob, for instance, is an ownership identity often generated by seemingly limited events, but determined by emotions that lend cohesiveness, and by the incapacity of other identities to satisfy expectations of ownership. The mob, while seemingly *ad hoc* and immediate, is a phenomenon with political longevity and utility that many individuals depend on and draw upon as a source of political power. Understanding the long-term political power of the mob is necessary to the understanding of the complete political calculus of many areas. Hobsbawm makes a convincing description of the evolutionary nature of the mob phenomenon, showing historical examples of changes from relatively spontaneous expression of shared frustrations and opportunism to a more sophisticated manipulation of the threat of mob violence for political leverage.

These points about the diffusion of property ownership and the particularization of power have been related to power within a national identity. Many of the individual policies may be at odds with the policy of the nation-state government and at odds with one another, but, in the aggregate, they constitute the nation's foreign affairs. Even the illegal identities add to the mixture of a nation's foreign dealings.

The particularization of power is a worldwide phenomenon. The challenges to a nation-state's government come not only from other nation-states, groups and individuals within nation-states, but increasingly from entities that are tenuously related, or not related at all, to a foreign state. Most of these operate within the bounds of existing national and international laws and ethics. Many, in fact are dedicated to the improvement of legal and moral regimes. The most well-known, such as the International Red Cross or Amnesty International, deal with other non-governmental organizations and directly with the highest levels of many state governments. These organizations are only the best known of thousands of organizations of every description that can claim international membership and exert partial or wholly independent supranational or transnational influence. Banks, because they hold the convertible wealth of many other owner identities, are some of the most powerful and least understood non-governmental actors internationally. Banks can translate the cohesiveness of one owner group into support for the project of another owner group. They can not only launder money – eliminating the connection between cash or commercial paper and the manner of its accretion – they can also launder group resolve, using the funds of one organization to support the aims of others.

Transnational criminal activity is one of the most dangerous growth industries of the post-Soviet world, and one that is currently under-recognized and ineffectively countered. In property analysis terms, an international criminal organization can have great power because it can maintain great cohesiveness of identity that can be translated by effective leadership into resolve for the purpose of gaining wealth. It can apply organizational and physical technologies to its enterprise and quickly reapply any wealth gained into the business of gaining more. The transnational criminal organization depends on very little population and no designated territory. It is in the business of gaining property and can gain property at the expense of legally constituted ownership systems.[18]

KNOWLEDGE AND TIME

> If Marx were alive today, he might fairly call education the means of production.[19] (Walter B. Wriston, from *The Twilight of Sovereignty*)

When a country invades another militarily, both face a set calculus regarding the amount of force they can bring to bear within specifiable amounts of time in given places. These decisions regarding where, when and how much, as difficult and consequential as history has shown them to be, are relatively simple decision-making scenarios for the application of force. Assaults against national ownership are decreasingly comprehensible in terms of resources that should be committed and time available. The physical threat of a nation-state military can be roughly understood in relation to the characteristics of physical technologies – the range and speed of an intercontinental missile, the march rate of a tank division. But cross-border migrations of populations, transnational crime, environmental degradation, violations of rights in foreign lands, harmful trade barriers, or the proliferation of threatening technologies are changeable challenges to ownership whose gestation period is difficult to know or articulate. The application of physical force in support of policy initiatives aimed at such threats is also likely to be sporadic, erratic, inconsistent and nebulous. Today, the power to influence behavior (or kill people) on a global scale has become more and more particularized. The most successful invasion of a country may be the aggregate result of thousands of disparate, independent actions orchestrated by no more than a popular idea, much less a national government.

The most difficult dilemma is the problem of rebounding property challenges. Part of a nation's power to conduct foreign affairs becomes particularized – falling to an array of individuals and organizations not committed to a national government's views. Much of this particularized power may support what the government characterizes as a property dispute. The State of Florida may oppose the mass arrival of Haitian migrants (suing the federal government for unrecompensed strain on infrastructure) while some Floridians work with international organizations to decry human rights abuses in Haiti and to make the United States government recognize the political oppression of Haitian refugees. Let's say that the United States government, after for some time following a policy of considering the Haitians as economic refugees and returning them home, changes its policy to allow mass Haitian migration to the United States under the determination that they are political refugees. At the same time, a majority of US citizens may oppose the entrance of Haitians to the country, regardless of how they are classified. The United States government, in this case, has determined that the priority property right that the American nation (as a discreet ownership identity) should protect is the right of the Haitian who is unable to exercise free use and enjoyment of his native land. The incremental deterioration of property rights belonging to the citizens of Florida is implicitly downgraded to a secondary priority based on the perceived relative suffering of the Haitians. In this case, the national executive translates concerns about a failed ownership environment into policy. The property concern then rebounds to affect the property ownership of Floridians. Rebounding property assertions and the particularization of foreign policy power will often be intertwined with painful and opposing emotions as to owner identities. In 1994, a yes vote by Californians in favor of Proposition 187, denying various state subsidized social services to illegally resident aliens in that state, caused a violent demonstration against a McDonald's® hamburger restaurant in Mexico City.[20]

Determining the gestation, variation, and interrelation of threats to national ownership is a leadership problem. Intelligence is knowledge in support of decision-making, and the organized acquisition of intelligence has become as central a feature of the modern state as has the military. In the United States, the intelligence function of the federal government is formally centralized in the CIA, but dozens of federal organizations add, in semi- or wholly independent ways, to the mountain of information decision-makers must digest. The Department of State, the Drug Enforcement Agency, the Commerce Department, the Environmental Protection Agency, and a myriad of others have informational responsibilities. There is no rule, or apparently even a tendency, within the federal government, to depend on the efforts of these huge organizations for foreign policy intelligence. Much of the government leadership's intelligence comes from private news organizations, analyses from academe, and from the opinions and observations of friends. In other words, the body of policy intelligence used to inform federal leaders about most issues is not far different from the policy intelligence available to other wielders of the particularized power discussed above. This is not due to quirks or failures on the part of the American president or any national head-of-state. However massive or efficient a system of policy intelligence, there is a fixed amount of information that can go into a leader's head in a given amount of time. For one thing, it is difficult to block some information in favor of others or even to decide the priority of sources. As a result, any of the leaders of the bits of particularized power that are partly or wholly at odds with the national policy of the United States, coming from within or without, may often have intelligence as good as, or better than that of the president.

In a democracy, understanding on the part of the national government of the views and commitments of the internal polity is supposedly a function of the political process. The fact of having succeeded through long electoral campaigns is evidence that elected officials are equipped with an understanding of owner cohesiveness. They supposedly possess an intuitive, artistic knowledge of the agreement, disagreement and depth of feeling within the population regarding key issues. Intelligence about diffusion, distribution, and expression of power comes from political awareness and astuteness. Intelligence concerning the particularization of power outside the nation, on the other hand, is a job that has fallen to specialized organizations. Still, Americans do not want the government looking for or maintaining political information on them. It is illegal for the United States' foreign intelligence apparatus to collect or maintain information on US persons (with limited exceptions).[21] At the same time, Americans expect the federal government to be fully cognizant of what is occurring in the outside world.

One of the by-products of the advances in information technology is what we might call the problem of rebounding political information. It is similar and related to the problem of rebounding property dispute mentioned above, and it makes setting the balance between citizen privacy and necessary collection about a dangerous world more and more difficult. The rebound happens in several ways. For instance: if the United States government were to decide to use propaganda in a foreign land in order to influence some group or government, the message may be picked up by the United States international media and related in the United States. Is the US government guilty of media tampering in the US?[22] What if the success of a foreign military intervention depends on cooperation with an international aid or human rights organization? If the military needs to secure information about the organization for security purposes and assurance of goodwill, are they then invading American privacy when the organization is principally American? Many foreign public media organizations are filled with the intelligence operatives of foreign countries. Counterintelligence efforts of the United States must at times attend to these individuals.

When these news organizations are tied intimately to media groups that provide public information in the United States, is the US government intelligence apparatus unethically involved in internal matters? Looked on as a property issue, the balance will involve the value of information itself as proprietary property, property rights related to citizen privacy, monitoring requirements about the maintenance of property rights globally, and competitive geopolitical considerations relating to protection of common national properties.[23]

The large, traditional American intelligence organizations are large mainly because of the imperatives of the Cold War. They oriented collection on a geopolitical scale, concerned with the ability of a major military adversary to take and hold the whole bundle of rights in land, or to completely deny the use and enjoyment of land. Secrecy of sources and methods of collection has been paramount to maintaining a full flow of correct information. Security regarding friendly communications and military forces was likewise stressed. When dealing with the world of particularized power, secrecy becomes a legal and practical burden that produces little competitive advantage in some cases. In reference to a crime organization or a violent political movement, secrecy of sources and methods may still be critical to following the course of their power. Most other power wielding identities depend heavily on open communication and on the creation of solidarity around ideas. They cannot afford much secrecy of communications. Since the power being exerted by non-governmental groups and individuals often depends on mobilizing adherents, there must be an openly publicized manifestation of effort. A free society gains strength from the free flow of information. The flow of information also improves as a result. Correspondingly, open source intelligence on political matters is now an important product of the United States and an important instrument and input for the many particles of power that are being exercised today.[24] Whether this information is considered a part of the national wealth, a function of leadership, or a basic element of power is unimportant. It is important that it has only recently been appreciated as an imperative source for national power at the federal government level.

The problem of intelligence in the post-Cold War world is a subject worthy of separate investigation. It is easy for us, however, to interpret intelligence as valuable private and common property.

It is likewise easy to understand the increased value of preferentially held information – proprietary information. More emphasis is being placed on open-source exploitation to avoid legal and practical pitfalls of government secrecy, and because it is so valuable in its own right.[25] Regardless of the growth of open-source information in support of national policy, the most dangerous threats to a state's sovereignty will continue to require monitoring by secret and expensive means. Particularization of power includes bad groups and individuals as well as good. The bad tend to be more liberal in their willingness to enforce their property pretensions through the use of force. They are also more likely to understand and manage the value of closely held information. For this reason, national governments, and even large non-governmental organizations, will probably invest more in information security and in attempts to gain the closely held information of others. The size and utility of general purpose armed forces may continue to decrease, but investment in intelligence gathering and information protection will increase.

WEAPONS AND TRESPASSERS

> God made man and Colt made him equal. (anonymous)

As was claimed in Chapter 1, every right that constitutes property is ultimately related to some form of enforcement or is subject to physical loss. Weapons are technologies that can physically change or preserve owner relationships. They can deter trespassers, they can deny use and enjoyment, they can gain possession, and they can intimidate or kill would-be owners. Since armed force is one of the most important instruments of power controlled by a national leader, the nature of weapons, and the difference between their usefulness for police or military applications, becomes especially relevant.

Strategic nuclear weapons threaten total ruination of property and mass killing of owner groups. Lesser war weapons are designed for the purpose of gaining or defending bare possession of geography. Such instruments reflect geopolitical dominance in foreign affairs thinking in that they can rarely be applied to protect or gain separable rights related to land and other things. In their direct use they effect the entire ownership control of designated land areas. If one wished to defend a right to subsurface minerals, or the right to an equal vote for people of a set minority, weapons of war are difficult to use without threatening the entire fee, that is to say, the whole bundle of rights in a territory. The rifle may be used to enforce the right of a minority student to attend a state university, and a tank can be used to prevent mass demonstrations in the national square, but in the aggregate, weapons like tanks and artillery and combat aircraft are inapplicable when particular rights in property, rather than the whole set of rights, are under challenge. And many large weapon systems are designed solely to defeat other large weapon systems. Big weapons can be used to back a threat or support extortion regarding a separable right in land, but in actual use they are obviously clumsy.

The gap between protection of select rights in land and protection of the whole basket of rights (the fee) is one way of distinguishing police from military activities. Police forces are designed and trained for the purpose of defeating threats to rights that are less comprehensive than loss of the whole ownership, less than the entire sovereignty. This is reflected in the difference in weaponry and organization as well. There is a firepower gap, narrowing perhaps, between police and military weapons. Although there is no exact line between the two, it appears to fall somewhere around the use of the crew-served machine-gun and certainly begins at the point of indirect fire weapons and bombs. This firepower differential follows the difference between the relative lawfulness within states and lawlessness among them. To the extent that the rule of law within a polity breaks down, the gap between the use of weapons appropriate for police purposes and those suited to military purposes often seems to close. In other words, military weapons are more likely to be used even when inappropriate or excessive in relation to the rights and duties being enforced or challenged. When military forces occupy an area, but their mission is not to take and hold terrain, their weapon set may be inappropriate to a task that is more akin to police work. With this distinction between police and military in mind, there are several aspects of weaponry that lend themselves to discussion of the enforcement of property rights on an international scale. Among these are legality, lethality, precision, and range.

One of the most controversial dimensions of the laws of land warfare is that of proscribed weaponry. International conventions against the use of specified types of weapons have seen mixed obedience, but their influence on military practices should not be discounted. If not for the international regime of agreements and resolutions against the use of chemical agents, it can be supposed that the world would have witnessed more frequent use of these horrific weapons. Infantrymen can be thankful for what success the international control regime on chemical weapons has enjoyed. The notion of a chemical battlefield means more gear to carry, more complicated training to endure, more uncertainty to suffer, and more fear to overcome. Many civilian populations, meanwhile, have been spared the lingering ecological nightmare of contaminated landscapes.

In part as a result of international legal proscription, chemical weapons have not changed warfare appreciably in the last half of this century, though this may yet change. The landmine, on the other hand, has. In many armed conflicts since the World War II landmines have inflicted the majority of casualties, not bullets, aerial bombs or artillery.[26] Moreover, serious civilian casualties are by far the result of indiscriminate or callous placement of landmines. Diplomats and human rights activists have finally turned their attention to the landmine and have targeted it in an effort to make the weapons taboo.[27] The majority of mines in many battle areas are of informal manufacture. Advancement of an international landmines protocol may seem a futile exercise since it would be directed at formal, law abiding industries, but would not reach a huge cottage industry that may be responsible for just as much civilian suffering. Should countries agree to a ban on weapons they feel they can afford and need while watching similar improvised weapons being used in spite of the ban? The answer is probably yes. It is understandable that international agreements proscribing the use of certain weapons are created among polities that are likely to obey. Outlaw groups or governments may not seem suitable targets of polite multinational diplomacy. But the secondary pressure of international opinion can nevertheless have an important influence on the behavior of outlaw entities who will still vie for a favorable moral image.

In a conflict where guerrilla use of home-made mines is the norm, the psychological environment may disfavor the use of anti-personnel landmines by a government force, no matter what the level of the mines' technical sophistication. Therefore, participation by that government in a generalized ban on anti-personnel landmines would seem reasonable on *realpolitik* as well as moral grounds. If there is a purely tactical doubt about a ban on landmines from the perspective of a regular security force, it is related to the protection of fixed, isolated installations of high economic value. Explosive mechanical sentries may efficiently protect pieces of modern infrastructure, such as electrical substations. Perhaps such sentries can in fact be made relatively safe for the general public. Thus some of the argument about landmines should turn on the method of their use and on the moral legitimacy of their employers, rather than solely on the nature of the weapon itself. Obvious in the case of the landmine is the direct relationship to rights in land. Landmines are regularly employed as a technological strategy for denying free use and access. Although they can be used to protect the value of real property, they can also retard land value long after a tactical military purpose is past.

The offensive use of the landmine by guerrilla forces must be described to appreciate the difficulty of separating legal military from criminal applications. In a traditional use, a guerrilla might cover a withdrawal route with landmines after having assaulted a town, a bridge, or a military outpost. The mines delay pursuit by enemy regular forces, allowing the guerrilla to escape. This kind of scenario, while genuine, doesn't describe the essence of the landmine in its potential role as the principal offensive weapon of a guerrilla force. The following scenario shows a common offensive use of the landmine in low intensity conflict. In order to leverage unspecific political concessions, guerrilla leaders decide to inflict continuous casualties on government security forces. In order to do so, the guerrilla plots routes along which landmines can be best employed, then conducts an assault on a town or a bridge or a military outpost as an inducement for enemy regular forces to pursue the retreating guerrilla and fall prey to the landmines. The government casualty is the ultimate physical goal of the operation. In such a case, the landmine is the offensive weapon whose employment is supported by the rest of the operation. A political objective is to be achieved by way of the psychological impact of continuous demoralizing casualties suffered by the security force. Is this a military use of a weapon, or is it more akin to terrorism? We might wish the control movement luck, but there is no prospect of seeing the end of the landmine as a primary casualty producer in future conflicts, especially by guerrilla forces. The landmine story serves, however, to demonstrate that the perceived morality of a weapon will continue to grow as an influence on its use, especially by government forces. This moral dimension of a weapon type continues to evolve into a legal dimension.

A policeman would normally not choose to use a hand grenade to kill a criminal in a crowd. The collateral effect does not permit it, even though the grenade might be effective for the immediate purpose of stopping the criminal. The policeman, even if he is a very precise shot with his pistol, will not attempt to shoot a criminal in a crowd because of the risk to bystanders.[28] A police sniper with a rifle might try to shoot a criminal under circumstances where it would be irresponsible for another policeman to fire a pistol. The same relationship of precision, morality and resolve in use applies to weapons of war. Nuclear deterrence worked because its use was appalling to the would-be users. The resolve required to use the nuclear weapon has not been great enough, in the context of historical circumstances (save one – the prospect of a 1945 homeland invasion of Japan) to overcome moral reluctance to its use. The nuclear weapon, a weapon of mass destruction, lacks precision, and is therefore morally unwieldy. The neutron bomb, a more precise nuclear weapon that would kill soldiers while supposedly doing minimal damage to the physical environment, was to be more useable because the moral threshold to its use was lower than a conventional nuclear weapon. It would therefore have presented a more credible deterrent to Soviet attack according to proponents of its use. In between nuclear warheads and police small arms, every weapon type involves a moral (and increasingly legal) disability that is based in part on precision.

The term lethality has some meaning beyond precision, although in most cases they are the same. Accepting that we can only be so dead, lethal weapons are equally lethal – but 'very lethal' carries a connotation of greater certainty. There are many technological devices that allow constraint in physical coercion or destruction of property. These are often referred to as non-lethal or limited-lethality weapons. They include the rubber bullet, water cannon, sound weapons, inventions that disable aircraft while on the ground or destroy runways, simple bulldozers, sticky goo-guns that render people immobile, blinding lasers, and many others. Each one, almost as part of its basic specifications, carries a moral limitation depending on the context of its application. The existence of this growing family of non-lethal weapons, and the energy with which the technology is being developed, speaks worlds about the intuitive difference between police and military relations to property. Non-lethal weapons tacitly admit not just that killing in a given situation is excessive, but that the people at whom the target is aimed have some rights associated with the place where the non-lethal weapon is being used. The weapons admit that the objective pursued by their user may be a temporary one, or perhaps involves less than an intention to take the entire fee.

One does not have to be a soldier to grasp the importance of the range of a weapon. If you have an artillery piece or tank cannon that can outdistance the enemy guns, you can destroy him before he comes in range. This is a fact of combat that is understood even at the boxing or karate level. Of course there are other factors, but there are few substitutes for being able to engage the enemy at a distance. Nothing may be more true than the old saw that one should not show up at a gunfight with a knife. Indirect fire weapons, even when not perfectly accurate, impede the use of weapons with a shorter range. If our archers can shoot farther than their archers, we are likely to take a greater toll on their swordsmen than they on ours. Today's big aircraft carrier is understood by many as a very long-range artillery piece. It can travel close enough at sea to unleash jets that can bring firepower to bear over a large portion of the earth's surface. Inter-Continental Ballistic Missiles (ICBMs) are the ultimate artillery perhaps, being able to reach all parts of the globe.

One thing is not often recognized about the range of weapons. If a distance gap exists in the coverage of one system over another, the gap creates initiative space for the enemy. Take a pure combat example. A small infantry unit may carry its own indirect fire support in the form of a few light mortars. These help cover the unit in the case that an opposing force has emplacements that cannot be defeated by the unit's small arms. If the enemy has a longer range mortar, he can suppress the small mortars of the infantry unit, unless that unit can call on field artillery support to suppress the enemy mortars, and so on. If there is a gap in coverage by either side, it will be reflected in the placement on the ground of the different systems and will give a marked advantage to whoever has the greater range. One side or the other, all else being equal, will be free to operate within the range of advantage. This fact of weaponry range can be applied by analogy to the moral characteristics, discussed in previous paragraphs, that derive from a weapon's precision or lethality. If a moral acceptability gap exists between one type of weapon and the next, escalation requires much more force of will, giving the opponent an advantage of initiative if that will is lacking.

For example, in 1990, a handful of radicals organized a group of between 1,000 and 1,500 protestors in the Tzutuhil Indian town of Santiago Atitlan in Guatemala. Unarmed, the crowd marched to a nearby army patrol base along the shore of Lake Atitlan and demanded that the detachment of soldiers leave the area. One or two of the soldiers fired on the crowd, killing several demonstrators. The shootings were widely characterized as a violation of human rights. The soldiers had not been prepared psychologically, trained properly, provided appropriate weaponry, or given necessary information regarding the villagers to confront the situation without firing their rifles. A moral gap existed between the weapons of the crowdspeople (knees and elbows) and the soldiers' small arms. This gap gave considerable initiative space to the organizers of the demonstration, who knew that the soldiers would either have to surrender and leave, or fire on the crowd, opening a new source for accusations of brutality. Positional advantage was taken of a difference in the relative coverage of weapons – only the gap was not in physical range, it was in moral acceptability. Had the soldiers been provided the training and physical wherewithal to control the crowd with non-lethal means, the radicals would not have had such a lucrative opportunity.

Even in the physical sense, effective range is the product of more than just distance. The accuracy and precision of a weapon is an ingredient of effective range. On today's battlefields, targets must be identified and fixed, and weapons users must receive target information quickly. This brings the problem of the covering range of intelligence systems. Ultimately, whoever has control of the greatest range of intelligence systems will secure the longest-range fires and will be in a position, other factors aside, of controlling any battlefield. Today, that means control of space-based systems. Similarly (only in relation to the moral range of weapons just described) social intelligence must be able to determine where different kinds of force can used and where gaps exist in the moral reach of competing weapons. This kind of intelligence must be able to distinguish the difference between military and police applications of power – between efforts to gain or dominate an entire fee and rights that are obviously less than the entire fee.

Weapons affect basic property rights. The right to deny access is frustrated and the right to free use and enjoyment is intervened when weapons fire is brought on a piece of property. Artillery fire obviously degrades property rights, and just as the longest range weapon impedes the use of lesser weapons, the endangerment of basic rights in land impedes expression of lesser rights. Try selling a piece of property in an area that is constantly bombarded, if not by artillery then perhaps by errant street gang pistol rounds. The price will be less than it would have been otherwise. The value of the land is reduced because the potential concert of rights that might be associated with the land is interceded by denial of the most basic rights. While this may seem obvious, stating the relationship of physical firepower to common rights in land allows consideration of the practical influence of most modern weapons and why it will become imperative to dominate control of the longest range technologies and possess weapons at every range, both physical and moral. It is also imperative to understand that the relationship between property value and weapons is not distantly theoretical. Connecting evidence is often immediate, available, and obvious. A few months after Abimael Guzmán (eccentric leader of the violent Peruvian revolutionary group Sendero Luminoso) was captured by the Peruvian government, prices for real estate in upscale residential areas of Lima began to soar. This had a wave effect on other real estate prices. Leftist radical bombing had for several years undercut the market value of homes and apartments. With the bombing over, general property values went up.

It is not an intention of this book to forecast what weapons will or will not be produced and which will dominate. However, seeing the relationship of basic property rights to subordinate rights and to the value of property, and considering the connotations of range, the author is compelled to conclude the following: whatever polity controls systems like those contemplated, say, by the US Space-Based Defense Initiative, will have an advantage in controlling lesser systems. It will in turn hold the advantage in winning property competitions that involve the use of lesser physical technologies.

The use of weapons has been stated in relationship to the will necessary to employ them, and it has been noted that the resolve needed to employ a precise weapon is logically less than the resolve needed to fire a weapon of mass destruction. It is not hard to envision a weapon that could be fired precisely at a finely identified target without intruding on the rights of most observers to the action. The weapon would not even have to be directed against a human life. It could coerce by threatening to knock out a single communication link or pipeline. It could threaten basic property rights in such a way as to influence all subordinate rights within the resolve of other would-be owners to use weapons in response. As has also been noted, when there is a gap between the level of weapon that can be employed, or the destructive consequences of the weapons, then cost-free coercion is made possible. More than just the ordnance delivering weapon, the idea of space-based defense or the domination of space systems flows from an understanding that future weapons will be broadly available. Just as with the particularization of power brought on by information and travel technologies, weapons control is also more diffuse than ever, as is sophisticated knowledge of their application and effectiveness. The achievable advantage of the United States and its close allies is in potential control of the longest-range systems. But even with control of the longest reaching and most technically advanced systems, there will remain range gaps, both physical and moral, that will allow maneuver room to opponents.

A report was produced in 1993 by the Center for Strategic and International Studies titled *The Military Technical Revolution* (MTR).[29] The document is the result of a six-month study that included the cooperation of several dozen experts on military matters. It provides a concise set of insights on the relationship of new technologies to the future of warfare and the future of US security challenges. It begins with an overview of national interests, stating that those interests will dictate the missions for US forces in the coming years, which in turn will determine what kind of military forces the United States requires. Included interests are protection of the US homeland, economic prosperity of Americans, democracy abroad, norms of behavior, and reputation. In their treatment of 'irregular warfare', the writers of *The Military Technical Revolution* seem to come from a bureaucratic experience given over to the development of large military technical systems. A skeptic might be swayed to think that the conclusions are obedient to a supposition that not much money can be made in weapon technologies oriented toward military operations other than open, maneuver war. 'Because military force is seldom decisive in irregular wars, the overarching political, social, and economic strategy for addressing those conflicts – in effect, the doctrine for irregular operations – becomes critical.'[30] It is by no means clear that military history teaches us that military force has seldom been decisive in irregular war, unless we simply define irregular war that way. It has to be remembered that it is the existence of irregulars and their violent actions that make us take note of the existence of an irregular war. An irregular enemy force is decisive to the existence of such a war. How can we say that failure or victory on the part of the enemy force has seldom been a decisive element? It is a mistaken lesson of Vietnam that the resolution of small, non-linear wars cannot be determined militarily. We forget that the North ultimately won the war with a tank thrust into Saigon and that defeat of the South Vietnamese army was the defining condition for victory over the South Vietnamese regime. We could easily say that deteriorated legitimacy and morale of the South Vietnamese government, combined with widespread participation in support of the Viet Cong, were the decisive factors. But, by similar logic we could say that military actions were not decisive in defeating Japan in World War II – that the determining factor was economic might of the United States. The authors of *The Military Technical Revolution* assert out-of-hand that 'The MTR can make only a limited contribution to irregular operations. In most cases, the roots of such conflicts are political, social, and economic in nature and do not admit easily to military solutions'.[31] If by 'military solutions' we are referring to the use of weapons and units appropriate for regular war then *ipso facto* the military technical revolution does not apply to irregular war. Perhaps then the conclusion can be made that the MTR will contribute little to prosecuting irregular war – if we could take the revolution where we wished. Unfortunately we cannot. It is curious that against the wisdom of Carl Von Clausewitz the CSIS study group so easily separated what is military from what is political.[32]

It does not carry logically that technology created for irregular war could not make a contribution to the prosecution of irregular war. This is true both of physical and organizational technologies.

The Military Technical Revolution defined the MTR as a 'fundamental advance in technology, doctrine, or organization that renders existing methods of conducting warfare obsolete'. What if the fundamental advance is innovative organization for irregular warfare, and the existing, obsolescent method of warfare turns out to be that kind in which *The Military Technical Revolution* says that MTR *can* make a significant contribution?

In April 1994, the US Army War College held a 'Fifth Annual Conference on Strategy' the topic of which was 'The Revolution in Military Affairs: Defining an Army for the 21st Century'. MTR had become RMA.[33] A spurt of papers on the subject was prepared for or as a result of the conference. One of the first was authored by Michael Mazarr, who had led the earlier CSIS study group.[34] In it Mazaar clarifies the MTR vision, citing Alvin and Heidi Toffler on a central guiding axiom.[35] 'No true revolution in military affairs is a narrowly military phenomenon. It is, in the most fundamental sense, the product of broad social and political transformation which gives rise to new military organizations and technologies.'[36] Mazaar's revolution, underway today, is in information, sensing, and precision strike technologies. These, he contends, demand substantial reforms in the existing methods of conducting warfare. Recommended reforms stress 'information dominance, synergy, disengaged combat, and civilianization'. Not everyone is impressed with the RMA. In a potent critique of the movement, A.C. Bacevich jabbed that 'however handsomely packaged, institutional advocacy of change almost invariably conceals a defense of orthodoxy'. Bacevich states:

> In truth, as currently touted by soldiers, the very concept of a Military Revolution is profoundly reactionary. Its true aim is to roll back the two genuine revolutions that have shaped war in the modern age, revolutions for which military professionals never devised an adequate response. The first of those revolutions was the advent of total war, culminating in the creation of nuclear weapons. The second – in large measure stimulated by the first – was the proliferation of conflict at the opposite end of the spectrum: terror, subversion, insurgency, and 'peoples war'.[37]

But Mazaar is explicit regarding the relationship of irregular war to the RMA:

> It is ... unsurprising that all four principles have always been true, to a greater or lesser degree, of irregular warfare. It was always non-linear, based on civilian political and socioeconomic factors; successful strategies to fight irregular war always deployed a high degree of synergy and civilian tools among their various political, military and economic elements. This suggests that future US military leaders will need more of the flexibility and innovativeness of thought characteristic of the great generals of guerrilla warfare, who have always looked to Sun Tzu, rather than Clausewitz for inspiration.[38]

In spite of great attention on the part of RMA strategic futurists of the important relationship between RMA and irregular warfare, Bacevich would say they are unresponsive to the real changes. Bacevich is perhaps as right as he is ungenerous. He suggests that the US military might only follow rules suited to its preferences: 'With politicians kept at some remove and the people observing appreciatively, generals will preside over neatly defined campaigns and battles, producing in short order and at tolerable cost the victories required to restore international comity. It is a vision of the Persian Gulf War replayed over and over again.'[39]

Property analysis exposes the revolution in military affairs in a different way. As ownership becomes more diffuse, and power more particularized, people will find ways to fight for and defend property that is not easily addressed in accordance with the existing state system. Few fights will be for the immediate taking, defense or recovery of the property fee, as was the Persian Gulf War in the most strikingly simple form. Property ownership is becoming chaotic. An armed force can have great success in enforcing and gaining specific property rights without having to share defining points of professionalism with the Western military model. For instance, an armed group, well-equipped with means for global electronic communication and travel, can suppress competition in a contraband trade, punish incompletion of contracts, protect the residences of their benefactors, and so forth. They can live the non-linear, synergistic, information-based, civilianized revolution. All the while, and while discussing the revolution, the United States military might deny that this armed group is professionally military, and could find it therefore unworthy of military attention. The revolution will be important to the military for the technologies that apply new things to the old wars. Any technology that changes the nature of the property – that changes what is being fought over, or that helps avoid the kind of war preferred by the United States military (where the United States military leaders would prefer to apply new machines) stands to be ignored.

High-end, interstate conflict may continue to demand the lion's share of technological resources. However, these geopolitical attractions are based on competitions for the entire ownership fee of set geographies. Not only future, but most current conflicts are or will be conducted to protect property rights short of the entire fee. These conflicts require their own organizational, physical and doctrinal inventions.

This chapter began by quoting a characterization made by Colin Gray that power was influence over behavior. Actually, his is a moderated, civilized definition. The power to destroy people affords the option to ignore people's behavior and go right to the purpose of power – property. Of course, Cline is talking about power to achieve human behavior that surrenders or shares property rights, or that submits to being chattel property. By adding property to the definition of power, we go beyond influence and behavior in our analysis, straight to what is being sought. In their exercise, attainment, or protection, preferential rights are the object of power. National power, its elements, and the instruments of national power (to include weapons), can be delineated in property terms. What remains is a more detailed showing, in property terms, of how power is used to attain and protect preferential rights. The next chapter, on strategy, moves toward that end.

NOTES

1. Hans J. Morgenthau and Kenneth W. Thompson, *Politics Among Nations: the Struggle for Power and Peace*, 6th edn (New York: Alfred Knopf, 1973), p. 117. 'We have spoken of the "power of a nation" or of "national power'" as though the concept were self-evident and sufficiently explained by what we have said about power in general. Yet, while it can be easily understood that individuals seek power, how are we to explain the aspirations for power in the collectivities called nations? What is a nation? What do we mean when we attribute to a nation aspirations and actions?... when we speak in empirical terms of the power or of the foreign policy of a certain nation, we can only mean the power or the foreign policy of certain individuals who belong to the same nation.' Ibid.
2. Colin S. Gray, 'Strategic Sense, Strategic Nonsense', *The National Interest* (Fall 1992), p.11.
3. The adjective 'strategic' should not be given more credit than it is due. We often suppose 'strategic' to have some logical relationship to the noun 'strategy', and thus a national strategy is related to a nation's strategic power. There is a usage problem disjoining the two terms, however. Military strategists try to enforce some semantic

discipline, but do so somewhat arbitrarily. An armored division may be designated as a tactical unit and a tank army as strategic – but it all depends on the context. The military staffs of some smaller countries may refer to a given battalion as 'strategic' because it can be committed throughout the national territory, is released at the national staff level, or is capable of making decisive changes in the course of combat actions. In US Army parlance, a third term, 'operational', is inserted between tactical and strategic. It is another difficult term because 'operation' and all of its derivatives – like 'operations', 'operative', 'operational' or 'operating' all have a variety of military meanings depending on the context of their use. Since the Second World War, 'operational' has gained honored space in the hierarchy of terms as it refers to a level of military art or knowledge. At the operational level, maneuvers are planned and executed that achieve or support strategic goals and that involve multiple units at the tactical level. Meanwhile, the US Air Force has become disenchanted with the adjective 'strategic'. The Persian Gulf War saw the B-52 strategic bombers flying tactical support missions while tactical fighters were doing strategic bombing. At the heart of its universal usage, 'strategic' carries the connotation of comprehensiveness – of being more than just military or local or short-term. For the US military, strategy does not lie atop the pyramid of decision-making. Above it is policy, a term reserved in professional subordination for the leadership expressions of the highest government officials. Outside military vernacular, strategy may still be found in the middle of the hierarchies used to describe decision-making. Vision/strategy/projects/tactics is a typical ordering.
4. Morgenthau and Thompson, *Politics Among Nations*, p. 117.
5. Determinism (*environmental determinism*, or *environmentalism*) caused a post-World War I reaction among geographers that was referred to as *possibilism*. French historian Lucien Febvre apparently invented the term. The possibilists stressed the power of human choice rather than environmental limitations to it. Although Mackinder himself swung toward the possibilists in his later thinking, the German translation of his Heartland Theory had great impact on German territorial acquisitiveness and on arguments that would bring the United States into World War II.
6. According to Mackinder's theory, control of the heartland, or central region, threatened the 'sea powers' meaning first Britain, and then the United States. N.J. Spykman (*American Strategy in World Politics*, 1942) picked up on the idea, but with a different thrust. He visualized the 'rimland' countries as being more important. These included Japan, Britain, India and the Mideast countries. He speculated that United States security depended on preventing the formation of an enemy coalition of rimland powers, or domination of rimland areas by the heartland (Russia). Necessity is the mother of invention, and Mackinder was as much innovative politician as innovative theorist. He sensed the strategic moment of the Heartland argument. Spykman, much less the politician, nevertheless recognized the durability of Mackinder's Heartland Theory and anticipated the American need for a post-war strategic vision. This, together with the intercontinental range of missiles, made the Heartland Theory a survivor. John E. Kieffer, in *Realities of World Power* (New York: D. McKay, 1952), picked up the geopolitical ball, explaining the East–West polarization using a power belt theory. Though equally as logical or illogical, Kieffer was nowhere as influential.
7. See Gerard Chaliand and Jean-Pierre Rageau, *A Strategic Atlas*, 2nd edn (trans. by Tony Berrett) (New York: Harper & Row, 1983). This atlas displays major geopolitical theories graphically and includes cartographic views of the world from various perspectives. 'Although it is sometimes excessively systematic, the geopolitical approach is stimulating; but it is so only if there is no lapse into geographical determinism and if all factors in the balance are taken into account.' Chaliand and Rageau's atlas presents many standard geographic features such as population, economic and natural resource distributions. It also shows a number of

8. Ray S. Cline, *World Power Assessment* (Boulder, CO: Westview Press, 1975).
9. John Spanier, *Games Nations Play*, 8th edn (Washington, DC: Congressional Quarterly, 1993).
10. These five elements, or components, of power are the same quantities as expressed earlier in the three-part reduction for analysis of the ownership environment – owners, rights, and ownership rules. Analysis of leadership falls under analysis of property owners. Technology is separately treated for the reasons stated in the text, and because technological change is such an important determinant of the rapid changes in the ownership environment that often cause conflicts.
11. *Resolve*, *morale*, *will*, and *cohesiveness* are closely related. The author has chosen to distinguish *cohesiveness* as the strength of a common identity as owners. The connotation is one of breadth and depth of emotion regarding a shared identity. A powerful feeling of solidarity as Americans gives an American president as a national leader, great potential power. *Resolve* and *will* carry a connotation more closely related to perseverance and willingness to sacrifice to achieve an end. They are less closely associated with strength of identity and solidarity. The meaning of *morale*, used especially by military people, seems to reside somewhere in between. One might say that the leader must translate cohesiveness into resolve in the face of a given project. If his organization, group, unit, or nation has high morale, the task is easy. The semantic differences are of secondary importance, and any overlap or lack of discipline in their use is of little harm to the principal points about national power.
12. See Joseph C. Goulden, *Truth is the First Casualty: The Gulf of Tonkin Affair – Illusion and Reality* (Chicago, IL: Rand McNally, 1969); Anthony Austin, *The President's War* (New York: J.B. Lippincott, 1971).
13. Some explanations of national power list the military as a basic element rather than as an instrument. When confronted by an international event or situation that requires or could benefit by the application or threat of physical force, the nation must arguably have some force on-hand. The technology, physical and organizational, of modern military force demands a development and procurement time so great that it is not feasible to wait for an enemy before determining to acquire a military instrument with which to respond. Also, the status of a nation-state seems so closely tied to the existence of a national military that the two concepts, state and military, often seem inseparable. The designation of military capacity as a basic element of power causes a new range of semantic problems, and twists arguments back in the loop of tautologies. For instance, does military power include police power? It is more than a semantic problem. Institutionally, many nations have national police or paramilitary forces under their defense departments. More important still is the question of intelligence. The capacity to know, under the rubric that knowledge is power, has fallen more and more to separate, civilian intelligence organizations. In many countries these apparatuses may be more significant than the military as supporting columns of the state. Some nations, meanwhile, have their entire intelligence apparatus under military control.
14. Geoffrey Blainey, *The Causes of War* (New York: Macmillan, 1973), p. 114.
15. 'Chapter 8, The Abacus of Power', ibid., pp. 108–24 passim. Blainey also writes, 'In peace time the relations between two diplomats are like relations between two merchants. While the merchants trade in copper or transistors, the diplomats' transactions involve boundaries, spheres of influence, commercial concessions and a variety of other issues which they have in common. A foreign minister or diplomat is a merchant who bargains on behalf of his country. He is both buyer and seller, though he buys and sells privileges and obligations rather than commodities. The

treaties he signs are simply more courteous versions of commercial contracts.' Ibid., p. 115.
16. Blainey, p. 149.
17. E.J. Hobsbawm, *Primitive Rebels: Studies of Archaic Forms of Social Movement in the 19th and 20th Centuries* (New York: W.W. Norton, 1959).
18. Graham H. Turbiville, Jr, 'International Organized Crime and Its Impact on US Interests'. Prepared for the National Strategy Information Center Conference, International Organized Crime, June 1993.
19. Walter B. Wriston, *The Twilight of Sovereignty: How the Information Revolution is Transforming Our World* (New York: Charles Scribner's Sons, 1992), p. 108. Wriston identifies technology as a culprit in the dispersion of power as well as a key to maintaining national wealth. 'If we are to compete in the global marketplace, we must constantly build and renew our intellectual capital. We have little or no control over the natural resources within our borders, but we do have control over our educational and cultural environment.' Wriston is optimistic, however, saying that the information revolution gives advantage to superior ideas, and that freedom has proved over and over to be a superior idea. When placed in an unrestricted open market by new technologies, good ideas hard are to restrict. 'The fax machine has become the pamphleteer of the late twentieth century.' Wriston also points out the real competitive importance of encoding and decoding. A state that does not master codes in the information age is highly vulnerable. Wriston calls this the single advantage in an information age that cannot be sacrificed.
20. Colin McMahon, 'Measures Racist Angry Mexicans Say', *Chicago Tribune*, 10, November 1994, p. 14, News Section.
21. A US Person is defined by executive order to be 'A United States citizen, an alien known by the intelligence agency concerned to be a permanent resident alien, an unincorporated association substantially composed of United States citizens or permanent resident aliens, or a corporation directed and controlled by a foreign government or governments'. Ronald Reagan, Executive Order No. 12333, 4 December 1981, 'Presidents Oversight Intelligence Board'. This can be found in *Compilation of Intelligence Laws and Related Laws and Executive Orders of Interest to the National Intelligence Community* (Washington, DC: US Government Printing Office, 1993), p. 645.
22. At their best, news organizations produce public intelligence. They survive on timely collection, analysis and dissemination of information supposedly useful for public decision-making, and they are sometimes the producers of the only intelligence available. Similarities between the news and intelligence industries are numerous enough that contact between the two is inevitable. The relationship between reporters and government intelligence agency personnel (in countries where they are not one-and-the-same) at least becomes one of mutual use. See *The CIA and the Media: Hearings Before the House Subcommittee on Oversight, Permanent Select Committee on Intelligence*, 95th Cong., 1st and 2nd Sess. (1978); see also, Lawrence J. Mitchell III, 'Espionage: The Symbiotic Relationship Between the Central Intelligence Agency and the American Press Corps', *Suffolk Transnational Law Journal*, 11, 41 (1987).
23. See Anne Wells Branscomb, *Who Owns Information?* (New York: HarperCollins, 1994). Branscomb correctly treats information in terms both of power and property. She asks, Who Owns Your Name and Address?, Who Owns Your Electronic Messages?, Who Owns Computer Software?, Who Owns Government Information?, and other questions that have direct bearing on the pace of the diffusion of ownership and the particularization of power.
24. The Internet is the realization of an old dream about universally shared global information. H.G. Wells, in one of his less well-known works, promoted the idea of a universal encyclopedia of knowledge and a worldwide common educational curriculum as an engine of world peace. Herbert George Wells, *World Brain*

(London: Methuen, 1938). Wells wasn't very optimistic about human nature or the use of information, however. 'Man reflects before he acts, but not very much; he is still by nature intellectually impatient. No sooner does he apprehend, in whole or in part, the need of a new world, than, without further plans or estimates, he gets into a state of passionate aggressiveness and suspicion and sets about trying to change the present order. There and then, he sets about it, with anything that comes handy, violently, disastrously, making the discordances worse instead of better, and quarrelling bitterly with anyone who is not in complete accordance with his particular spasmodic conception of the change needful. He is unable to realize that when the time comes to act, that also is the time to think fast and hard. He will not think enough.' Ibid., p. xi.

25. An oddly relevant historical analogy can be found in Hagen Schulze, *The Course of German Nationalism* (New York: Cambridge University Press, 1985). In one section, Schulze describes the energy generated in 1848 Berlin over news of the revolution in Paris. 'Public opinion immediately entered a stage familiar to the early history of all revolutions: that of widespread excitement and general exasperation, when opportunities for general outbursts are cultivated, without giving the police occasion for effective counter-attacks. "The public places", wrote a contemporary observer, "the reading-booths ... presented an unusual appearance as overcrowded political meeting places ..."', ibid., p. 7. The dawn of new communication technologies and the widespread, poorly censored or monitored use of public communications gives hint to the importance of the Internet.

26. See generally, The Arms Project of Human Rights Watch and Physicians for Human Rights, *Landmines: A Deadly Legacy* (New York: Human Rights Watch and Physicians for Human Rights, 1993).

27. In December 1993, the United Nations General Assembly passed a resolution calling for a ban on the export of anti-personnel landmines. The United States, describing the UN action a 'first step', is going further, formally urging a number of countries to join in banning the export, sale or transfer of mines for three to five years. During that time, negotiations on a permanent ban and monitoring arrangements would be conducted. For a comprehensive report on the worldwide status of the anti-personnel landmine see *Landmines: A Deadly Legacy* (New York: Human Rights Watch and Physicians for Human Rights, 1993) *Landmines* covers landmine technology, use, production, clearance problems, existing legal prohibitions, and the peculiar difficulties of victim care. *Landmines* quotes a Defense Intelligence Agency analysis, saying 'landmines are an affordable weapon for the entire range of military organizations, from terrorist groups to large, well-equipped armies' and 'will continue to be a significant element in armed conflicts at all levels of intensity well into the foreseeable future'.

28. Precision of a weapon is not quite the same as its accuracy. An accurate weapon will hit where it is aimed and if aimed at the same exact point over and over, will keep hitting it. A precise weapon is one that only hits and effects what it is intended to hit and nothing else. The idea of accuracy and precision are related in that an inaccurate weapon is also imprecise. However, a very accurate weapon might also be imprecise. A nuclear weapon aimed at a factory in Siberia might hit dead-on no matter how many times it were sent, but it could not be expected to harm only the factory.

29. Michael J. Mazaar, *et al.*, *The Military Technical Revolution* (Washington, DC: Center for Strategic and International Studies, 1993).

30. Ibid., p. 48.

31. Ibid., p. 54.

32. 'We see, therefore, that war is not merely an act of policy but a true political instrument, a continuation of political intercourse, carried on with other means.' Carl Von Clausewitz, *On War*, ed. and trans. Michael Howard and Peter Paret (Princeton, NJ: Princeton University Press, 1989), p. 87. This is perhaps the most

quoted phrase from *On War*. The section of *On War* that follows regards the diverse nature of war, and in it Clausewitz retreats a bit, giving war more semantic distance from politics: 'the less intense the motives, the less will the military element's natural tendency to violence coincide with political directives. As a result, war will be driven further from its natural course, the political object will be more and more at variance with the aim of the ideal war, and the conflict will seem increasingly political in character.' Ibid., p. 88.

33. Curiously, the term RMA as well as the general range of concerns, apparently has at least one root in Soviet military theorizing. See, for example, N.A. Lomov, ed., *Scientific-Technical Progress and the Revolution in Military Affairs: A Soviet View*, trans. the United States Air Force (Washington, DC: US Government Printing Office, 1979).
34. Paul Bracken and Raul Henri Alcala, *Whither the RMA: Two Perspectives on Tomorrow's Army* (Carlisle, PA: Strategic Studies Institute, 1994); Jeffrey R. Cooper, *Another View of the Revolution in Military Affairs* (Carlisle, PA: Strategic Studies Institute, 1994); Michael J. Mazaar, *The Revolution in Military Affairs: A Framework for Defense Planning* (Carlisle, PA: Strategic Studies Institute, 1994); Steven Metz and James Kievit, *The Revolution in Military Affairs and Conflict Short of War* (Carlisle, PA: Strategic Studies Institute, 1994).
35. Alvin and Heidi Toffler, *War and Anti-War: Survival at the Dawn of the 21st Century* (Boston, MA: Little, Brown, 1993).
36. Mazar, *The Revolution in Military Affairs*, p. 2.
37. A.J. Bacevich, 'Preserving the Well-Bred Horse', *The National Interest* (Fall 1994) pp. 43–9.
38. Mazaar, *The Revolution in Military Affairs*, p. 28.
39. Bacevich, 'Preserving the Well-Bred Horse', p. 48; Bacevich may be right about the reactionary tendency of military thinking, but his is not the whole story. Margaret Wheatley's *Leadership and the New Science* (San Francisco: Berrett-Koehler, 1992) has become a popular leadership text among some American military instructors. 'Intentionally or not, we work from a worldview that has been derived from the natural sciences. But the science has changed.' Ibid., p. 6. Understanding non-linear, seemingly chaotic processes is the most important new direction in military leadership.

5
Strategy, Access and Extortion

> Strategic culture ... is very much the product of geopolitical factors as they are locally interpreted.[1] (Colin Gray, from *The Geopolitics of Superpower*)

We defined national strategic power as an interweave of the following factors – cohesiveness of identity, ideology, leadership, technology, and the wealth enjoyed by a people and applied to gain or defend property. In this chapter, strategy is a decision process that supports ownership.[2] Plans and efforts of a government to attain or maintain worldwide property ownership, or to attain or maintain strategic power, are discussed under the rubric 'national strategy'. 'National strategy' means a course of action (tied to objectives and resources) taken by a government to gain or defend property. However, leaders of every property-owning or property-claiming identity in the world will apply a strategy, even if the scope of desires and efforts does not seem to merit the modifier strategic. Wealth applied to foreign policies is not all applied toward goals of the government. Strategies of individual citizens and groups of citizens can also be considered part of the country's strategy or as an expression of the country's power. The cohesiveness of identity, ideology, leadership, technology, and wealth of Americans is only partly the product of anything the United States government does, and these same quantities are threatened by factors that the United States government may be inadequate or indisposed to deal with. Therefore, 'national' strategy must be distinguished from a 'nation's' strategy, the latter being more ambivalent, multidirectional, unmapped, and probably more important than whatever the national government does.

Recent debate over United States national and military strategy highlights this possible drifting away of government policy from a nation's purpose and efforts. Venerable theoretical determinants of US military strategy, particularly those involving geopolitics and annihilation warfare, impede the adoption of needed innovations. Strategic thinking appropriate for success in the context of major military confrontations has made the prosecution of less-than-critical contests more difficult. It is instructive to note that Colin Gray, whose definition of power began the preceding chapter, wrote a 1988 book entitled *The Geopolitics of Super Power*.[3] In it, Gray favorably invokes the influence on American security policy of Mackinder's Heartland and Nicholas Spykman's Rimland theories. Reading his book less than a decade later makes one strain to remember the strategic context in which Gray's advice was so plausible. 'Even without a great statesman at the helm – though with policy makers who are, one hopes, familiar with the ideas of Halford Mackinder and Nicholas Spykman – Americans should be able to remember that the Soviet Union is going to be an enemy for a long time to come; that Soviet power needs to be distracted by major military tasks on the ground in Eurasia; and that Soviet seapower should be denied access at will to the world's oceans.'[4] There may yet be a ring of truth there, but the inertia of this thinking creates a mismatch between the theoretical underpinnings of American strategic policy and the kinds of challenges that the United States most often takes up.

Neither Mackinder nor Spykman wrote of geographic areas as property with divisible rights. They mentioned cultural data as entries on lists of factors – like population or strategic materials, but their geopolitics assumed that whole geographies were lost or gained in gulps. Strategic materials and populations were obtained or subdued through territorial control. It is a whole-fee approach to property inspired by litmus test sovereign entities. Perhaps the threat posed by the Soviet heartland is not gone forever, and anyway, more states exist that seem interested in gobbling up other lands. This fact demands respect. Geopolitics is by no means an empty subject. However, it is the world of diffuse ownership and particularized power that promises to occupy the majority of spies and diplomats day-to-day. Most places demand a strategy whose theoretical roots show all the knotty twists of property relationships. In fact, the United States has at times formulated property-oriented strategies, usually a version of land reform. Land, or agrarian, reform has been variously embraced by the parties to many conflicts throughout the world. Even admitting these property strategies we can ascribe unevenness of results to incomplete understanding of the ownership environment.

NATIONAL STRATEGY OF THE UNITED STATES

> Our national security requires the patient application of American will and resources. (from the US *National Security Strategy of Engagement and Enlargement*, 1996)

United States national security strategy, and the military servicing of that strategy, has been the object of a dialectic irony – one that bedevils Fukuyama's thesis about the end of history arriving with the triumph of liberal democracy. The United States has successfully exported principles that have caused the diffusion of ownership and the breakdown of traditional sovereignties. Ownership rules worldwide have been turned in the direction of free trade and constitutional social contracts. During the process, the United States' war machine evolved in a world of nation-state contests. Bipolar, nuclear superpower competition lengthened the historical relevance of these whole-fee military strategies against which American might was shaped. Meanwhile, the global ownership environment continued to change in a way that would leave the whole-fee strategies inappropriate for the defense of most national property rights. This is the thrust of the discussion that follows: that the world ownership environment, changed in good measure by American success, has left the American military (and others) unmatched to ownership challenges that the country faces. There is no petulant insistence that the old ways be immediately changed wholesale. Although this book tends to paint things otherwise, large battles involving capital-intense forces contesting sizeable geographies will remain a dangerous possibility for the foreseeable future. Nevertheless, there will be a far greater number of important contests for which traditional military answers are not appropriate.

Geopolitics has been a dominant intellectual influence in contemporary United States foreign policy. This point is expertly argued by Geoffrey Sloan in *Geopolitics in United States Strategic Policy, 1890–1987*.[5] Sloan weaves together American geopolitical theorizing, geopolitical expressions in US policy, and the geopolitical determinants of other policy traditions. He recognizes a remarkable intuition displayed by America's best-known geopolitical theorist, Nicholas Spykman. As geopolitician, Spykman claimed that the power of a state was strongly related to its location and its physical features. His geographic focus, and what distinguished his work from Mackinder's, was what he called the Rimland of Eurasia. Playing on Mackinder's Heartland theory, Spykman asserted that 'who controls the Rimland rules Eurasia; who rules Eurasia controls the destinies of the world'.[6] Spykman's observation may seem gratuitous coming as it did in 1941. Anyone might have stumbled across a threatening presence or two on the outer edges of the Eurasian landmass. But what Spykman stated as the consequence of this geographic observation set in motion what is a beautiful example of the far-reaching impact pure theory can have on strategy. Spykman stated that the rimland powers of Japan and Germany would, after the end of the war, become allies of the United States to counter Russian expansion.[7] He had maintained that Soviet foreign policy aims, as Russia's before, were to break out of the heartland to warm water ports, and ultimately, to dominate the world. Understandably, his predictions were not universally well received at the time. Spykman died in 1943, and as the coming end of the war exposed the need to reappraise strategic threats in a changed world order, Spykman's geopolitics quickly gained influential weight. His observations were stated in the context of power balancing within the state system. World domination was a viable end in a zero-sum game of dominators. All this had a natural appeal to the strategy-oriented.

Sloan points out that Spykman's reputation suffered vilification as the 'American Haushofer'.[8] The conclusions Spykman asserted or implied from his interpretation of geography – that the United States should not seek to destroy Germany and Japan, but only to change regimes and preserve the countries intact as allies – appeared to be in amoral if not immoral consonance with disgraced enemies. Consequently, neither Spykman nor geopolitics would enjoy the open recognition during the early years of containment strategy that they perhaps deserved.[9] Sloan indicates that Henry Kissinger called for an explicit geopolitics, but that he did not mean a theory of spatial and historical causation. He meant power equilibrium. Of course, treatment of states and regions as discrete geographic entities among which power could be balanced was always both precondition for and effect of geopolitical thinking. (Obviously, geoproperty, in which owner identities and ownership slices are not delimited by boundaries and governments, would seem a generally confusing theoretical environment for the balance-of-power practitioner.)

In 1986, the United States Congress passed The Department of Defense Reorganization Act (the Goldwater–Nichols Act). It stipulates that the President of the United States annually send to Congress a comprehensive report on the country's national security strategy.[10] The Act orders that the annual report include a description and discussion of the following:

(1) The worldwide interests, goals, and objectives of the United States that are vital to the national security of the United States.

(2) The foreign policy, worldwide commitments, and national defense capabilities of the United States necessary to deter aggression and to implement the strategy.

(3) The proposed short- and long-term uses of the political, economic, military, and other elements of the national power to protect or promote national interests and achieve goals and objectives.

(4) The adequacy of the capabilities of the United States to carry out the national security strategy, including an evaluation of the balance among the capabilities of all elements of the national power to support implementation of the strategy.

(5) Such other information as may be necessary to help inform Congress on matters relating to the national security strategy of the United States.[11]

Early versions of the official *National Security Strategy of the United States*, the document prepared annually by the president to comply with the aforementioned Act, show the influence of geopolitical thinking in the explanation if not the construction of US foreign policy. President Reagan's 1988 report, written just before the close of the Cold War, presents an enlightening contrast to President Bush's 1993 report.

In 1988, the essential 'objectives' of the United States were summed as peace, security, and freedom. The report states that the

> first historical dimension of our strategy is relatively simple, clear-cut, and immensely sensible. It is the conviction that the United

> States' most basic national security interests would be endangered if a hostile state or group of states were to dominate the Eurasian landmass – that area of the globe often referred to as the world's heartland. We fought two world wars to prevent this from occurring. And since 1945, we have sought to prevent the Soviet Union from capitalizing on its geostrategic advantage to dominate its neighbors in Western Europe, Asia, and the Middle East, and thereby fundamentally alter the global balance of power to our disadvantage. ... The national strategy to achieve this objective has been containment, in the broadest sense of that term.[12]

Thus the official security strategy of the United States asserted a continuity with past national goals and policies (although President Reagan's interpretation of 'containment' was far more forward-leaning than President Carter's had been). It ratified the geopolitical slice of foreign affairs scholarship. Also in introductory paragraphs, national 'values' (human dignity, personal freedom, individual rights, the pursuit of happiness, peace and prosperity) were tied logically to 'an international order that encourages self-determination, democratic institutions, economic development, and human rights. The values were to be translated into national interests and objectives. The interests were defined as:

(1) The survival of the United States as a free and independent nation, with its fundamental values intact and its institutions and people secure.

(2) A healthy and growing US economy to provide opportunity for individual prosperity and a resource base for our national endeavors.

(3) A stable and secure world, free of major threats to US interests.

(4) The growth of human freedom, democratic institutions, and free market economies throughout the world, linked by a fair and open international trading system.

(5) Healthy and vigorous alliance relationships.[13]

The document states that the major 'objectives' in support of national 'interests' are to:

(1) Maintain the security of our nation and our allies.

(2) Respond to challenges of the global economy.

(3) Defend and advance the cause of democracy, freedom, and

human rights around the world.
(4) Resolve peacefully disputes which affect US interests in troubled regions of the world.
(5) Build effective and friendly relations with all nations with whom there is a basis of shared concern.[14]

The president's document did not present a very clear hierarchy of terms with respect to values, interests, policies goals, or objectives. This has to be forgiven in light of bureaucratic birthright of any such document and the cloudily synonymous nature of the available vocabulary. A good sense of national strategy still emerges from a generous reading of the report. Starting with the Constitution as the guide, the US government states that Americans should be safe, free and prosperous. The United States has looked at the rest of the world and, in general, concluded that it would be advantageous if other peoples were prosperous, safe and free as well. Though not always observed in the specifics, this has been a noble slice of national identity and the wellspring of considerable power. The government in 1988 also concluded that there was a single major threat to United States' wealth, safety and freedom – the Soviet Union. The resulting particulars were clear. The United States would defend Western Europe against the Soviet Union, even if it meant using nuclear weapons, and the military would seek physically to defend the United States rather than expose its territory to nuclear attack as part of a theory of mutually assured destruction. The United States would also support not only governments, but revolutionaries who were struggling against Soviet surrogates or were opposed to its ideological corollaries. In short, the United States was officially dedicated to fighting and winning the Cold War. The spirit reflected in the 1988 National Security Strategy (NSS) had been evolving over the previous several years, and was distinct from the tone and spirit of security policy of the previous decade. By 1988, the United States was no longer tied to massive offensive reaction as a strategic defense.

In addition to the required annual National Security Strategy, another major strategy document was published in 1988, the report of the Commission on Integrated Long-Term Strategy.[15] The commission was co-chaired by Fred Ikle and Albert Wohlstetter. First, it recommended that the United States emphasize a wider range of threats than the two that had dominated policy and force planning for decades prior.[16] Instead of concentrating on the extreme cases of a massive communist attack through Central Europe or all-out nuclear war, the commission called for the ability to make discriminate military responses to lesser, but still major confrontations in other areas. In essence, the report recognized the kind of dangerous physical and moral gap that was discussed in the previous chapter on strategic power. It stated that by focusing so exclusively on Armageddon scenarios, other challenges could be mounted by the Soviet Union that would be very costly, but would nevertheless not stir the resolve of United States' allies into a unified or effective response. 'To help our allies and to defend our interests abroad, we cannot rely on threats expected to provoke our own annihilation if carried out. ... We must diversify and strengthen our ability to bring discriminating, non-nuclear forces to bear where needed in time to defeat aggression. ... To help deter nuclear attack and to make it safer to reduce offensive arms we need strategic defense. ... We will need capabilities for discriminate nuclear strikes to deter a limited nuclear attack on allied or US forces.'[17]

The report also lamented a deteriorating American technological lead, and proposed a further strengthening of the ability of the United States to not only contain, but to confront the Soviet Union at all levels below all-out war. The introduction refers to 'the next twenty years' and 'the long haul'. It and its 1988 companion, the NSS (which followed the commission report) are especially informing in light of the timing of their appearance. Five years earlier, in March of 1983, President Ronald Reagan 'addressed the American people and said that it was time to turn the technological might of the nation, not to inventing ever more deadly offensive weapons, but instead to creating new instruments for peace and stability'.[18] This meant the earnest development of the Space Based Defense Initiative, or Star Wars. The primary defense strategy documents in 1988 followed through on a course that had been set near the beginning of the Reagan presidency. They announced a long-term policy of technological, all-level, all-places competition against the Soviet Union. Considering the accelerated changes in the Soviet Union beginning in 1989, it is difficult to believe that the strategic gauntlet of expensive, unyielding, detailed competition thrown down by the United States did not count among the causes of the Soviet Union's demise, or at least its moment. During the following five years, the strategy statements of the United States would reflect the caution, relief, uncertainty and opportunity of watching the main enemy melt away.

Writing the National Security Strategy in 1993 was a different challenge than in 1988 since Cold War containment of and competition with the communist empire could no longer serve as an azimuth. The 1993 document featured arms control and limiting the proliferation of nuclear weapons, control of illicit drug trafficking, halting environmental degradation, advancement of free market global economics, fostering democracy worldwide, responding to straightforward aggressions, and building coalitions with allies to achieve all of the other goals.[19] The Russians were not entirely off the scope yet. They still held the ability to destroy American land, had not left Cuba completely, nor had they withdrawn troops from much of the former Soviet empire. The national strategy document reflected on the possibility of a resurgent Russia, but the direction was one of greater specificity in describing the actions to be included in the government's strategy to provide for the general welfare and secure the common defense.

The first National Security Strategy of the Clinton administration was due for publication in the spring of 1994. However, differences of vision between the Departments of Defense and the Department of State delayed internal administration acceptance of a unified strategy document. An April draft placed new emphasis on non-traditional security concerns like global climate change, the spread of AIDS, population growth, and mass migration. The Department of State oriented on the use of diplomacy to address human and environmental concerns while the Department of Defense sought to retain a geopolitical construction.[20]

In this debate within the Clinton administration we see the recurring post-Cold War clash between the two strains in United States foreign policy. The difficulty of arriving at a reconciliation between the realist and idealist traditions lies partly in the artificial distance of vocabularies between the two perspectives, as well as in misguiding aspects of both. The geopolitical perspective tends to overly simplify classification of foreign lands according to physical geographical aspects. This can lead to poorly prioritized national interests. Oil, the possibility of oil, distance in terms of missile ranges, jet engine minerals, or sea lane choke points consume analyses, while other values, less visible on the map, are obscured still further. Many geopolitical measurements are created within the hypothetical context of international war. Thus, places gain importance and priority because of their contribution in the exceptional case of global conflict. Other lands, whose property may have far greater value, and whose problems insinuate greater risk to the value of neighbors' properties, go overlooked. In this century, Panama has been a nearly compulsory geopolitical reference in all descriptions of US strategy – Mexico an unusual one.

On the other hand, the moralist approach is subject to the accusation of being naive, at times even silly. It, too, simplifies problems, not recognizing their competitive nature. Humanitarian aid, for instance, is immensely satisfying to the collective Calvinist conscious, but it often generates superficial action that denies the validity and even the existence of violent politics. It is understandable that the argument of humanitarian purpose would effervesce within the United States administration when it did, irrespective of the supposed ideological leanings of the Clinton policy team. The fall of the Soviets and the resultant geostrategic supremacy of the United States virtually vacated the possibility of an all-consuming war, and gave more room to moralist policy arguments. *Realpolitik* could no longer dispatch moralizing voices by invoking the urgency of mortal competition.

A Clinton administration national security strategy document titled *A National Security Strategy of Engagement and Enlargement* was finally published in July 1994.[21] It recognized post-Soviet complications in penning a national strategy. Goals had to be coherent and broadly shared if there were to be much hope of mobilizing public support. Protection of the natural environment was highlighted and will probably remain a visible part of future US national security statements. Economic integration was emphasized and isolationism rejected, though the document downplayed the United States' role as a world policeman. Militarily, it called for an ability to win, in concert with regional allies, two nearly simultaneous major regional conflicts (MRC). The Persian Gulf and the Korean Peninsula are the regions alluded to. In a section dealing with when and how to employ US military forces, the president's statement asserts that the United States will use force decisively, unilaterally if necessary, in those specific areas where United States vital or survival interests are involved. Vital or survival interests are defined as 'those of broad, overriding importance to the survival, security and vitality of our national entity'. Once again, the strategy had fallen into a, perhaps forgivable, tautology. Survival interests are those of importance to survival? Is stemming illegal immigration vital or not? Would protecting the Amazon rain forest be a survival interest? It appears that while national security documentation might provide insights regarding the probable decision paths of national leaders, we are really left a know-it-when-you-see-it understanding of what vital national interests are.[22]

Comparing recent United States governments' national strategies according to their corporate understanding of national interests, we are likely to find that the verbiage rises to a common level of abstraction that takes away distinguishing edges. We can nevertheless discover a controversial change of vision tied to owner identity. The Bush administration stated the premier national interest this way:

> Foremost, the United States must ensure its security as a free and independent nation, and the protection of its fundamental values, institutions, and people. This is a sovereign responsibility which we will not abdicate to any other nation or collective organization.[23]

President Clinton's first national security strategy betrayed something significantly different:

> The US government is responsible for protecting the lives and personal safety of Americans, maintaining our political freedom and independence as a nation and providing for the well-being and prosperity of our nation. No matter how powerful we are as a nation, we cannot secure these basic goals unilaterally ... Therefore, the only responsible US strategy is one that seeks to ensure US influence over and participation in collective decisionmaking in a wide and growing range of circumstances.[24]

The international direction of collective identity taken by the Clinton administration is apparent. Of course, it may be in the selfish national interest of the United States to at times encourage international cooperation in security matters, but the Clinton 1994 national security strategy displayed something more about the administration's core beliefs. We began to see how closely the United States might follow this enlarged sense of owner identity. The US president went to the United Nations for approval to enter Haiti with military forces, not to the US Congress.[25] Public displeasure and an historic shift of party control from Democrats to Republicans in the 1994 mid-term congressional elections leaned United States policy back away from this kind of enlargement. Many United States congressional leaders felt disillusionment with United Nations capability and legitimacy after the debacle in Somalia in 1992. For better or worse, the public fecklessness of world government helps determine America's definition of what 'we' means for the formulators of US foreign policy. Geoproperty suggests that national government strategies are decreasingly complete reflections of their people's global efforts. The United Nations, unable to reconcile the property conflicts of contending member states in this century, is even less competent to address the disparate property issues of the next.

All of the basic elements of national strategy found in the major United States strategy documents can be usefully considered in property terms. For instance, outlines in *A National Security Strategy of Engagement and Enlargement* about what the United States should do – about the need to enlarge the community of democratic nations, protect the environment and promote economic integration – are easy to express in property terms. We would simply say that the United States seeks to expand acceptance of its ideology regarding rules of ownership, ensure that other possessors meet ownership duties (according to the accepted rules), and increase the value of property through open trade. There is an evident efficiency in so stating the problem. In the examples used above, we note that simple investigation of items of national interest may often prove infertile. By addressing other elements of the ownership environment, such as attitudes about the collective identity of owners, we can perhaps more easily define the points of potential disagreement.

We might arrive at the following, dysfunctional conclusion: the difference between a 'Reagan–Bush' and a 'Carter–Clinton' vision is not in the goals or identification of national interests, but rather in the way to achieve them (national interests remaining the same while the route to secure them is adjusted). Such an analysis could be comforting, especially to those who believe that national interests have an immutable quality and that consistency in their interpretation lends strength. The conclusion, however, is misleading in the extreme, even while it is true. The important change is not in the generalized statement of high-toned values. It is in the vision regarding for whom the national property is to be protected, and according to whose formula of ownership. Put bluntly, the first Clinton administration policy documents appeared to call for the nation to share its sense of ownership more widely and to relinquish some decision-making regarding the protective mechanisms supporting that ownership. Is this the same as surrendering sovereignty? Without a doubt. Is it bad, either for the United States or the rest of the world? Before hardening an answer, we should first look at an area of great consequence in the construction of national strategic vision – the development of national military strategy.

National strategy – the reconciliation of ends, ways, and means in service of the national ownership – must take careful account of the physical power the nation can muster to underwrite its objectives. The military strategy must service the national objectives and national objectives should not be established that are beyond possibility of attainment. So in the case of the US it is valuable to trace how military statements of support to the national strategy have changed or tried to change with the end of the Cold War. The United States armed forces have not adjusted enough.

UNITED STATES MILITARY STRATEGY

> I say that, in my judgement, those are able to maintain themselves who, from an abundance of men and money, can put a well appointed army into the field, and meet anyone in open battle that may attempt to attack them. And I esteem those as having need of the constant support of others who cannot meet their enemies in the field, but are under the necessity of taking refuge behind walls and keeping within them. (Niccolò Machiavelli, from *The Prince*)

American military theory has drawn from an eclectic mix of thinkers such as Antoine-Henri Jomini, Carl Von Clausewitz, Alfred Thayer Mahan, Emory Upton, Giulio Douhet, William Mitchell, Basil Liddell Hart and others. Jomini, for example, was influential for his structured, geometric approach to organizing a battlefield. Clausewitz proffered psychological aspects of war and the concepts of war as an instrument of policy. Clausewitz, a nineteenth-century strategist who died before his famous *On War* was first published, became especially influential in American military thought after the Vietnam War. Mahan, an Annapolis graduate of 1859, promoted seapower to assure open maritime commerce. He applied Jomini's concepts of concentration, interior lines and logistics to naval deployments. Major General Emory Upton argued, at the turn of the century, that civilian government should not interfere with operations of the army in the field. His admiration of German staff organization and professional schooling also had a lasting impact. Giulio Douhet, an Italian General of the 1930s, advocated massed bombing against enemy centers of industry and population, and outlined the three-dimensional aspect of air war. He argued that air power alone could win wars – a view that has seen some recent adherents. US General William Mitchell taught centralized control of air assets to take advantage of the fundamental nature of air warfare. British officer and historian Liddell Hart (critical of Clausewitz) suggested an indirect approach to victory on the battlefield. Of all these, Clausewitz has been the most influential in recent years, at least on the military population.[26]

As the Vietnam War drew to a close, the 1973 Arab–Israeli conflict offered a war fought to Clausewitzian specifications. It provided a basis for recapturing traditional military doctrine that had been obscured during the Vietnam decade. It was a refreshing example of maneuver by mobile, armored columns unhampered by the confusion of part-time combatants, civilian populations, urban complexity, or for that matter, even foliage. In 1976 a new English translation of Von Clausewitz's *On War* rekindled interest in the fundamentals of strategy. *On War* quickly became a bible for tank and cavalry commanders predisposed to weighing description of the military problem in terms that celebrated the predominance of their role.[27]

Reinvigorated was a strong interest in the design and conduct of campaigns and large operations (operational art) and a conviction among US military planners about the efficacy of overwhelming force to achieve strategic objectives. As Clausewitz said, 'war is an act of force, and there is no logical limit to the application of that force'.[28] Not only did the absence of the Vietnam distraction allow US military professionals the freedom to refocus on a preferred calculus of open warfare, Vietnam itself offered important strategic lessons. Slow escalation in the application of force, failure to fix the enemy, failure to secure support at home, failure to achieve the strategic offensive – these became Vietnam lessons to be avoided in future contests. But the post-Vietnam rebirth of operational art must be identified together with its earlier European roots; it not only boasted a German guru in Clausewitz, but also a Germanic hubris that arrived hand-in-hand with geopolitics.

This hubris can be explained by reference to another, less well-known German strategic thinker, named Hans Delbruck.[29] Delbruck was not a military professional, but a civilian historian. During his lifetime, Delbruck's scholarship and methodology were dismissed in Germany. Strategic wisdom in the late nineteenth century was the property of the German General Staff and the Prussian General Staff College. There, strategy professors adulated Frederick the Great. An author and philosopher, Frederick had also been a military strategist whom the General Staff looked upon as a paragon.[30] Modern day historian Arden Bucholz attributes to the mainstream German military thinking of the day a one-sided interpretation of Carl Von Clausewitz. 'To that generation Clausewitz seemed to have captured the essence of the wars of unification: war was an act of violence carried to the utmost bounds. The destruction of the enemy fighting force by battle was the only valid goal.'[31] This supposedly Clausewitzian reading of Frederick's Military Testament was interpreted to support the Prussian School approach of annihilation battles, but Delbruck alone noted a completely different lesson in Frederick's writing. 'Frederick had always regarded battle as an evil to be undertaken only in necessity, as Clausewitz himself had pointed out.'[32] Delbruck felt that Frederick's strategy had to be understood in terms of the social and technological conditions prevailing in Frederick's day. Delbruck suggested instead an attrition strategy that would wear Germany's enemies down and allow its leaders to leverage advantage in political negotiations. His uninspiring advice was to not look for a decisive victory, thereby avoiding decisive defeat or the loss of resources.[33] German failure in World War I would be debated in reference to Delbruck's annihilation option to the German General Staff's obsession with seeking the decisive battle. While many Germans agreed during the interwar period with Delbruck's 'I told you so', the German penchant would prevail. And where in Delbruck's pallid criticism was there sufficient room for the dark Hegelian esteem of war for its own sake?

For the United States, the Delbruckian lesson is not so much that the United States should today seek attrition rather than decisive strategies in military confrontations. The lesson is that the United States will not be given many opportunities to apply the favored Clausewitzian strategies because most opponents will take Delbruck's advice. Smart foes will not seek victory in decisive battle against the Americans. They will apply violence to erode resolve, constantly leveraging ruthlessness against weariness, fear, and moral self-constraint. In this way attrition becomes synonymous with interminable extortion. A strategy of permanent violence appears in which no final uniformed, tanked, maneuver battle is offered to the Americans. It is terrorist guerrilla war generalized. If American impatience and anger draws US military might out of its holster, it will not find a final objective. Either there will be no Baghdad to go to, or if a target seems to exist that promises a satisfying military closure, it will be too distant given the confines of the same American impatience and moral self-constraint. Wealth and value will be extracted violently and piecemeal from a United States that is hoping for that situation where American military advantages are insuperable. Worst of all, at some point the whittling away at US warring strength, and the ability to recognize its proper occasion, will make traditional defeat of American forces an attractive possibility.

Recent US military manuals incorporate the experience of the Persian Gulf War, especially the notion that to win efficiently the US must apply decisive force in simultaneous attack throughout the entire battlespace.[34] In other words, instead of just a synchronized set of events and maneuvers, attacks against the enemy will be mounted in priority, all over, as much as possible, in a furious overlapping rhythm. This improvement (made possible by new technology) on the tried-and-true Germanic basics is appropriate in view of the large force-on-force battles that might yet have to be fought. It has nevertheless been partially mocked by the transformation in the strategic environment. Peacekeeping, humanitarian assistance, nation assistance, and the like have been harder for the US military to embrace within its doctrine.[35] These tasks are treated as extraordinary – even as they are becoming a central part of national security strategy.

Soon after the immensely successful application of US military power in the Persian Gulf, Chairman of the Joint Chiefs of Staff, General Colin Powell offered a proposal for a 25 per cent defense spending downturn to a 'Base Force' level as a hedge against Congressional demands for more dramatic expenditure reductions. One critic of the Base Force was Congressman Les Aspin who considered the proposed reduction as too timid and out of touch with the changed world.[36] With the subsequent change from the Bush to the Clinton administration in January 1992, military strategic planning was placed on hold. While the President delayed in promulgating security policy guidance, newly appointed Secretary of Defense Les Aspin began a 'bottom-up review' to assess the threats to the nation and to determine military force structure. The review was designed in good part 'to rationalize reductions in the $120 billion range over the Bush administration's defense spending plans for 1995–99'.[37] The result was a force structure design that would purportedly deter nuclear attack and meet the needs of prosecuting two major regional conflicts (MRC) almost simultaneously. The same collection of general purpose forces needed for two MRCs would provide the military resources for smaller-scale conflicts or crises.

The smaller-scale challenges to security (those that are not MRCs) include black market trading of nuclear material; weapons proliferation in all its dimensions (including weapons of mass destruction in the hands of rogue states, terrorists and organized criminals); conflict over scarce resources and environmental values; ethnic and religious conflict; spread of uncontrollable viruses and other diseases; the transnational linkages of crime, drug trafficking and its stormy marriages with terrorism and insurgency; illicit electronic capital movement; migration and illegal immigration; famine; mob violence and spontaneous ungovernability. Unrestrained by borders and the traditional protocols of the international system, these dangers threaten a nation-state system poorly prepared to deal with non-governmental global dynamics. United States military doctrine and force structure are designed almost exclusively around traditional concepts of overwhelming conventional force to achieve decisive victory – an unlikely formula for success against most of these threats.

The long list, just summarized, of 'other' dangers invites another list. Typical military tasks in what the US Army briefly took to calling Operations Other than War (OOTW) include surveillance and investigation; intelligence gathering, reporting, and analysis; negotiation and mediation; patrolling, traffic control, monitoring transportation of goods, local security, search and seizure of contraband; medical care, supervision of internees and prisoners of war, humanitarian aid, evacuation and relocation of refugees, warding undocumented migrants; construction, mine clearing or other ordnance disposal, route maintenance, force security; and, still, combat. If the list resonates of police more than military responsibilities, it should come as no surprise that most of the tasks present themselves in conflicts for which no decisive battle, annihilation strategy is remotely appropriate.

Is there, then, an inconsistency between the dangers and related tasks that the United States faces, what the US national leadership plans to do about them, and the resources that are programmed to do the job? Les Aspin's bottom-up review stated:

> our emphasis on engagement, prevention, and partnership means that, in this new era, US military forces are more likely to be involved in operations short of declared or intense warfare. Events of the past few years have already borne this out, as our armed forces have been involved in a wide range of so-called 'intervention' operations, from aiding typhoon victims in Bangladesh during Operation Sea Angel, to delivering humanitarian relief to the former Soviet Union under Operation Provide Hope, to conducting the emergency evacuation of US citizens from Liberia during Operation Sharp Edge, to restoring order and aiding the victims of the civil war in Somalia during Operation Restore Hope.[38]

The Pentagon did not complete a final version of a National Military Strategy (NMS) during 1994. Each year the NMS is designed to address existing and potential military objectives in the national strategy in terms of military capabilities, but in 1994 the job of publishing a military strategy was burdened by the same clash of perspectives that delayed the national strategy. One 1994 NMS draft began with what can easily be taken as a combination of complaint and warning: 'But let there be no doubt: military forces exist – are organized, trained, and equipped – first and foremost to fight and win America's wars.' One might read between the lines – 'We'll do all this other business because we are told to, but it's not our job'.

Army strategist William Mendel writes that the warfighting structure of the United States is definitely good for what it is good for – fighting and winning America's wars. Mendel points out, however, that the dominant doctrine of annihilation warfare has left little tolerance among military leaders for the idea of expanding the specialized force structure that deals with missions that are not war.[39] US military leaders have insisted that 'these capabilities [missions] could be provided by the same collection of general purpose forces needed for MRCs, so long as the forces had the appropriate training'.[40] In spite of repeated use by US National Command Authorities of conventional force structure (and doctrine) to accomplish police-type missions, results have been mixed.

The ambiguous results of the Somalia mission cast a shadow across the Rwanda humanitarian crisis operation, Support Hope, through the summer of 1994. US Agency for International Development and United Nations officials with the High Commissioner for Refugees were dismayed over what they saw as a gap between what the White House promised and what the US military delivered. 'The Americans came in full of plans and promises to put everything right, and as soon as they came in, they started talking about getting out', said a senior relief official.[41] The Rwanda crisis, Haiti intervention, and Cuba refugee crisis were nearly simultaneous events. One could not help but impact on the others even if only to the point of straining physical resource planning. But Joint Chiefs of Staff Chairman John Shalikashvili, who replaced General Colin Powell, expressed the essential military attitude: 'My fear is we're becoming mesmerized by operations other than war and we'll take our mind off what we're all about, to fight and win our nation's wars.'[42] Civilian defense leadership was showing its frustration as well. Secretary of Defense William J. Perry said: 'My job is managing an army, not a Salvation Army.'[43] Irrespective of these complaints, it is becoming obvious that US national leaders will continue to attempt to apply military resources to resolve or at least influence violent struggles that do not reach the status of one of the 'nation's wars'.

LOW-INTENSITY CONFLICT

> The revolution will not be televised, but the proceedings will be available online. (anonymous, on the Internet)

Mainstream US military leaders have long dismayed of missions in which the enemy is poorly defined, part-time, informal, or maybe non-existent. The Cold War forced some institutional organizational responses such as the Vietnam-driven growth in the Special Forces. By the 1980s, 'Low Intensity Conflict' became the doctrinal container for most of whatever was not heavy unit maneuver warfare.[44] LIC was the subject of doctrine writing for more than a decade, but was always a disfavored title. 'Low intensity' was an appropriate modifier to the extent that the ratio of metals to men (that is, the relative capital investment in *matériel* technologies) was lower than in a mechanized conventional war. The overpowering connotation, however, was always one of relative unimportance to the United States. But what was low intensity for the United States was a question of survival for some directly involved ally – this was the common complaint from abroad. A favorite analogy likened the comparative intensities to the effort of providing a breakfast meal of ham and eggs. Like the chicken, the United States was involved and contributed. Like the pig, other countries were committed. Thus the term fell on hard times, and was ineffectively replaced by Operations Other Than War (OOTW), although the latter term encompassed more explicitly such things as multinational peace operations and disaster relief. The newer title proved as debilitating as the old in that it replaced a connotation of unimportance to the country with one of irrelevance to the soldier. By mid-1997, Army leaders were attempting to chase 'OOTW' out of the lexicon.

Regardless of the heading under which consideration of irregular-type armed struggles are pegged, the United States, especially since the end of the Vietnam War, has resisted giving full attention to them. Bacevich's critique (see Chapter 4, p. 141) that the United States military has failed to come to grips with the two major revolutions in military affairs of the twentieth century (nuclear war and revolutionary war) has some merit. His is a crucial observation in face of America's apparently interventionist mood. Finding the right mix of doctrine, strategy, and forces for military interventions other than war is fundamental for the success of 'engagement and enlargement' policy objectives.

Under pressure from representatives of a broad domestic political spectrum, President Clinton toyed with the idea of intervening in Bosnia. He concluded that in order to intervene with any chance of success, sufficient domestic support, a consensus of European allies, a clear immediate objective, and an achievable, acceptable end-state (preferably one that did not include another permanent presence of United States troops in foreign territory) were prerequisites. These prerequisites did not materialize, but the military was deployed anyway. Looking at this situation in property terms we can see a link between national objectives, military strength, and other components of strategic power, especially national will. If the United States were to go into a place like Bosnia with military force and gain basic possession of terrain, then turn that possession over to whomever it felt were rightful owners, could the United States then leave, or would possession soon revert? Does the United States have the national will to meet all the duties that America's political leaders assume for it? Is it sufficient to outlast opposing wills or to cause other peoples (in this case we might suppose the Clinton policy team had in mind the Serbs) to suffer such that their resolve be broken? The United States might wish to give basic possession of land to some group, but it must also want to establish a stable system of rules regarding that ownership and a stable psychological environment regarding who has what rights in what land. Land itself and its basic possession is only a starting point. Then we must consider the competing identities and strength of identity of would-be owners to all parts of the concert of rights related to the land. We must consider what kind of legal regime and what kind of ideology regarding ownership is to apply. All three areas, i.e. rights in the geography, identity of owners, and the system of ownership rules, must be addressed en route to political stability. In 1995 President Clinton had promised a one-year deployment of American forces to Bosnia. In 1997 he was insisting to European allies that the American contingent would be withdrawn in mid-1998. Had the necessary changes in the ownership environment been made to assure that ancient hatreds would not re-ignite?

On occasion, the construction of stability in all three dimensions of the ownership environment, sometimes called nation building, has been a military mission. The military has not only had to secure basic possession against a hostile claimant, it has been asked to establish the social conditions that would allow its own withdrawal. Occupations of Japan, Korea, Taiwan, and part of Germany are the largest US examples in the twentieth century. The US military held possession, but also organized a restructuring of the ownership regime, changing ideology and creating owners. In the Japanese case, the goal was not stabilizing ownership claims among competing nations as might be the case in an area such as Bosnia. Instead, the question was one of making the population of Japan more owner and less owned; in other words, democratizing.

Militarily, more and more attention is being paid to concepts like 'operations other than war' or 'conflict termination'. It has become obvious that post-combat environments demand actions incompatible with combat. The attitudes appropriate to secure possession of terrain or to achieve basic physical safety are combat attitudes. Soon, however, police attitudes are needed to consolidate basic civil and property rights. Initial entry of the US military into Somalia was humanitarian. Government motivation was one of duty to prevent widespread, needless death. It was soon obvious that the problem was one of competitive ownership within the Somali geography. Powerful Somalis did not even consider the starving population to be property worth shepherding (since to do so was to invite a future demand for participation as owners). Indeed, long-term stability might have been achieved by the extermination of the weaker identities. The United States applied foreign military force in an attempt to ensure that human beings would at least be fed. In a favored end-state, the starving would be accepted not just as beings worthy of compassion, but as co-owners of Somalia. For this result, rules of shared ownership would have to have been established in the minds of Somalis generally. In no way could this be achieved in the time foreign forces were present, or were the forces placed in Somalia appropriate for the task.

Somalis who were able to exert physical force against their countrymen in the absence of foreigners did not recognize a duty of ownership to the extent of servicing humans as a chattel property worthy of investment, much less empathy. Somalis display a resolve that allows them to eliminate other would-be owners. Westerners, especially Americans, responded to the plight of starving Africans in the way they might respond to baby seals at risk to bludgeoning by hunters. There is a tendency to treat people, especially 'tribal' people, as an anthropological patrimony that should be cared for humanely. We assert the same kind of rights that the Society for the Prevention of Cruelty to Animals or Greenpeace asserts. We expect other nations to meet their duty of caring for their people as though we had a correlative right not to have our sensibilities offended. In strategic military terms, such an attitude can be a formula for permanent presence and ultimate failure, and it may be fundamentally inhumane. If we are to create the conditions that will allow us to withdraw the military after asserting force in a situation like that in Somalia, we must transform into owners the people we go to aid. To do so, we must understand the rights and duties being disputed, and we must create a legal and psychological environment in which our will is accepted without the need for permanent coercion. This is why Noyes argued that human rights should not have to be protected under property concepts – because we should not fall into treating people as property with the duty of their care residing in other human owners. Instead, we should make owners. To the extent this is accepted, it may mean that in many instances of humanitarian aid, a humanitarian intervention will require lengthy occupation if the project is to be any more than a temporary anesthetic for collective sympathetic pain. If we are not willing to stay for a long time to police, judge and teach, we probably should not start at all, especially if we have to use soldiers on whom we have spent time and money trying to imbue with the spirit to kill.

LAND REFORM

> Many years of observation in the developing nations ... have convinced me that in these vital areas the most important economic and political question is: who owns the land?[45]
> (Chester Bowles)

Attention to property matters has not been wholly absent from US strategic thinking. With regard to contexts that are describable as 'low intensity' or 'other than war', the most recurring property theme is land reform. The attraction of land reform (usually 'agrarian reform') as an adjunct to US military strategy has ebbed and flowed during the twentieth century. One unfortunate factor is that the political left has promoted many land reform schemes during a century in which geopolitical advantage has been associated with polarized ideologies. That is to say, land reform ideas have often been discredited as benefitting an ideological and strategic enemy. Land reform is a label given to a wide array of property-focused strategies for resolution of political struggles. The results have been mixed and depend ultimately on subjective measures. Their history is relevant to the current theme, but land reform is not prescribed here as the key to strategy. Too many land reforms have been bad ideas. Their reduction following the particular rights and duties associated with land usually bares the statist consequences of most initiatives.[46]

All strategies, and especially those that are aimed at attaining objectives going beyond immediate physical possession, are land reform strategies in a sense. Their essential flaw is a presumption that land is the dominant source of wealth and therefore political power. Lost is a full understanding of the nature of property. Property, even real property, is not the thing. It is the concert of rights, associated with the thing, that regulates relationships between people. Strategies that begin with a complete understanding of the preferential rights and duties of all owner interests are more likely to succeed than any strategy that only envisages a limited slice of rights related to the land. It is safe to claim that every land reform project so far attempted has suffered from unexpected and unintended effects of tinkering with forces and relationships that were incompletely understood.

That successful political strategies can be based on property ownership is difficult to question. A review of the history of Israel is enough to dispel doubt. The initial strategy of the Zionists was one of simple land purchase combined with efforts to make that land productive enough to support further settlement.

> The Zionist leadership concentrated energies and resources on the acquisition and settlement of land and the furtherance of agriculture. Much land was reclaimed from swamp or desert. Most of the lands acquired were purchased in large tracts from absentee private Arab proprietors. The mandatory administration itself controlled over a quarter of a million acres classed as state domain but it leased only a minute portion of this to Jewish agriculture. By the late 'thirties Jews held little over a quarter of a million cultivable acres, approximately twice the area they had owned in 1920. In 1939, about five percent of the total land area of the country was in Jewish ownership.[47]

As regards the creation of Israel, the other elements of the ownership environment were considered from the outset. The British sponsors considered national identity and cohesiveness.

> Underlying the British concept of the national home was the assumption that Jews and Arabs would become integrated within a broader Palestinian national identity. The British goal was to promote neither Jewish nor Arab sovereignty as such, but a polity of Palestinians. The Hebrew and Arabic languages, it was assumed, would afford the two peoples the means of separate cultural expression while the English language would provide a bridge for their political integration.[48]

The British understanding of the ownership possibilities was perhaps not well reasoned, since Arab nationalism was inchoate while an historical basis for a Palestinian identity existed among the Jews. The strength of a cohesive Jewish owner identity associated with the lands of Judea was matched against the underdeveloped cohesiveness of Arab identities. Today, with Palestinian identity catching up, the conflict is marked throughout by conspicuous property issues like homestead settlements on the West Bank of the Jordan, or autonomous rule in the Gaza Strip.[49]

The early Zionist strategy was a property strategy, but it is hard to fit it within the rubric of land reform. Nevertheless, misinterpretation of important elements of property ownership is a shared error in predicting effects. For instance, the concert of rights that constitutes land ownership includes the right to divest. This single characteristic of ownership can probably be blamed for half of the whole failure of land reforms in this century. If a peasant is given redistributed land, he will sell it unless he can afford to be the owner and wants to be. Therein lies the essential debility of a majority of land reform ideas. If a plan includes incentives for the peasant to stay on the land – seed credits, extension service advice, technical capitalization – the government is in effect entering the agricultural economy in a pervasive and very expensive way. Even with all necessary aid having been provided to the small farmer, there is little a government can do to assure the value of food staples. The next logical step is price support buying by the government, or other interventions into the market mechanism. Pressures build towards re-redistribution of ownership portions, in new mortgages, resale to original owners, and so on. In order to avoid the immediate frustration of the reapportionment, reform regulations tend to include tenure requirements such as residence during a fixed minimum number of harvests before the occupant receives title. In these cases, not only is part of the ownership retained by the government, but the government has created a new form of serfdom. As with most government intrusions, the process is subject to corruption and to loopholes that allow the black market sale of quit claims, false appraisals, and so on.

In order to influence the lives of any large number of persons, an agrarian reform necessarily involves overarching central government control of prices and movement of labor. If successful on a large scale, agrarian reform can slow a process of urbanization that, however painful, may be necessary to shift an economy away from subsistence farming. Nevertheless, forced reapportionment of rural terrain has on occasion supported strategic interests. Accordingly, land reforms sometimes appear at the outset to be good ideas even to the anti-statist. A quote from the United States military governor of Korea in 1945 says everything:

> The program of Military Government included taking over all Japanese properties as rapidly as possible for the benefit of the Korean people, relieving labor from the conditions of absolute servitude under which it has existed for the last forty years, returning to the farmers the land which had been wrested from them by Japanese guile and treachery, and giving to the farmer a fair and just proportion of the fruit of his sweat and labor, restoring the principals of a free market, giving to every man, woman and child within the country equal opportunity to enjoy his fair and just share of the great wealth with which this beautiful nation has been endowed.[50]

In post-World War II Korea, the land reform measures were taken by a military occupation force that had followed another foreign occupier. Probably the most important policy impetus was a desire to undermine the appeal of socialist and communist arguments within a large rural population. In this case, large tracts of virtually ownerless properties were available for redistribution.

In the case of the American occupation of Japan, the number of pure owner-cultivators was increased from 52.8 per cent of the total farming households in 1946 to 61.8 per cent of the total in 1950. Pure tenant households dropped from 28.7 per cent to five per cent.[51] In the process, one million former landlords were dispossessed. Rights in land had been purchased by the central government by instruction of the Supreme Command Allied Powers. The plan had its roots partly in pre-war academic appreciations of a relationship between feudal tenure systems in Japan and the power of militarist elites. General MacArthur's directive to the Japanese government stated in part:

> In order that the Imperial Japanese Government shall remove economic obstacles to the revival and strengthening of democratic tendencies, establish respect for the dignity of man, and destroy the economic bondage which has enslaved the Japanese farmer for centuries of feudal oppression, the Japanese Imperial Government is directed to take measures to insure that those who till the soil shall have a more equal opportunity to enjoy the fruits of their labor.[52]

It is difficult to claim that these land reform efforts led to the economic successes of Korea or Japan. Many other factors weigh in. At least they did not prevent economic development, and perhaps the redistribution of wealth broadened the base of material expectations. Both efforts seem to have had a direct effect on elections that favored pro-United States elements. One observation is essential. These reforms were externally imposed; in one case they were imposed on a defeated enemy, in the other on a country that had been previously occupied by a foreign army. The possibilities for reform were made available by the prostrate condition of previously dominant owners.

A look at the southern Mexican states shows the central place of property matters in rural conflicts of an internal nature. There, imperfections in land reform measures (finding their spiritual and bureaucratic roots in the history of the Mexican Revolution) are now showing their consequences. 'Amid indecisive efforts to achieve a solution to the political-military conflict in this state [Chiapas], the struggle for land is heating up.'[53] For some peasants the fight is over communal, *ejido* land that was supposed to be parceled out under a 1992 reform. Others complain about *ejido* land that was taken out of agricultural use to make a wilderness preserve. Nearby coffee plantations owned by foreign absentee owners are now the objects of armed squatting. 'And in response to eviction threats from the government and the ranchers – who are calling for Army intervention – the peasants claim that the land belongs to them and they will not abandon it, "even at the price of death."' Land pressures are creating a sense of desperation in a peasant population that has been encouraged to remain on the land and is unprepared to leave it. Add to this the contiguity of oil-rich regions and hydroelectric infrastructure on which the greater Mexican economy depends. Add, too, the leadership energy of outsiders who know how to focus the peasants' desperation and leverage the threat of violence against the government. A formula for extensive organized violence is evident.

> Mexico's land reform has left an ironic legacy. Though intended to benefit the *campesinos*, the reform actually made the land of the beneficiaries less productive than that of the non-beneficiaries. To the Mexican nation, this is a serious setback. Half of the country's agricultural land, which is in *ejidatario* hands cannot improve its productive capacity because *ejidatarios* cannot efficiently utilize it and because productive non-*ejido* farmers cannot acquire it.[54]

The above quote comes from a 1974 study on the political effects of land reform. The difficulty of which the author speaks was precisely the reason for the 1992 reform of the revolutionary land reform. What was seen at least partially by the proponents of the 1992 effort (not discounting the involvement of particularized greed in some cases) is that land, though it maintains special emotional attachments, is a commodity subject to market forces. In fact, the separable rights associated with the land are subject to market forces. Every disregard of and every act of defiance against those forces will eventually charge a price. That is what has been happening in Chiapas, and it is why strategies, whether government, personal, corporate, military or otherwise, should be determined as best as possible in accordance with the details of the ownership environment.[55]

Returning briefly to the direction of US strategy in these matters, one can see the powerful effect of entrenched military thinking. Perseverance and restraint are at least superficially recognized as principles in operations other than war. This recognition is explicit not only in the national strategy documents, but in the US Army's keystone operations manual. However, a revealing difference in tone can be noted between the 1994 National Security Strategy of Engagement and Enlargement and drafts of the 1995 update. The shift seems one of impatience and lowered expectations. To be added in 1995: 'the very heart of America's power is military force'; 'The efficient and rapid way in which our military conducted the recent operations in the Persian Gulf, Haiti and Rwanda can leave no doubt about their current readiness and strength'; 'No outside force can impose on any society what is, in the end, its own responsibility, perhaps only giving a fractured society a window of opportunity to sort out its own affairs.' Americans may recognize patience and perseverance as important ingredients for attaining some objectives, but recognition doesn't provide the quantity. Environments where complicated owner relationships need adjustment simply do not lend themselves to blitzkriegs. Police work means suspects and trespasses, rather than enemies and invasions. Unfortunately there is a growing world of overlap between what is police and what is military. Of all the sociological settings in which this overlap is seen, none is more telling than urban areas, urban violence being a subject whose real nature the US military has avoided assiduously.

COUNTERING URBAN VIOLENCE

> A major difficulty ... is the deeply entrenched military opinion, that goes back many centuries, that cities are places where battles should not be fought. Consequently, when it occurred in urban areas, conflict tended to be regarded as an unfortunate aberration to be avoided in the future, rather than an example to be analyzed so that lessons for the future could be drawn.[56]
> (G.J. Ashworth, from *War and the City*)

In a book titled *New Visions for Metropolitan America*, Anthony Downs outlines some government policy strategies for large cities in the United States. Downs presents a full matrix of options that includes such things as expanding minority membership in local police forces, decriminalizing the use of drugs, and expanding suburban school access to inner city children.[57] Elements on the strategy matrix reflect the full range of government program-based thinking about how to tackle the problem of what may be a growing urban underclass. Taken together, the strategy suggested by Downs as a preventive to urban violence is reminiscent of some broad-based socioeconomic program approaches to rural counter-insurgency. As Downs points out, such program approaches require a substantial redistribution of wealth, a requirement often unsupported by political realities. Moreover, many argue that such social programs generally do not work, that they create an addiction to programs that entrench dependency on government, robs human dignity and instills resentments that fuel the culture of violence even further.

Whatever the validity of arguments that favor such government programs, trends of violence in the United States do not appear positive. Major Third World cities can expect to muster less public program funding than cities in the United States, and so the supposedly enlightened control of violence by way of social engineering will remain an unrealized dream.

Meanwhile, intermittent outbursts of violence and a growth in criminal organizing will continue. Existing military literature, even of the most recent vintage, addresses the question of urban violence in terms of conventional combat, or in terms of insurgency.[58] Military doctrine sees such environments as unique principally because of the nature of the terrain and due to the need for specialized rules of engagement and detailed intelligence.[59] The need for measured responses aided by specialized weapons is also highlighted.

In the United States, defense industries are paying more attention to non-lethal weapons and technologies such as sticky foams, anti-sniper radar, and other advanced surveillance devices.[60] At the strategic level, the direction of the best urban counter-violence can be expected to follow architecture, as in the examples made earlier in Chapter 3. Architectural technology has proven successful in containing rioters and can thus limit the options of opposing groups intent on managing mob behavior. We can expect defense planners to survey urban landscapes using a methodology that keys on architectural phenomena both to anticipate violence and to control it. In most of the world, the architectural control strategies will not resemble the massive capital investment made by Los Angeles businesses to immunize their downtown area, but they will reflect existing conditions of urbanization. For instance, in many cities, the form and dynamics of the public transportation system guide the development of any impending mass demonstration. Security forces not only monitor and adjust aspects of the transportation system, they can create temporary architectures that restrict, canalize, diffuse or otherwise confound potentially violent events.

The closeness of shantytowns to target crime areas, to high value real estate, or to vulnerable public service nodes can all be analyzed according to courses of action available to anti-state actors. In addition, the specifics of property ownership, as detailed in land title registries and other ownership instruments, can be studied. This may suggest a rational distribution of financial responsibility for strategic defense costs, and provide information about the value and vulnerability of target areas, and reveal outlaw profit motivations.

Beyond the promise that management of the built terrain holds for counter-violence, security forces should address the sociological phenomenon of the excluded populations. Governments will seek new means of opening shantytowns to the presence of the state. These should pay particular attention to such things as the psychology of the abandoned child, and intimidation by criminal organizations that dries up publicly provided information. At the physical, tactical end of the equation, the particularization of power will be translated into more and more ways to trespass. We can predict, for instance, that the tank will be reinvented. Just as the machine-gun has been incorporated into the urban scene so will the use of improvised armored vehicles be employed to confound the architectural defense strategies just outlined.

Several trends are likely to influence the look of future urban violence. One is the use of children, another the use of the mob. Another is the trend toward architectural responses (and legal counterparts) in response to the fear of urban masses and of criminal organizing. Yet another, and perhaps the most difficult, is the confusion of purposes, identities and methods of groups that are variously revolutionary, anarchist, and criminal. In the past 20 years there have been many outbreaks of urban guerrilla war around the world, and they were mostly failures. But while prominent guerrilla movements failed, many street gangs and more formidable criminal organizations thrived. Somewhere between the failed urban insurgencies of Montevideo or Lima and the durable drug organizations of Cali or Sinaloa is a growing format for violent competition against established authorities.

This violent hybrid does not have to be a single thing with a coordinated leadership. It can be just the coincidence of several forms of anti-state violence feeding on the disruptive capacity of each other and on the fear that the concert of violence produces. Geopolitics, in spite of its escapes into the theoretical heartland of immense forces, may yet be a valid school of thought for untying the complex mathematics of modern disorder. However, for this new geopolitics to be useful, architecture and land ownership must be understood in their full complexity. We remember that the single most important defining aspect of urbanness is high concentration of people. A natural starting point for conflict is the increased pressure on ownership portions. Thus we see (as a simplified example) that a population of abandoned children, seeking new ownership identities and associations, links itself to criminal groups that define territory along market competitive lines. These are outlaw groups. That is to say, they defy and manipulate the establishment system of ownership. It is no surprise that they learned violent formulas from a generation of failed revolutionaries. Like the new gangsters, violent leftists of the twentieth century sensed and engaged the resentful energy of have-nots. Unlike leftists tied to critical, dubious theories about property, the violent entrepreneurs poised to stir the twenty-first century are simply out to get more of it. The last word in this chapter's title is extortion. It is violence that can be applied in the absence of war, in the absence of revolutionary strategy, with or without a political goal, and regardless of any correlation of forces. It is an always-available strategy option for any mix of identities, and it is aided by every advance in communications and information technology. It is supremely flexible in that some form of violence can be leveraged against almost any vulnerability.

As urban violence evolves, so do the measures for countering it. Based on what amounts to urban geopolitical mapping, architects have become, in the urban context, the new military engineers – modern counterparts to the designers of the fortified cities of the early seventeenth century.[61] Some will argue that broad social programs aimed at the socioeconomic causes of economic marginalization offer a more sane and humane approach to the problem of urban violence. Meanwhile, if the owners cannot control the weather, and despair of controlling their enemies, it is at least an attractive recourse to try to control the terrain. Thus, a unique feature of urban geopolitics may be the manipulation of the geographic factors of conflict.

As evidenced in the above discussion of new trends in urban violence, one of the most useable aspects of a property appraisal of conflict is clarification of the overlapping frontier between what are military and non-military applications of power. The US military cannot define itself away from the problem; it will be forced into police-like missions.[62] One reason is the United States' relative lack of national police or paramilitary units. Aside from debate as to whether recent United States' non-war military deployments were successful (or could have been more successful had there been a different force structure) there is a corollary, more powerful trend that is likely to reshape the US military. It is the evolution of legal strictures that formally define the details of legitimacy of US military efforts. Most intriguing is that these legal restraints are now in the process of being internalized and exported by the American military itself. Called Operational Law, the growing body of legal restrictions on military activities has far-reaching strategic implications. These include changes in force structure, military education, intelligence collection, and the realistic determination of national objectives.

Before exploring in the next chapter the curious balance of overwhelming force and legal restraint in the US military future, one unanswered question from this chapter remains. Should the United States surrender decision-making regarding the use of force to international or multinational bodies? This author concludes not. US military strategy, inspired by geopolitics and the Realist school of international relations theory, can be described in part by the word access – access to raw materials, access to the Gulf, denying Russian access to warm water ports, securing access for free trade. Territorial occupation has had less weight as an American imperial habit, but a country of traders intuitively understands access as a most important property right. Occupation is another thing. Occupation means application of cultural rules. It means exercising and imposing all the minutiae of property ownership. It is human rights in detail – what distinguishes one culture from another.[63] It is a police question, and the US does not share police goals or ethos with Saudi Arabia, or China, or France. The US will in too many cases face its soldiers with moral and legal dilemmas if decision-making regarding operations-other-than-war are relinquished to international organizations.

Finally, to help restate the differences in strategy that a property focused analysis suggests, consider the following ledger:

Bismarck	*Delbruck*
annihilation	attrition
decisive battle	negotiation

seek surrender	extort
whole fee	property slices
terrain mapping	land-title registries
military	police/constabulary
unit maneuver	control architecture
federal initiative	particularized power
national identity	diffuse ownership
state system	non-state actors
United Nations	Internet
geopolitics	geoproperty

The left-hand column alludes to the mainstream of strategic thinking, the sweep of United States strategy in the twentieth century, and a dominant mentality in international studies and foreign policy. The world in which this construct has relevance is not going away; it will not be replaced by what is listed in the right-hand column. The things in the right-hand column are real and growing, nevertheless. Some may wish to believe that the habits used to study and resolve the older problems of the left-hand column suffice for the other. They are wrong.

NOTES

1. Colin S. Gray, *The Geopolitics of Superpower* (Lexington: The University of Kentucky Press, 1988), p. 51.
2. Strategies are, in the broadest sense, ways or courses of action for achieving something. A strategy is usually associated with a theory. For instance, in international economics, a developing nation's import substitution strategy might be based on acceptance of the theory that infant industries need protection until they are strong enough to compete with international companies. For the purposes of this book, strategy is more than just a course of action in service of a theory. Strategy must bind together and reconcile objectives, courses of action, and resources. That same marriage of elements can be attributed to good decision-making at any level of bureaucratic, geographic, or financial importance. The corporal as much as the general, the mailroom clerk as much as the CEO (Chief Executive Officer), defines goals, decides how to reach them and assesses the resources available to do the job. Thus the tying of the word 'strategy' to the idea of a decision process distances the word from its connotation of size and importance. In this book's introduction, the author stated that 'strategic' was used for its connotation of relative importance and global reach. Since strategies (decision-making processes involving ends, ways, and means) are needed for projects that are less than strategic, no necessary link between the noun 'strategy' and the adjective 'strategic' is to be assumed.
3. Gray, *The Geopolitics of Superpower*.
4. Ibid., p. 199.
5. Geoffrey R. Sloan, *Geopolitics in United States Strategic Policy, 1890–1987* (New York: St Martin's Press, 1988).

6. Nicholas J. Spykman, *The Geography of the Peace*, ed. Helen R. Nicholl (United States: Archon Books, 1969). See also David Wilkinson, 'Spykman and Geopolitics', in *On Geopolitics: Classical and Nuclear*, ed. Ciro Zoppo and Charles Zorgbibe (Boston: Martinus Nijhoff, 1985).
7. Sloan, *Geopolitics*, p. 19.
8. Ibid.
9. Actually, Spykman called Haushofer's writing 'metaphysical nonsense'. Spykman was also adamant about not assigning too much weight to simple geography as a guide to policy. 'The formation of policy is not to be simplified into one all-inclusive generality like geography. They are many; they are permanent and temporary, obvious and hidden; they include, besides geography, population density, the economic structure of the country, the ethnic composition of the people, the form of government, the complexes and pet prejudices of foreign ministers, and the ideals and values held by the people.' Spykman, *The Geography of the Peace*, p. 7. Spykman's conception of power is still rigidly framed by the official action of states in a state system and only casually tries to incorporate technological change.
10. United States Congress, Goldwater–Nichols Department of Defense Reorganization Act of 1986, PL 99-433, 1 October 1986, Section 104.
11. Ibid.
12. Ronald Reagan, *National Security Strategy of the United States* (Washington, DC: The White House, 1988), p. 1.
13. Ibid., p. 3.
14. Ibid., p. 4
15. The Commission on Integrated Long-Term Strategy, *Discriminate Deterrence* (Washington, DC: US Government Printing Office, 1988).
16. The commission report gives an excellent summary of US Cold War strategy – 'The strategy can be stated quite simply: forward deployment of American forces, assigned to oppose invading armies and backed by strong reserves and a capability to use nuclear weapons if necessary'. The report notes that the strategy had had considerable success and asserted that the commission did not propose that the strategy be replaced, only that it be revised. Ibid., p. 5.
17. Ibid., p. 2.
18. Department of Defense, *Strategic Defense Initiative: Progress and Promise* (no publisher information or date provided), p. iii.
19. George Bush, *National Security Strategy of the United States* (Washington, DC: The White House, 1993).
20. Although one might remark on the strategy differences taken by the Reagan and Bush administrations compared to the Carter years, or on the differences of vision between the Clinton and Bush administrations, the strategy documents indicate more continuity than change. A concluding paragraph from the report of the Commission on Integrated Long-Term Strategy in 1988 is enlightening. 'We live in a world whose nations are increasingly connected by their economies, cultures, and politics – sometimes explosively connected as in the repeated vast migrations since World War II of refugees escaping political, religious, and racial persecution. It is a world in which military as well as economic power will be more and more widely distributed and in which the United States must continue to expect some nations to be deeply hostile to its purposes.' Administration strategy writers could have as easily written these words in 1994 or in 1984.
21. William J. Clinton, *A National Security Strategy of Engagement and Enlargement* (Washington, DC: The White House, 1994).
22. Not just with regard to the United States do we see the difficulty of distinguishing abstract concepts in the formulation of national strategy. The Brazilians, for instance, have formally defined their national objectives as 'interests and aspirations, vital and optional, that in a given phase of its historic-cultural evolution, the nation seeks to satisfy'. Vital national interests that are expected to endure throughout the

period of Brazilian history are termed 'Permanent National Objectives'. Superior War School, *Basic Manual* (Brazil: Escola Superior de Guerra, 1992), p. 24. Of these Permanent National Objectives there are six – Democracy, National Integration, Integrity of the National Patrimony, Social Peace, Progress, and Sovereignty. Integrity of National Patrimony, for example, is defined as 'Territorial integrity inherited from our forefathers and enlarged by those increments resulting from the evolution of technology or international law, examples being the territorial seas or airspace; integrity of the public lands, natural resources and the natural environment to be preserved against predation; integrity of the cultural-historical patrimony, represented in language customs and traditions, to wit, preserving the national identity.' Ibid., p. 27. Sovereignty refers to 'maintenance of national intangibles, assuring the capacity of self-determination and to live together with other nations in terms of equality of rights, not acceding to any form of intervention in internal affairs, nor participating in like processes in relation to other nations. In essence, it is the search for its own destiny; and as well sovereignty signifies supremacy of the juridical order of the State throughout its territory.' Ibid., p. 28.
23. George Bush, *National Security Strategy of the United States*, p.3.
24. William J. Clinton, *A National Security Strategy of Engagement and Enlargement*, p. 6.
25. On 19 September 1994, US combat troops entered Haiti, a country steeped in tyranny and kleptocracy. The 20,000 US troops spearheaded by the Army's 10th Mountain Division had the mission of returning to power the elected Haitian President Jean-Bertrand Aristide and to oversee the transition from the government of *de facto* President Emile Jonassaint. As US forces were reinforced by troops from perhaps 24 other nations, the US occupation mission was to give way to a United Nations multinational force of about 6,000 (about 3,000 of these were to be US troops).
26. See Peter Paret, ed., *Makers of Modern Strategy: from Machiavelli to the Nuclear Age* (Princeton, NJ: Princeton University Press, 1986); see also Arthur F. Lykke, Jr, ed., *Military Strategy: Theory and Application* (Carlisle Barracks, PA: US Army War College, 1989).
27. Colonel Harry G. Summers, Jr, used Clausewitz's principles of war to frame a critical analysis of US policy in Vietnam. Harry G. Summers, Jr, *On Strategy: The Vietnam War in Context* (Carlisle, PA: Strategic Studies Institute, 1981).
28. Von Clausewitz, *On War*, p. 77.
29. See Arden Bucholz, *Hans Delbruck and the German Military Establishment: War Images in Conflict* (Iowa City: University of Iowa Press, 1985).
30. Ibid., p. 4.
31. Ibid., p. 6.
32. Ibid., p. 9.
33. The history of Soviet military thinking includes a similar debate. Marshal Mikhail Tukhachevskii best represents the decisive battle school of Russian military thinking that reached its apex during the interwar period of this century. For Tukhachevskii and his followers, the future of war was mobility and firepower. Defense was deemed senseless as one could not defend against the new weapons of future war. The objective had to be destruction of the enemy forces by a series of strikes into enemy territory (Germany in mind). On the other side was General-Major Alexandr Svechin. For Svechin, attrition strategies were sensible and perhaps the only path to victory. A resolute attack could consume incalculable resources and, as a rule, would not be justified by operational gains. Attacking troops run the risk of having lines of communication interdicted or of suffering flank attacks. Therefore, in the opening phase of a war it is more expedient to keep on the strategic defensive. War can be waged at the same time on economic and political fronts while gradual, favorable change is sought in the relationship of military forces. Of course, Svechin was looking from a Russian perspective, Delbruck a German one. Svechin taught a

flexible generality about attrition and annihilation strategies. For him they were debatable, adjustable, and blendable quantities whose relative measure depended on the situation at hand. The balancing of strategies became part of 'operational art'. See Jacob W. Kipp, 'General Major A.A. Svechin and Modern Warfare', in *Alexandr Andreevich Svechin: Strategy*, ed. Kent D. Lee (Minneapolis, MI: East View Press, 1992). Dr Kipp argues persuasively, *inter alia*, that the American military strategy in the 1990 Gulf War fit the strategic model that Svechin called attrition. But this is almost the opposite application of the term attrition that this author seeks. It can, after all, be argued that the Gulf War exemplifies the decisive battle philosophy of a Tukhachevskii. Strategy has been delimited as a blending of ways, means and objectives. The objective from the outset of the Gulf War campaign, the resources mustered to accomplish the objective, and the methods chosen were all geared toward decisively destroying the Iraqi Army and physically removing it from Kuwait. Whatever the mixing of diplomacy and economic leverage, it is difficult to assign the English word attrition to such a military undertaking.

34. For example, see Department of the Air Force, Air Force Manual 1-1, *Basic Aerospace Doctrine of the United States Air Force* (Washington, DC: Department of the Air Force, 1992, Vols. I and II). 'One way a commander can exercise operational art is through a strategic air campaign that directly attacks an enemy's centers of gravity. Providing these centers are accurately identified and can be struck effectively at a tempo that maximizes psychological shock, the campaign may be decisive through air action alone.' Ibid., Vol. II, p. 129; 'The principal means for the application of military force is combat – violence in the form of armed conflict.' Department of the Navy, *Fleet Marine Force Field Manual (FMFM) 1, Warfighting* (Washington, DC: Headquarters, US Marine Corps, 1989), p. 20; 'We must be ruthlessly opportunistic, actively seeking out signs of weakness, against which we will direct all available combat power. And when the *decisive* opportunity arrives, we must exploit it fully and aggressively, committing every ounce of combat power we can muster and pushing ourselves to the limits of exhaustion.' Ibid., p. 61. 'The objective [of a campaign] is the employment of overwhelming military force designed to wrest the initiative from opponents and defeat them in detail.' Chairman, Joint Chiefs of Staff, *Joint Publication 1, Joint Warfare of the US Armed Forces* (Washington, DC: Joint Chiefs of Staff, 1991), p. 47.

35. Only in the 1993 version of *Operations* were 'operations other than war' given a chapter at the end of the manual – but with a different set of principles. Overwhelming force and decisiveness gave way to perseverance and restraint. The tendency in Joint and service doctrine is to treat low intensity conflict (more recently operations other than war) as a thing apart from 'normal' or traditional warfare; but commanders would use force structure designed for conventional war to support unique tasks such as nation assistance, countering illicit drug trafficking, and peacekeeping.

36. Harry E. Rothmann, *Forging a New National Military Strategy in a Post-Cold War World: A Perspective from the Joint Staff* (Carlisle, PA: Strategic Studies Institute, 1992); see also, Dennis M. Drew, 'Recasting the Flawed Downsizing Debate', *Parameters* (Spring 1993), p. 39.

37. Colin S. Gray, 'Off the Map: Defence Planning after the Soviet Threat', *Strategic Review* (Spring 1994), p. 33.

38. Les Aspin, *Report on the Bottom-Up Review* (Washington, DC: US Department of Defense, 1993), pp. 8–9.

39. See, generally, William W. Mendel, *A Joint Command for Engagement Policy* (Ft Leavenworth, KS: Foreign Military Studies Office, 1994).

40. Les Aspin, *Report on the Bottom-Up Review*, p. 29.

41. R. Jeffrey Smith, 'Spooked by the Shadow of Somalia, the Pentagon is Ready to Pull Out of Rwanda After Delivering Much Less Than the US Promised', *The Washington Post National Weekly Edition*, 12–18 September 1994, p. 16.

42. Ibid.
43. Ibid.
44. See Department of the Army, *Field Manual 100-20, Military Operations in Low Intensity Conflict* (Washington, DC: Department of the Army, 1990) which superseded *Field Manual 100-20, Low Intensity Conflict* (1981) which superseded *Field Manual 100-20, Internal Defense and Development* (1974); see also *Field Manual 7-98, Operations in a Low Intensity Conflict* (Washington, DC: Department of the Army, 1992). None of these texts mentions property as an issue or focus. They address urban environments cursorily and they mention organized crime briefly in the context of narcotics trafficking. A 1994 draft of the updated *Field Manual 100-20* is titled *Operations Other Than War*, and while it incorporates Peace Operations, it maintains much of the Vietnam counter-revolutionary war flavor of its predecessor manuals.
45. Quoted by Thomas Melville, *Guatemala: The Politics of Land Ownership* (New York: Free Press, 1971), p. xi. Chester Bowles was a former US Ambassador to India.
46. This assertion depends, of course, on one's point of view. For leadership interested in centralizing and securing state power, land reform has had a record of successes. Economic advantage, individual liberty and upward mobility have not fared as well. As Professor Powelson expressed, 'The most disheartening conclusion ... may be that whenever a reformer (such as a king, a government, or a revolutionary junta) has changed the land tenure system by fiat, he, she, or it has retained a substantial portion of the rights instead of yielding them to the peasant'. John Powelson, *The Story of Land*, p. x.
47. Noah Lucas, *The Modern History of Israel* (New York: Praeger, 1975), pp. 111, 112.
48. Ibid., p. 114.
49. In 1997, Yasser Arafat publicly supported the death penalty for Arabs who sold land to Jews. See 'Arafat Defends Death for Sellers: Penalty for Arabs Called Response to Israeli Land Confiscation', 22 May 1997, *Associated Press*, http://www.dallasnews.com/~dmnews/international-nf/int229.htm.
50. Gary L. Olson, *US Foreign Policy and the Third World Peasant: Land Reform in Asia and Latin America* (New York: Praeger Publishers, 1974), p. 42.
51. Ibid., p. 28.
52. Ibid., p. 24.
53. Alonso Urrutia, 'Seized Estate's Mixed Population Cited', Mexico City, *La Jornada*, in Spanish, as translated in FBIS-LAT-94-240, p. 25. See also José Gil Olmos and Elio Henriquez, 'German Owners Criticized', as translated in FBIS-LAT-94-240, p. 27; Julio Cesar Lopez, 'Local Links Indicated', as translated in FBIS-LAT-94-240, p. 29.
54. Hung-Chao Tai, *Land Reform and Politics: A Comparative Analysis* (Berkeley: University of California Press, 1974), p. 475; for an apologetic survey from the same period see Peter Dorner, Land Reform & Economic Development (Kingsport, TN: Kingsport Press, 1972).
55. A sadly ironic article comes from a land disgraced by the 1930s land reforms of Stalin. The author of the article may be speaking only for a pro-Western minority, but his message is relevant if not universally accepted. The problem of production has been a problem of ownership by farmers. Most peasants still work on communist collective and other state farms. A growing minority own their farms, but the problems of mortgages and capitalization are still out of reach for most would-be family farmers. G. Nikolayev, 'Why Can't Russia Feed Herself' and 'Private Land Ownership is the Pivotal Problem of Reform', *New Times International*, No. 18, April 1993.
56. G.J. Ashworth, *War and the City* (New York: Routledge, 1991), p. 92. Ashworth cites Yi-Fu Tuan, *Landscapes of Fear* (Oxford: Blackwell, 1979), p. 112. 'It is difficult to draw a clear distinction between defense against external threats and that against internal insurgency. Such distinctions have rarely been drawn in history. City walls were intended as much to keep citizens in, and accounted for, as to keep

enemies out. The wall had a practical, as well as symbolic, jurisdictional purpose, enabling the urban authorities to exercise a control over the movement of goods and people, and thus served police, customs, fiscal and immigration purposes (as such flows could be channeled through the limited number of gates which would be opened and guarded at specific times). Thus the distinction between police and military structures was generally blurred, with the same forces being called upon to perform both functions. Indeed, the only distinction between the modern situation – especially in countries with the Anglo-American aversion to paramilitary police forces – and that which prevailed in most countries until the last century, is that the military now operate "in support of the civil power", whereas previously they were frequently the only effective instrument of that power.' Ibid.
57. Anthony Downs, *New Visions for Metropolitan America* (Washington, DC: The Brookings Institute, 1994), p. 176.
58. Jennifer Morrison Taw and Bruce Hoffman, *The Urbanization of Insurgency* (Santa Monica, CA: RAND Arroyo Center, 1994).
59. See T.R. Milton, Jr, 'Urban War: Future War', *Military Review* (February 1994), p. 37.
60. Barbara Starr, 'Pentagon Maps Non-Lethal Options', *International Defense Review* (July 1994), p. 30.; see also Steve Coll, 'Britons Turn Their Cameras on Crime: Is This the Way of the Future or an Orwellian 1984 Come True?', *The Washington Post National Weekly Edition*, p. 19, for a description of the growing industry of public video-surveillance systems.
61. Two Spanish-language studies, *Manual de Métodos Geográficos Para el Análisis Urbano, Chile* (Manual of Geographical Methods of Analysis, Chile) (México, DF: Instituto Panamericano de Geografía e Historia, Comisión de Geografía, Comité de Geografía Urbana, 1988); and Nelly Amalia Gray de Cerdan, *Territorio y Urbanismo: Bases de Geografía Prospectiva* (Territory and Urbanism: Bases of a Predictive Geography) (Mendoza, Argentina: Consejo Nacional de Investigaciones Científicas y Técnicas, 1987) are examples of a nascent, operationalized geopolitics for urban conflict. In *Manual de Métodos*, mapping has been done of Santiago, Chile that includes the type and age of construction, value of homes, and many other aspects of the urban terrain and properties. The methodology, using transparent map overlays in an effort to gain insights about urban problem areas, is reminiscent of Intelligence Preparation of the Battlefield (IPB). IPB is a methodology used by United States military intelligence officers as part of a commander's decision-making process in conventional, mostly rural, warfare. The Latin American geopolitical style of analysis not only promises to show potentially conflictive areas and urban targets in broad graphic terms, but perhaps can predict the most probable unfolding of events in the case of violent crises. *Territorio y Urbanismo* also delves into the application of geography-based modeling for the description of urban social problems and the rational determination of social programs. These works are a very short step from a full-fledged urban geopolitic.
62. Perhaps persons who are neither police nor military can best describe the intangible but profound distance between military and police mentality and the organizational preparations that attend the difference. One such description is Bob Shacochis' 'The Immaculate Invasion', *Harper's* (February 1995).
63. 'Human Rights: Never Heard of Them', *The Economist*, 12 June 1993. Problems rising to the surface at the United Nations 1993 Vienna Conference reveal that at the UN no agreement exists about what human rights are. 'The draft document, ground out after endless confabulations, is a sad thing that reveals the depth of disagreement.' The article notes that fewer than half the UN members have ratified The Convention Against Torture and that many countries fear UN meddling in their internal affairs. The UN has a Center for Human Rights in Geneva and rapporteurs who observe what goes on in certain countries, 'but none of this is treated with much respect: reports are publicized by the Security Council when it finds it politically convenient to do so – as with Iraq – but not otherwise'.

6

Operational Law and Law Enforcement

> We don't know what our job is, what our mission is, and for how long it's supposed to last. We've just been instructed not to shoot anybody.[1] (Private First Class Matthew Knopf, on his Instructions for the Haiti Intervention)

Cumulative legal developments may obligate, as a practical matter, the creation of a United States expeditionary police force distinct from, if not separate from, the mainstream military. The standardization of legal constraints on military operations parallels and defines the differences between 'pure' military missions and the myriad things that are not the warfare of uniformed nation-state armies. This standardizing of constraints is rooted in multiple legal traditions including public and private international law, laws and regulations on intelligence gathering, laws regulating property compensations, and laws directly related to the proper role of the armed forces. Taken together, these sources express the American cultural understanding regarding human and property rights – that is, regarding the regime of ownership rules. The extent to which this legal regime fashions or delimits military operations defines what separates those operations from classical international war. The legal regime offers formal evidence that contested property is by consensus less than the whole bundle of rights taken with physical possession of terrain. Now it is clear that the US military itself recognizes and codifies this consensus. US military interpretation of the whole regime of laws that apply to military operations is called operational law and is defined by the military as:

> That body of domestic, foreign, and international law that impacts specifically upon the activities of US forces in war and operations other than war ... It is a collection of diverse legal and military skills,

focused on military operations. It includes military justice, administrative and civil law, legal assistance, claims, procurement law, national security law, fiscal law, and international law.[2]

The term 'operational law' was coined in the aftermath of Operation Urgent Fury, the invasion of Grenada in 1983.[3] At that time, military lawyers at the United States Army Judge Advocate General's School began a reassessment of the legal advice and support due military commanders.[4] The long-term result may be a profound change of direction in the practice of military law.[5] There is now an accelerating military professional interest in operational law that goes beyond the Army JAG Corps.[6] National Security Law is now in its own right a rapidly expanding branch of civilian legal studies. Growth in the stature of military operational law is a response to the same environmental factors that led to the development of the doctrinal rubric Operations Other Than War (OOTW).[7] An institutional phenomenon, operational law (like OOTW) reflects the changing nature of sovereignty, the increasing reach of legal norms into military affairs, and the great variety of missions assigned to military organizations. Operational Law is a manifestation of Geoproperty's moment. Its evolution is not inevitable in a dialectic sense, but it is the direction of international trends. The Army's Operational Law Handbook is a veritable bible of 'do's and don'ts' whose scope and power is scarcely informed by anything Clausewitzian.

There is no intention here to teach any part of operational law, extol its application, or even to advocate its growth. The objective is to reveal a message that the growth of operational law offers regarding the nature of today's military operations, particularly operations that are not war. Simply put, most OOTW are constabulary or social service activities, and the United States will ultimately manage them as such. OOTW missions involve the protection of rights and the enforcement of duties. That is to say, what makes an operation 'other than war' is the fact that its objectives and legitimacy are embedded in existing ownership regimes. They do not seek to take territory, do not seek to change whole fee control from one independent sovereign to another. The most controversial upshot of this not-war military employment may be creation by the United States of a police expeditionary force distinctly different from its warfighting units. Such a force can be more readily made suitable by training, indoctrination, and structure to deal with a wide range of non-combat, near-combat, and non-linear combat missions now given to combat units.[8] Creation of a dedicated police-military force component would free warfighting elements of the US armed forces to prepare for the conventional warfare challenges that the National Security Strategy documents continue to highlight.[9] This advantage – that warfighting muscle might be freed from the bulk of constabulary and social service duties – will ultimately convince US military officers to support the creation of such a force. Rededication of warfighting units to the challenges of winning high-stakes maneuver wars will be the primary selling point among US officers. For the most senior US political leaders and for intervention planners, a separate force would represent a closer alignment of capabilities with what may be the greatest non-technical aspect of the aforementioned Revolution in Military Affairs. This aspect is the reach of legal norms (the acceptance of shared ownership rules), domestic and international, into activities being undertaken by United States armed forces. Of less immediate concern, but perhaps greatest long-term consequence, the alignment of force structure with the details of legal imperatives may help preserve the intangible weight of American moral exceptionalism. In other words, keeping combat forces at a distance from most interventions, and designing a separate force more responsive to the legal requirements of operations other than war, may service the sense of moral legitimacy which lies at the base of United States initiative as a world leader. Creating an expeditionary police force may also make easier judgements regarding the practicability of deployments since entering and subduing an enemy armed force will not be capabilities or objectives of the organization.

The reasonableness of the assertion that the United States will be obligated to field a force of international policemen depends in part on clarity regarding what is not asserted. First, no claim is made that there is a sharp, observable boundary (created either by the legal regime or by political norms) between what is being described as 'Operations Other Than War' and war. This itself is an area for political and legal argument. Neither the current growth of operational law for OOTW (nor the predicted creation of a separate structure within the armed forces) need follow existing doctrinal boundaries. OOTW is not a whole or integral concept: it is a grab-bag of missions that are usually distinguishable from linear, maneuver war, or are officially distinguished from war for political reasons. The three factors mentioned above – changes in the nature of sovereignty, the reach of legal norms into military affairs, and the gamut of missions assigned to the military – are the overriding determinants of the changes predicted in the structure of American forces. Any changes will be pragmatic responses, not reactions to legalisms or because there is a bold line separating one type of warfare from another.

Second, the author does not claim that dedication of force structure to international police jobs will excuse US combat units from application to problems described as OOTW. The development of force structure designed specifically to meet the needs of OOTW will become an increasingly attractive option, but the definitional overlap alluded to in the previous paragraph assures that some OOTW missions will continue to demand the assignment of warfighting units. Nevertheless, an impressive majority of missions subsumed by OOTW are unmatched to the organization, equipment, and spirit of combat units. This is becoming obvious, as legal norms increasingly set not just the limits of permissible actions, but training and attitudinal parameters as well.

Third, nothing here suggests that operational law is only applicable to OOTW. Operational law will continue to grow as an influence among warfighters and in the prosecution of pure combat. In almost every American military venture, legitimacy of presence, goals, results and methods all interrelate. Legitimacy and legality are intimately tied, so it follows that the degree of legality in the design and execution of any mission will have its effect on mission success.[10] In OOTW, however, an existing reign of laws is more likely to define the limitations within which legitimacy is achievable or claimable. An objective of many OOTW is to leave an enduring rule of law – without the requirement of constant physical coercion. Within this framework of logic regarding the nature of OOTW we can predict the dominance of military police and military legal specialties. What immediately follows is an analysis that shows how imperatives of formal legality are supplanting traditional military considerations. The presentation flows from an example of extreme American military legal carefulness, to the reasons for that care, and finally to its consequences for the future of the US military. The initial illustration of matured operational law comes from military counterdrug operations along the United States border with Mexico.

Joint Task Force 6 in El Paso, Texas identifies and prepares US military units to support civilian law enforcement agencies in the counterdrug effort in the southwest border states. The units plan their counterdrug activities meticulously, with legal considerations paramount. Constraints leveled against the domestic use of the federal military by the Posse Comitatus Act are strictly interpreted so that the professional image of the military remains intact and the command is protected from legal attack.[11] Individual units from around the country, whether engineer, ground radar, or another element, will brief their operations plan through the entire chain of command to include a general officer. Some tactical consequences of this legal preoccupation are prominent. During a mission pre-brief, given months before commencement of the mission itself, the intelligence officer (J-2) will advise on intelligence analysis. For a typical reconnaissance mission, say to detect marijuana cultivation areas or cross-border transport activities, the J-2 will tell the participating unit to carefully prepare visual map overlays. Fortunately, the Intelligence Preparation of the Battlefield (IPB) techniques used to guide weather, enemy, and terrain analysis in combat operations are also useful for this kind of OOTW. The J-2 may require the unit to produce hydrology, ground elevation, and road network overlays from maps and other information available. These relate to the normal needs and patterns of marijuana production. The usual crop will be within a certain distance of a road and an irrigation source, and below a given altitude. However, the J-2 will then say that the most important overlay, an overlay that must be accurate – is the private property overlay. Trespassing is illegal and dangerous.

The J-2 will warn the audience to give special attention to the briefing given by the command's JAG officer. There are other factors to be noted regarding the nature of private versus public property and about constraints to intelligence gathering that the unit can include in the intelligence graphics. The legal officer will explain, for instance, that Federal Bureau of Land Management (BLM) land may be federal property, but that private citizens lease use and access rights, thereby giving the land characteristics of private property. The JAG will also talk about architectural structures, and perhaps point out that a structure may still have the legal character of a dwelling no matter how odd or dilapidated it appears. Therefore, the military unit cannot stake it out (domestic surveillance is an activity forbidden to the military) or search it. This then turns to advice that the range fans for visual or radar observation be limited to exclude such structures. The Task Force JAG officer then advises that the unit leaders pay special attention to the command's Environmental Protection Agency liaison officer. The EPA briefing could add yet other legal considerations to the map overlay. Perhaps the unit will need to include a wildlife refuge or a protected archeological site. Again, the map overlays take a legalistic shape.

THE 'US PERSON'

> No State shall make or enforce any law which shall abridge the privileges or immunities of citizens of the United States; nor shall any State deprive any person of life, liberty, or property, without due process of law; nor deny any person within its jurisdiction the equal protection of the laws. (from Section 1, Amendment XIV, of the United States Constitution)

The lawyer's briefing to the participating units at JTF-6 is not a short one. The next subject may be about the 'US Person', and it is in this briefing that we see the powerful and exceptional American tradition of owner identity. The owner is not just the owner of private land or specialized private rights in land. Every citizen enjoys ownership rights throughout and everywhere in the national space. 'Persons', even without regard to their status as citizens, have been recognized as owners also, even if not of the entire set of rights due full citizens. Americans have by and large agreed that 'we the people' has to include more than one status – that the cohesiveness of national identity (by force of arguments about the nature of rights, and the pragmatics of an immigrant culture) demands inclusive interpretations of constitutional principles. It is unlikely that soldiers receiving the mission pre-brief will have ever heard of the term 'US Persons' or its consequences, but it too has mappable features that translate America's vision of owner identity into tactical restrictions.

A 'US Person' is defined by executive order to be 'a United States citizen, an alien known by the intelligence agency concerned to be a permanent resident alien, an unincorporated association substantially composed of United States citizens or permanent resident aliens, or a corporation directed and controlled by a foreign government or governments'.[12] US Person status engages a range of constitutional protections including those relating to illegal government searches, invasion of privacy, and warrantless arrests. It is an example of a self-imposed dilution of sovereignty and preferential citizenship rights. For many law enforcement purposes, the rights accruing to United States citizens have been extended beyond citizenship and beyond US borders. This can have direct and immediate consequences for a US military unit when involved in a police-type mission. Military intrusion into civilian police powers is constrained by the Posse Comitatus Act, and although the statute has many exceptions, its basic intent is to exclude the US military from domestic police activities. JTF-6 takes a broad interpretation of the executive order defining the US Person. In that spirit, and guided by the intent of the Posse Comitatus Act, the command is cautious, presuming anyone within the United States but outside a certain distance from the border to be a US Person. It may also presume that anyone heading toward Mexico from the interior of the United States is a US Person. Rules that might seem relevant only to the intelligence agencies or the Immigration and Naturalization Service thus become significant for soldiers at the tactical level. Along the southwest border of the United States, the military does not search, arrest, detain, question, or follow any US Person. Naturally, this limits the scope of the military role.

Whether or not tactical intelligence overlays display legal limitations is of secondary importance. The point is that enemy, weather and terrain are junior worries compared to the limitations imposed on the soldiers' actions by the concert of civil and property rights protected by law. These worries are translated into graphically illustrated tactical planning factors. They, in turn, have strategic consequences. We can anticipate the problem of a US Person, for instance, complicating possible future deployments of a near-international character.

One dark cloud on United States' near horizon is Cuba.[13] Castro's fall from power may yet be a number of years distant, and there are a few analysts who doubt that changes will be abrupt or violent. If there is a period of violent instability, however, it will attract thousands of US Persons intensely interested in steering the outcome. A United States military intervention would be conducted in the most muddled citizenship environment in the nation's history.

It should not be lost on anyone who doubts the importance of this problem that actions of the US government in detaining Cubans have already invited legal challenge.[14] These court actions, in turn, have and will continue to have a direct effect on military missions and orders. In the southwest, JTF-6 has succeeded in mounting hundreds of missions supporting local law enforcement because it made an absolute priority of legal discipline. JTF-6 based this legal discipline on careful interpretation not only of applicable laws, but of the effect that the violation of the spirit of those laws would have on the legitimacy of the military presence. Because parties to any Cuban conflict will have immediate access to mainline US news media and to US courts, the link between legality and legitimacy of military actions will be constantly and quickly tested. The military must be especially attentive, in advance, of the institutional consequences of their rules of engagement. Support for many OOTW associated with a Cuban crisis will have a geographical origin in southern Florida. Many missions themselves may be focused on southern Florida. In addition, many service members are Cuban-American. To avoid damage to its image and morale, the military will need more than careful writing of rules regarding the immediate use of force. A Cuba contingency could require legislative tooling as to all the police attributes of the organizations involved. Military units may be well advised to extend the spirit of the Posse Comitatus Act to US Persons in Cuba as well as in Florida.

RULES OF ENGAGEMENT (ROE)

> Hence it comes about that all armed Prophets have been victorious, and all unarmed Prophets have been destroyed. (Niccolò Machiavelli, *The Prince*, 1513)

Of all the areas associated with operational law, ROE may be the most popularly recognized.[15] 'ROE are the commanders' rules for the use of force.'[16] They 'define the mission by limiting the use of force in such a way that it will be used only in a manner consistent with the overall military objective'.[17] Commanders in OOTW want to be completely confident that the orders they give regarding the use of weapons are legal, practical, provide sufficient security for the soldier, and allow the accomplishment of the mission. A mission may require multiple ROE instructions to correspond with varying phases of a deployment, different geographic locations and even different levels of classification. ROE problems demonstrate the relationship of operational legality to strategy. Force must be used in a manner consistent with the strategic objective. If the ultimate objective is the rule of law, military behavior must satisfy public expectations about the legitimate use of force. These expectations reside not only in the population of the deployment locale, but in the US population and worldwide. Usually, ROE instructions are not difficult to establish. If no condition of warfare exists, it is unlikely that an American commander will issue an ROE instruction other than one prohibiting the soldier from using a weapon for other than self-defense or to protect against the imminent loss of life of another person. There will be details in the ROE defining the readiness condition of weapons (loaded, charged, holstered, etc.), and there may be special or classified ROE regarding a particular group that soldiers can presume to be enemy.[18] However, lacking a uniformed enemy, ROE will almost inevitably tend toward the pattern of instructions extant in police departments across the United States. These police rules were not developed in a legal vacuum. They are the product of case and statutory law, criminal and civil, which over time have come to reflect the expectations of the citizenry regarding government use of force. The ROE that military lawyers give to American commanders in OOTW are an evolved expression of American legal culture.

Major Mark Martins, instructor in the International and Operational Law Division of the US Army JAG school and an authority on rules of engagement, concluded that the present method of imparting ROE to individual soldiers and Marines relies too heavily on what he terms a 'legislative' model of controlling behavior.[19] As Martins puts it, there is a resulting failure to account for the cognitive limits of humans under stress. When the shooting starts it is easy to forget the rules. Martins' recommendation is a 'training model' which would include training scenarios designed to reinforce the standing rules across the spectrum of potential conflict. Martins notes that the present method of imparting land force ROE struggles to sort rules according to their purposes.[20] The method

> also struggles to draw a sharp conceptual line between war and peace. Combatant commands draft and disseminate wartime rules in the same manner as they do peacetime rules; however, the rules

themselves differ to reflect the increased justification for using force in wartime operations. Wartime ROE (WROE) permit US forces to open fire upon all identified enemy targets, regardless of whether those targets represent actual, immediate threats. By contrast, the PROE merely permit engagement in individual, unit, or national self-defense – the sole legal ground for international use of force during peacetime.[21]

As Martins states in the introduction to his thesis, there are two dangers inherent in ROE instructions. The first is that soldiers will respond tentatively to an attack. A classic example of this tentativeness is provided by the failure of Task Force Smith, the first unit to see combat in the Korean War. Before the North Korean Army engaged the unit, officers at all levels were describing Task Force Smith's mission as a 'police' action. Commands did not publish ROE as they do today, but the characterization of the operation as a police action was enough to misguide soldiers into inaction when under attack.[22] The second danger is that the soldier will be too aggressive. As an example, Martins uses the courts martial of an Army specialist for the negligent homicide of a Somali during Operation Restore Hope.[23] Martins argues that the importance of ROE to the success of military deployments requires a basic change in the training of soldiers.

Martins points out that current soldier training emphasizes wartime ROE and not peacetime ROE, and that the training depends on a clear distinction between war and peace. Martins' analysis about the practical difference between a legislative model and a training model is surely correct. Merely describing the right way to disassemble a weapon or to assault a hill or to organize a motor pool is no substitute for practice in those things. ROE is not different in this respect.[24] Police departments across the country now involve peace officer candidates in marksmanship training that stresses target identification and ROE in simulated situations based on real, controversial cases. Difficulty arises from the recommendation that American combat soldiers receive training that allows them to employ, by way of situational and repetitive training, a whole range of ROE from peacetime to wartime. Many will argue that the soldier can be trained for one or the other and that training toward restraint is the more demanding. It seems at best ambitious to train a warrior for an immediate and violent response and to simultaneously train him to employ a precise and legally supportable self-defense. We hope a qualified law enforcement officer will be better trained in ROE than the average combat soldier. The combat soldier must spend training time on mastering the effective functioning of a larger variety of weapons, unit maneuvers, equipment and combat skills. The police officer must spend relatively more time on legal considerations involving the application of force.

We can summarize the implication of the ROE debate as follows: There is a need to prepare soldiers both to be warriors and to be peace officers. It is hard to train and indoctrinate them to be both simultaneously. Effective ROE discipline is essential to the accomplishment of strategic objectives in most OOTW. Therefore, the training set that participants in most OOTW must receive will be distinct from the training needed by the combat soldier. This in turn implies the design of a separate force that can train under a distinct doctrinal regime.[25] Yet currently it is administration policy to 'use the same collection of general purpose forces' for both conventional war and OOTW.[26]

While ROE mostly focus on immediate physical relations with people, questions surrounding property can have a longer-lasting effect on peace, stability, and legitimacy. Discussion of JTF-6 activities along the Mexican border region already raised the subject of property. There the prominent property issue was trespassing, but operational lawyers are concerned with a variety of property issues. Reimbursement claims for property damaged or seized by US forces was a key concern in the after-action reviews of operation Urgent Fury.[27] At least when it came to claims, the JAG corps could rely on a large body of experience, including many Reforger training exercises in Germany. More recent deployments have raised the complexity of the property element of operational legal practice. A paragraph from an after-action report on Operation Restore Hope to Somalia is illustrative:

> Humanitarian assistance operations presented questions of how to handle public and private property. When US forces arrived in Somalia, there was no functioning government. Resolution 794 gave US forces authority to use 'all necessary means' to facilitate the flow of relief supplies. In effect, the US was a de facto occupying power during Operation Restore Hope. US and coalition forces, therefore, had authority to perform some or all functions previously performed

by the former government. Consequently, the right of coalition forces over former government property was superior to the rights of others. Public property, once determined as such, could be seized to support the JTF mission if it was susceptible to direct military use. Real property (of the former government), airfields, ports, and other facilities were used without paying rent or taxes. Moveable property that was susceptible to direct military use, such as road construction materials, was seized. Private property was not confiscated, but it could be requisitioned if necessary for the maintenance of the 'occupying army'.[28]

Coalition forces in Somalia also had to deal with related contraband issues and with the property issues imbedded in the weapons confiscation program. It must be remembered about these property problems that viable private claims can generate future suits in US courts – and there will always be a population of lawyers ready to enter them. As a result of the United States' emerging intervention policy, the country could build a flood of future federal cases. Commanders understand that the equitable resolution of property claims is an integral and necessary part of maintaining support for or tolerance of US presence.[29] It is intuitively understood that questions associated with damage to private property have a volatile emotional content, so the time and money are well spent to ameliorate the condition of those whose property has been affected. Important legal distinctions, such as the difference between confiscation, seizure and requisition, guide property and contract issues.[30] Cuba again offers some difficult legal issues for any intervention there. Real estate on the island is still claimed by members of the Cuban exile community or by non-Cubans who had acquired property before the communist revolution in 1959. Many of these properties are highly valuable and have been possessed for decades by groups and individuals favored by Fidel Castro. Some situations are more complicated than others. A few mansions, for instance, have been given over to foreign governments as embassies. Depending on mission scope, an intervention in Cuba might require a legal preparation of the area of operations that includes not only a detailed overlay of public and private property, but also an historic overlay based on land title registry documents (or the Communist system equivalent).

PSYCHOLOGICAL OPERATIONS (PSYOP)

> The insolence of authority is endeavoring to substitute money for ideas. (attributed to Frank Lloyd Wright)

> Let us come back to the superiority of arms as opposed to learning, a subject long in dispute, and debated this way and that from each side of the question, and among other arguments that have been put forward, learning insists that, without its help, arms cannot endure, since warfare too has its laws, which must be obeyed, and laws fall under their jurisdiction. To this, arms replies that, without it, laws cannot endure, because it is with arms that republics defend themselves, and kings maintain their thrones, cities protect themselves, highways are kept safe and open, the seas are cleared of pirates, and, in short, without arms, all republics, kingdoms, monarchies, cities, and all highways both on land and on sea would be subject to the severities and disturbances that, so long as it last and is free to exercise its powers and privileges, always accompany war. And, clearly, whatever costs the most is, and must be, most highly valued. One rises to learned eminence at the cost of time, sleeplessness, hunger, nakedness, tired brains, weak indigestions, and other such matters, which I have to some extent already discussed, but to achieve a good soldier's goals costs everything required of the student, but so much more intensively that comparisons are impossible, for at every step the soldier is at risk of losing his life.[31] (Cervantes, from *Don Quijote*)

Legal influences reach past the use of force in dealing with people, and past tangible property – into the management of ideas. At one level we note that international law (and the arguments made about international law in international forums) is a premier format of international propaganda. Justifications for all actions are couched in international legal arguments, and propaganda at levels below that of the international forums is likely to rest on a foundation of international legality if it is to have much longevity. At times, proof of obedience to international law is less important because domestic laws are perceived to be more rigorous or better enforced than international law. The military lawyer and the propagandists wish to be in sync, and to be assured of this synchronization, either the

PSYOP officer must be made completely aware of all angles of relevant international foreign and domestic law, or the international lawyer must be made aware of the relevant propaganda objectives and techniques.

A second level of involvement of the legal expert with the purposeful use of ideas relates to the legality of the activity itself. Several rules and regulations constrain United States government propaganda.[32] If black or gray propaganda is to be used, then the activity is better conducted within the protective confines of a secret intelligence organization.[33] In such a case, the legal adviser must be knowledgeable about relevant laws, regulations and orders governing intelligence activities as well as PSYOP. The lawyer must also be able to discuss the indirect practical effects on the news media.[34] Here, the legal issues identified with PSYOP meld with those surrounding the public affairs offices and command information activities. Legal issues arise about what news agencies will gain access to areas, persons, and documents under military control. Also contentious are restrictions placed on coverage, and what copyright laws might attend some products – all need increasingly sophisticated legal support.[35] These questions fuse the legal treatment of public affairs offices and PSYOP units in many types of deployment.[36]

Both levels of professional legal involvement in the management of ideas presage an increasing need to marry legal educations and approaches to the informational instrument of power that the military commanders are, for better or worse, given to employ in Operations Other Than War.

THE ARTILLERYMAN AS POLICEMAN

> This is not the time to cast aside the lessons of Clausewitz and the concepts of operational art, but there is obviously room for innovation as we structure our forces for the 21st century. (William W. Mendel, from *A Joint Command for Engagement Policy*, 1994)

Several identifiable organizational tendencies also carry legal dimensions that push the United States toward the development of a separate OOTW force. Included are interagency collaboration, international peace operations, growth of non-governmental and private voluntary organizations (NGOs and PVOs – hereafter called NGOs), and habitual deployment of units holding specialized OOTW expertise. At least three of these tendencies are wrapped in unique legal considerations.

'The interagency'

The term interagency is now heard used as a noun, but this usage is as much exhortation as it is reference to an existing thing. It invokes concerted effort by all US government agencies that can contribute to or have a stake in the outcome of a government project. At the level of the United States unified commands, the military has become an interagency actor, and operations, especially OOTW, include multiagency activities. Representatives of the CIA, DEA, FEMA, the EPA and others will have permanent liaison personnel assigned to the military staff. As military operations, deployments and temporary organizations (joint task forces usually) tend away from active combat, the interagency relationships become broader, more numerous, and more essential to the accomplishment of the mission. Civilian agencies' personnel rarely fall subject to military disciplinary laws, and every civilian agency brings along its individual statutory mandate. The civilian agencies are generally created and funded for peacetime pursuits and must follow laws and regulations pertaining to a peacetime legal regime. We can say that almost every increment of increased collaboration from a civilian agency to a military command restrains the project by some new set of legal considerations. Each new legal entailment further distances the military force from being able to apply its original combat design.

International peace operations

President Clinton's administration has shown remarkable deference to collective international decision-making in security affairs. The National Security Strategy of Engagement and Enlargement expresses an unequivocal change regarding the attainment of national security goals, stating, 'We cannot secure these goals unilaterally'.[37] President Clinton underlined and ratified these expressions by seeking approval from the United Nations, rather than from the United States Congress, for the 1994 intervention in

Haiti. It remains to be seen if the United States government will continue to thus honor the United Nations, or if Haiti represents a unique usage. It does appear that United States participation in collective security measures will remain at a higher level than in the past.[38] Like the interagency, collective security participation brings a formidable range of legal entailments. The categories of peace operations – peacekeeping, peace-making, peace enforcement, and related terms – are still unsettled. Significant differences exist between United Nations, United States, and other national parlance. Many, if not most, military deployments that occur under a peace operation label, however, will have a police character. In this regard, it is informative to review comments from Canadian military writers. The Canadian military has participated actively in collective security endeavors, and Canadian officers claim some doctrinal authority as to the nature and workings of international peace operations. In the following excerpt, Canadian Army officer and peace operations expert David Last refers to a form of peace operation he calls 'constabulary intervention'.

> The constabulary role can be carried further, once segregation has been effective and in place for a while. Shots can be treated as criminal matters, for resolution by the civilian police, reinforcing the norm that shots by either opposing force are not to be tolerated under the cease-fire. There are two interesting examples of this occurring. In the first, two shots were reported. A young soldier claimed to have returned fire when shot at by a UN patrol. In response to the protest, the UN used Australian civilian police to investigate the incident, treating both the UN and the opposing force as potential suspects. The forensic evidence exonerated the UN, and was presented to the opposing force for subsequent action against the individual guilty of careless discharge of a weapon.
>
> In the second case, the accusation was made not by a soldier, but by the commander of an opposing force unit. It was alleged that several shots were fired from a heavy machine-gun at a specific time and place. UN observers should have heard the shots and seen the tracers, but had not. There was some suspicion that the accusation was false, with the aim of embarrassing the UN or the other side. The incident was escalated to UNFICYP headquarters, where staff officers demanded a full civilian police investigation, with interviews of all witnesses. The accusations were withdrawn.

>In these two cases, the soldiers on the scene acted as policemen, maintaining a stable and orderly background against which combatants come to rely not on force of arms, but on recourse to the adjudication of a neutral third party. Research has shown that this is the main impact of effective police practices, which rely on presence and assertion of a positive influence more than on coercion. Constabulary intervention, then, is the classic tool of peacekeeping forces at the tactical level for maintaining a stable segregation of forces once an effective cease-fire is in place.[39]

The above excerpt is offered to highlight the police nature of many multinational peace operations. Debate over the prognoses for success in these collective security enterprises aside, the character of 'engagement' is one in which legality and legitimacy are expressly tied.

NGOs

The work of NGOs (Non-Governmental Organizations) often may be essential to the successful outcome of an operation. However, relations between a US military force, or a US-led international military force, and NGOs may not always be cordial or fluid. Some NGOs will hold negative prejudices against the US military, and will be unwilling to reciprocate duties. In Somalia, for instance, some NGOs resisted the disarmament of gunmen who were extorting the NGOs in protection rackets.[40] The problem of the status of NGOs in many OOTW situations awaits juridical clarification. For example, where does an NGO gain authority for its presence in a 'failed state' situation? When there are parties to a conflict as defined in the Geneva Conventions, the International Committee for the Red Cross will in almost all cases attempt to secure authorization for its presence from all sides of the conflict in order to establish neutrality. Some organizations, Doctors Without Frontiers, for instance, reject any requirement to request permission. When does one of the parties to the conflict, or an intervening power, have a right to expel such an organization? Or, to what extent are members of an NGO subject to the civil and criminal jurisdiction of an intervening command? Poorly considered decisions about these issues might not withstand the criticism of other NGOs on which the commander could come to depend.

Habitual deployment of OOTW-ready units

OOTW specialized forces may already be a reality. The US Army's 10th Mountain Division, home-based in Fort Drum, New York, sent 5,100 soldiers to Homestead Air Force Base in Florida to give assistance in the aftermath of Hurricane Andrew in 1992. It deployed 7,300 troops to Somalia in 1993. Tenth Mountain troops were sent to Panama early in 1994, and later the division sent nearly 8,600 soldiers to Haiti for Operation Restore Democracy.[41] Partly because the unit has gained specialized OOTW expertise and has exercised interagency and inter-organization networks, the division appears to have become the country's default fire brigade. United States Special Operations Command, meanwhile, has assumed sole responsibility for a number of OOTW mission areas. Its limitations relate mainly to the large scope of deployments required for many types of interventions.[42]

The United States Coast Guard

The United States Coast Guard provides one model of an organization having military capabilities and wartime combat responsibilities, but whose missions and mandate are police in character. Protection of life and property of those at sea is the essence of United States Coast Guard efforts, but the Coast Guard mission list reads like a description of operations at sea other than war. It encompasses maritime law enforcement, international ice patrol, fisheries patrols, search and rescue, aids-to-navigation, marine environmental protection, boating safety, port safety and security, military readiness, marine inspection, and waterways management. All of these require seamless interagency coordination, and internalized domination of relevant legal constraints and obligations. 'The CG does not have a Judge Advocate General (JAG) Corps. All lawyers, including those who practice operational law, are line officers. As such, these lawyers are tied to non-legal billets in other mission areas throughout their careers.'[43] Coast Guard legal expertise, in other words, is not an add-on, adjunct, or 'force multiplier'.[44] It is woven into the institutional body of knowledge necessary for accomplishment of the Coast Guard mission. This integration of legal training and police training is natural when compared to the relationship of many district attorneys or district prosecutors' offices with police departments across the United States. The intimate relationship helps to confirm public trust that the rule of law is being served by the public force. The United States Coast Guard has been trusted with a range of duties that covers many of the missions falling under OOTW, to include restoration of domestic order on land. Under its broad statutory mandate, the Coast Guard provided assistance to federal agencies to quell the widespread looting on St Croix after Hurricane Hugo had ravaged the island. The president also used his legal authority to order the Coast Guard to suppress violence and restore law and order on St Croix.[45]

This section on 'Operations Other than War' asserted at the outset that post-Cold War changes in sovereignty, increasing reach of legal norms, and the large variety of mission types given to military organizations spurred doctrinal experimentation by military lawyers. Not highlighted, but contributing to the large mission mix, is increased American willingness to intervene militarily in foreign lands. A recent book by Richard Haass titled *Intervention* lends perspective.[46] Haass had been assigned to write a speech on the subject of intervention that was to become President George Bush's final major public statement on national security issues.[47] The book itself is a defense of the propositions expressed in the speech and provides an elaboration of the theoretical and practical context in which it was written.[48] Haass does not waste ink on national self-doubt or moral circumspection. He frames the controversy as when, where, why, and how to intervene. Whether or not the United States has a right to intervene is finessed behind the assertion that isolationism is no longer possible for America.[49] In brief, *Intervention* represents and formulates the details of a currently dominant attitude about America's role in the world and about how the military is a primary tool of that role. Reading between the lines we can see that the American military may have to be able constantly and simultaneously to respond to a long gamut of missions. Coinciding with this acceptance of United States international crusading is an acknowledgment that the federal military will be applied in domestic support operations almost whenever and wherever it can be of help. The message is clear. The US military will engage in a lot of OOTW. But, what is military?

There is a semantic pitfall in the debate over the appropriate use of American military forces in interventions and other OOTW. It is the duality of meaning of the word military. For many 'military' thinkers, the term has a substantive content that evokes war between nation states and their uniformed armies. In American English, however, 'military' also refers to any organization or resource controlled by the United States Department of Defense. Calls for military participation, or military help, or military involvement, or even the use of military force, do not necessarily mean a call for military approaches, or military art, or military ethic in their ontological sense – only in the bureaucratic sense. On the one hand, is a special professional purpose in time of war, on the other, is an institutional expediency. Fortunately, and unfortunately, the ontological 'military' fosters obedience to superiors, and denial of unsuitability or inability to accomplish an assigned mission. A trap is set against the traditional military ethic. Any order given to the military (that is, to a military commander in the Department of Defense) is treated as a military mission. The request is to be obeyed, the mission can and will be accomplished. Nevertheless, the mission given may have been a military one only in the bureaucratic sense.

The essence of police operations is enforcement of the law, whereas in war, violence is applied in an almost extra-legal context. This, then, is what the growth of operational law reflects – recognition that legal norms provide operational parameters. We must now go one step further and recognize that legal norms should also inform the establishment of mission goals, methods, training, and resource management. The consequences of not making major institutional changes in response to this legal reality are readily visible. At one end, warfighting units may lose the spirit of combat. At the other end, police missions will be inexpertly accomplished, perhaps leaving commanders vulnerable to lawsuits. More than a failure to use the right tool, mistakes in law enforcement can undermine internal morale of the force, and public morale toward the force. The British, for instance, experienced the police dilution of military identity in Northern Ireland in the late 1960s. British military doctrine applied in Northern Ireland grew out of touch with the expectations of the legal regime, and therefore became illegitimate politically. 'In short the use of troops in public order disputes in what might be termed the traditional aid to the civil power role, had, for a variety of reasons, become politically unacceptable in Britain by 1969.'[50]

Because of attention by US military JAG officers to the evolution of National Security Law, the United States military is not losing track of American legal expectations. However, there may be a gap in the practical obedience to legal expectations because of inertia in force structuring. Ongoing missions and reactions to US military conduct will continue to shape operational law. New cases will be argued and new precedents set, and most are likely to further limit commanders' powers in OOTW. US military actions in Haiti are yet to be analyzed, but conditions are appropriate for the establishment of some demanding new legal parameters.

Haiti's former military rulers earned widespread enmity not only in Haiti, but also in much of the international community. The military-controlled government was the object of severe and repeated criticism from human rights groups, other non-governmental aid organizations, and major news media organs hoping to improve conditions in Haiti. As such, a quantity of goodwill toward the international intervention existed. It is understandable that they would be generous in underplaying or overlooking collateral and incidental violations of civil rights that the international force might feel obligated to commit in order to bring Haiti a semblance of democratic order. However, the record of United States command behavior, and the way it is presented, can quickly shift toward the appearance of arrogant disregard for human rights.[51]

> As we establish order, we must understand that we have temporarily taken over Haiti's sovereignty and that our actions have long-term political consequences on a society which will shape such actions to suit its needs. Sovereignty will be restored as work proceeds on a desired end state of a new political order that respects human rights, individual liberty, the constrained use of force, the rule of law, and the right of people to freely express themselves and organize politically ... The critical test of legitimacy will be the shape and effectiveness of the judicial system and the police ... One of the lessons learned in Panama is that you cannot take thugs and make them into law-abiding and respected police. The society will reject them and their morale will diminish.[52]

The police and judicial performance of the United States in Haiti may prove excellent. A substandard performance may avoid detection. Either way it may have little effect on the long-term prospects for Haitian democratic development. More important is the pending challenge of the Cuban transition. The US military was already dealt the questionable role of warden to tens of thousands of Cuban would-be immigrants. In view of the much greater strategic ramifications that Cuba's troubles will have for the United States, it seems the United States would want to ensure correct alignment of forces with the expectations and demands of the civil legal regime. The dubious maintenance of refugee prisoners by an American army was in 1994 a political time-bomb that hardly troubled the American public conscious. It was, nevertheless, only a puff compared to the legal and logistic explosion that a full-blown Cuban crisis will represent for the American military (even in the absence of combat missions).

The many individual legal considerations brought together as operational law have a combined strategic influence. The sweep of this growing body of law will generate mission attributes that traditional combat units are ill-disposed, ill-equipped, and ill-advised to master. (Extreme shortage of appropriately trained soldiers led the 10th Mountain Division to use their few MPs to give crash courses to artillerymen on how to police.) If US civilian leaders and military commanders are successfully to conduct OOTW on a broad scale they will be forced to operate within the bounds of operational law. For many OOTW challenges this will require a way of thinking that is foreign to combat doctrine and education. Therefore, invention of a new organization attuned to the legal basis of its actions will be the offspring of necessity.[53] This is the little implication of operational law. The larger implication follows the argument made in the previous chapter regarding strategies. Occasions for applying pure military power to take, retain or recover simple possession of land diminish as property becomes more diffuse, as rights and duties become more widely shared and recognized, and as potential enemies learn to circumvent the ability to take possession. In their place is a continuum of property problems that requires the right mix of force and legality. As indicated in the discussion of weaponry, any gap in the moral applicability of a weapon creates a vulnerability to extortion. National Security Law and its junior partner, Operational Law, are a recording of the moral distances. They provide a map of the moral ranges in the use of different kinds of force. They describe the applicability of the use of different kinds of force to different property rights. They fill the gray area between what is police and what is military. The strategic advice is avoidance of paralysis in the use of force to defend national interests. It is a warning that national interests must be more carefully detailed in terms of property and more precisely protected by weapons and organizations that can apply the right amount of force in the right instance. A corollary implication may be equally important. If warfighting units and strategies are used too often in situations for which they are inappropriate, the warfighting part of the military will lose moral credibility with its own population (perhaps as the consequence of mishaps along our own borders), and it could also lose combat credibility internationally.

NOTES

1. Jack Kelly and Judy Keen, 'Like Somalia, Goal Difficult to Define', *USA Today* (20 September 1994), p. 1. Private Knopf was one of the US soldiers on the invasion force to Haiti.
2. International and Operational Law Division, *Operational Law Handbook* (Charlottesville, VA: The Judge Advocate General's School, 1994), p. A-1. (The *Operational Law Handbook* is now used both at the JAG School and at the Army War College in Carlisle, PA, as a text reference. At the War College it has replaced *Theater Planning and Operations for Low Intensity Conflict Environments: A Practical Guide to Legal Considerations*.)
3. See David E. Graham, 'Operational Law – A Concept Comes of Age', *The Army Lawyer* (July 1987), p. 9. 'Lest there be any doubt, OPLAW is a *new* concept. It is not simply a modified form of international law, as traditionally practiced by Army judge advocates, dressed up in battle dress uniform and given a catchy name.' Ibid. 'By its nature, OPLAW transcends normally defined military legal disciplines and incorporates, for the first time in one legal regime, relevant substantive aspects of international law, criminal law, administrative law, and procurement-fiscal law.' Ibid., p. 10.
4. A foundation had already been laid within the Judge Advocate General academic community for the construction of operational law doctrine. Department of Defense Directive 5100.77 of 10 July 1979 required all US forces to abide by the law of war. (In 1977, President Carter had signed the 1977 Protocols to the Geneva Conventions.) As a result, the international law division of the JAG school gained status and positions, though the scope of interest remained fixed on law of war issues. Shortly before the Grenada intervention, Joint Chiefs of Staff Memoranda 59–83, of 1 June 1983 (and a later memorandum – MJCS 0124-88, 4 August 1988), required lawyers to provide advice on both restraint and the right to use force, and to assist in operational plans and orders. These instructions, as well as FORSCOM Message, Subject: Review of Operations Plans, 29 October 1984, provided the official mandate on which operational law doctrine was developed.
5. Although the *Operational Law Handbook* includes national security law as one of its elements, it is also correct to conclude that operational law is a practitioner by-product of national security law. National security law has become a major area of legal study, like domestic law or tax law, that is individually recognized by the American Bar Association. More than 80 law schools in the United States now offer some course work in national security law. This body of legal study reflects legislation and court decisions that have shaped all aspects of national defense during the past half-century. It is an area of study that involves scholars, policy-

makers, and legal practitioners well beyond those in military uniform. The development by military lawyers of military operational law doctrine was an unavoidable consequence of this larger academic movement. Rather than just relating operational law principles based on experiences from military deployments (although this is important), military legal faculty must prepare unit JAG officers to incorporate the lessons of national security law into their military practice. The future of military law is now tied in great measure to the evolution of national security law. The range of this discipline can be seen in the contents of one of the major national security law texts. See, e.g., John Norton Moore *et al.*, *National Security Law* (Durham, NC: Carolina Academic Press, 1990). Material in Moore's text covers 1,200 pages in 28 chapters ranging from international conflict management to emergency preparedness.

6. As part of its annual senior service college curriculum, the Army War College at Carlisle, PA, now offers a 30-hour advanced course to prospective senior officers and civilian leaders on legal aspects of defense and military decisions. At the Command and General Staff College at Fort Leavenworth, KS, the follow-on generation of military leaders is now offered a 30-hour elective on operational law.
7. See Chapter 5, note 35.
8. See William W. Mendel, *A Joint Command for Engagement Policy*, p. 19.
9. William J. Clinton, *National Security Strategy of Engagement and Enlargement* (Washington, DC: The White House, 1994), p. 1.
10. 'Legitimacy' also has a formal definition in US Army doctrine. Field Manual 100-5 defines it as 'The willing acceptance by the people of the right of the government to govern or of a group or agency to make and carry out decisions'. *Field Manual 100-5, Operations*, note 5, pp. 13–14. For an in depth analysis of the importance of the attainment of legitimacy in some OOTW (and the relationship of legitimacy to other factors) see Max G. Manwaring and John T. Fishel, 'Insurgency and Counter-Insurgency: Toward a New Analytical Approach', *Small Wars and Insurgencies* (Winter 1992), pp. 272–310.
11. 18 United States Code § 1385, Posse Comitatus Act. The Act states, 'Whoever, except in cases and under circumstances expressly authorized by the Constitution or Act of Congress, willfully uses any part of the Army or Air Force as a posse comitatus or otherwise to execute the laws shall be fined no more than $10,000 or imprisoned not more than two years, or both'. As understood, the Act provides no exception for use of the military just because the requestor is a civilian federal agency, say the FBI. The Act is also understood to refer to personnel assets only, not equipment or facilities, and it is not regarded as having any extraterritorial application.
12. Ronald Reagan, Executive Order No. 12333, 4 December 1981, 'President's Oversight Intelligence Board'. Can be found in *Compilation of Intelligence Laws and Related Laws and Executive Orders of Interest to the National Intelligence Community* (Washington, DC: US Government Printing Office, 1993), p. 645.
13. See Edward Gonzalez and David Ronfeld, *Storm Warnings for Cuba* (Santa Monica, CA: Rand, 1994).
14. Andres Viglucci, 'Repatriation of Rafters Is Blocked', *Miami Herald* (26 October 1994), pp. 1A, 5A.
15. The 1993 FM 100-5 virtually elevates ROE to an operational principle under the term restraint, which is defined briefly as applying appropriate military capability prudently. *Field Manual 100-5, Operations*, p. 13-4. At the time this book was being written, some military doctrine writers considered using the term RUF or Rules for the Use of Force. RUF would be the more appropriate term for non-combat situations. ROE would apply to combat rules of engagement.
16. *Operational Law Handbook*, p. H-1.
17. Ibid.
18. ROE can become complicated. Note the experience with ROE by Joint Task Force

Los Angeles that was formed to respond to the 1992 riots in that city. 'Arming Order Levels' were established as part of the ROE. They ranged from Arming Order (AO) I to AO-VI. AO-I meant rifle at sling, bayonet scabbard on belt, bayonet in scabbard, pistol holstered, baton on belt, ammunition controlled by the officer or NCO in charge, and weapon chambers empty. AO-VI meant rifle at port, bayonet scabbard on belt, bayonet fixed, pistol in hand, baton on belt, ammunition controlled by the officer or NCO in charge, and weapon chambers locked and loaded. It is understandable how the after action report might conclude 'The JTF experienced problems with the application of the arming order levels. Most notable was the inconsistent application of the guidance'. Center for Army Lessons Learned, 'Operations Other Than War Volume III: Civil Disturbance', *CALL Newsletter* (Nos 93–7, November 1993), p. 26.
19. Mark Martins, *Rules of Engagement for Land Forces: A Matter of Training, Not Lawyering* (Master of Laws Thesis, The Judge Advocate General's School, United States Army, 1994).
20. These purposes are policy, legal, and military. Ibid., p. 18.
21. Ibid., p. 19.
22. T.R. Fehrenbach, *This Kind of War: A Study in Unpreparedness* (New York: Macmillan, reprinted US Army Command and Staff College Press, 1994), p. 100.
23. Martins, *Rules of Engagement for Land Forces*, p. 10; A description of the problems of designing and implementing ROE in a humanitarian relief operation are described in F.M. Lorenz, 'Law and Anarchy in Somalia', *Parameters* (Winter 1993–94), pp. 27–41. See also Jonathan T. Dworkin, 'Rules of Engagement: Lessons from Restore Hope', *Military Review* (September, 1994), p. 26.
24. 'Lessons: a. Commander must possess a clear picture of the threat and make an assessment of soldier experience and their level of training and discipline. b. Realistic threat training is essential, so that commanders and first-line leaders are better able to strike the balance between threat level and safety. Predeployment training on the proper ROE is a must.' Center for Army Lessons Learned, 'Operations Other Than War Volume III: Civil Disturbance', p. 26.
25. Martins' logic can be reconciled with this point. Combat soldiers still need a modernized approach to training regarding ROE that are appropriate to warfighting conditions and when they are about to be involved in operations that are or approach OOTW. Careful ROE instructions are not enough, and Martins' suggestion that the problem of ROE be incorporated more thoroughly into training habits cannot be discounted.
26. William W. Mendel, *A Joint Command for Engagement Policy*, p. 12, footnote 44.
27. Graham, 'Operational Law – A Concept Comes of Age', p. 10. Graham refers to a quip made regarding the state of operational law at the time. 'You can only tell the CO he can't shoot the prisoners so many times. You reach the point at which, when the boss has run out of beans and bullets, has certain equipment requirements, and has the locals clamoring to be paid for property damage, you have to be prepared to provide the best possible legal advice concerning these issues as well.' Ibid.
28. Center for Army Lessons Learned, *Operation Restore Hope: Lessons Learned Report, Operations Other Than War* (Ft Leavenworth, KS: US Army Combined Arms Command, 1993), pp. XIV–36.
29. 'Legitimacy is built on adherence to law, and promise keeping. On the micro level, human rights and subordination to civil authority are the keys to legitimacy. Supporting activities include payment of personal and property damage claims, on time payments for goods and services, proper coordination with civil/military authorities prior to going into an area, and providing a POC [point of contact] for the populace.' Robert L. Swann *et al.*, 'Role of the Judge Advocate Under the New FM 100-5, Operations', *The Army Lawyer* (December 1995), p. 33.
30. For a full definition of these terms, and a review of the significant field of contingency contracting (contracting in the early stages of a military deployment)

see Elyce K.D. Santerre, 'From Confiscation to Contingency Contracting: Property Acquisition on or Near the Battlefield', *Military Law Review* 124 (Spring 1989), p. 111.
31. Miguel de Cervantes, *The Story of That Ingenious Gentleman Don Quijote De la Mancha*, trans. Burton Raffel (New York: W.W. Norton, 1995), p. 254.
32. For a list of relevant legal limitations, see *Operational Law Handbook*, p. G-1.
33. Black propaganda purports to emanate from a source other than the true one. Grey propaganda does not specifically identify its source. White propaganda is disseminated and acknowledged by the sponsor, or an accredited agency of the sponsor. Ibid., G-1.
34. For debate about the constitutional and practical relationship between the news media and intelligence organizations, see generally *The CIA and the Media: Hearings Before the House Subcommittee on Oversight, Permanent Select Committee on Intelligence*, 95th Cong., 1st and 2nd Sess. (1978).
35. In May 1992, DOD and major news organizations reached agreement on guidelines that apply to media coverage of US military forces engaged in armed conflict. These rules are listed in *Operational Law Handbook*, p. PAO-1.
36. The question arises why a command would want to call any unit a PSYOP unit if the command plans to acknowledge being the sponsor of the propaganda it disseminates. The term PSYOP carries enough pejorative connotations that the presence of such a unit would itself seem poor PSYOP.
37. William J. Clinton, *National Security Strategy of Engagement and Enlargement* (Washington, DC: The White House, 1994), p. 6; see also, William W. Mendel, *A Joint Command for Engagement Policy*, p. 27.
38. Debate about the creation of an independent United Nations military force is related by Barry M. Blechman, 'The Military Dimensions of Collective Security', in Roger A. Coate, ed., *US Policy and the Future of the United Nations* (New York: The Twentieth Century Fund, 1994), pp. 81–8. United States' enthusiasm for this idea may have passed, but the call to establish standardized courses, curricula, and educational aids for training earmarked units has not. At the Training and Military Education Conference of the American Armies held at Ft Benning, Georgia, 15–17 November 1994, military delegates from around the hemisphere voted to recommend that the School of the Americas be used to provide common preparation for international peacekeeping operations.
39. G.M. Reay and David M. Last, 'Building Peace in the Age of Fragmentation', *Canadian Defense Quarterly* (March 1994), p. 7.
40. F.M. Lorenz, 'Law and Anarchy in Somalia', p. 39.
41. Paulette V. Walker, 'Gone Again', *Army Times* (31 October 1994), p. 12.
42. William Mendel suggests providing the Special Operations Command with the structure needed, in the form of a Joint Engagement Command, to accomplish the kinds of missions that the 10th Mountain Division has recently been asked to accomplish. William W. Mendel, *A Joint Command for Engagement Policy*, p. 11.
43. *Operational Law Handbook*, p. E-1.
44. The notion of the force multiplier is hard to escape when dealing with organizations whose primary mission is to support a combat unit. 'Operational Law specializes in the "military strength" component of the elements of national power, and the OPLAWYER can walk the commander up to the line between peacetime engagement and conflict. In this manner, law becomes an arrow in the "quiver" for commanders, and can be used as a force multiplier.' Ibid., p. B-2. Unfortunately, the idea may be irrelevant or counterproductive in many types of OOTW.
45. Ibid., p. E-2.
46. Richard Haass, *Intervention: The Use of American Military Force in the Post-Cold War World* (Washington, DC: Carnegie Endowment for International Peace, 1994).
47. Speech delivered by President George Bush at the US Military Academy, West Point, 5 January 1993. Relevant excerpts can be found in Richard Haass, *Intervention*,

ibid., at Appendix F, p. 199.
48. Haass summarizes a number of recent US interventions and proposes a list of types that includes deterrence, preventive attacks, compellence, punitive attacks, peacekeeping, warfighting, peace-making, nation-building, interdiction, humanitarian assistance, rescue, and indirect use of force. Reconciling Haass' list with the way in which military missions have been doctrinally organized by the US military takes a little effort, but there is no contradiction. The range of actions that makes up 'engagement' in recent foreign policy parlance is obviously broad. Chapter 3, 'The Vocabulary of Intervention', *Intervention*, pp. 49–66.
49. Also swept aside is the reasonable doubt that the peacetime engagement and nation assistance promoted as the centerpiece of our post-Cold War foreign dealings is effective or useful. On this point see Benjamin C. Schwarz, 'A Dubious Strategy in Pursuit of a Dubious Enemy: A Critique of US Post-Cold War Security Policy in the Third World', *Conflict & Terrorism* (October–December, 1993), p. 263.
50. Stephan Deakin, 'Security Policy and the Use of the Military – Military Aid to the Civil Power, Northern Ireland 1969', *Small Wars & Insurgencies*, 4 (Autumn 1993), p. 224.
51. See Larry Rother, 'Legal Vacuum in Haiti Is Testing US Policy', *New York Times* (4 November 1994), p. 32. The *Times* article addresses the detention without trial and without right to counsel of both Haitians and supposed US citizens by US military authorities. The article suggests that this particular human rights story is just beginning.
52. Gabriel Marcella, *Haiti Strategy: Control, Legitimacy, Sovereignty, Rule of Law, Handoffs, and Exit* (Carlisle Barracks, PA: US Army War College, 1994), pp. 2–7, passim.
53. The author does not favor creation of a national police similar to the Gendarmerie, Carabiniere or border troops of other countries that would have continuous application within the United States. Limitations on the use of national armed forces within the boundaries of the United States should be applied strictly – more especially to a paramilitary organization with police capabilities and orientation. The existence of such a national force would tempt federal leaders to use it to solve perceived domestic problems. This is an unattractive aspect of the prediction that the US will create a separate interagency structure to deal with low-intensity conflicts. At the same time, it should be recognized that the US will continue to be faced with overseas situations that call for a militarized police force.

7
New Things, New Owners, New Rules

> Immobility and a state of equilibrium in a system of human factions seem to be an illusion which is shared only by pacifists and backward political scientists. (Alexander Svechin, from *Strategy*, 1992)

In Chapter 3, the grand sweep of geopolitical tradition was rejected in favor of the detailed mapping of the urban land title registrar and the city planner. This, it was argued, better matches a world in which ownership is diffuse, power is particularized, and man-made landscapes are constantly redefined by physical and organizational innovations. Like the geopolitician's map, the charts of the urban planner focus on morphology, but unlike the geopolitician's renderings, they express the legal import of the physical form. The pipe is not just a pipe, it is an easement. Rights and duties are mapped along with the form. After all, to the extent terrain is man-made, the form generally evolves to reflect the relationship of rights and duties – not vice versa.

We do not, however, want to totally discredit the effort of the geopoliticians to seek powerful, global and graphically satisfying explanations of conflict. The shape of continents and oceans was not of man's design. Major conflicts have been waged to secure the advantages that possession of select global real estate has conferred. As Chapter 5 insisted, geopolitics has been and remains a theoretical lighthouse for twentieth-century military strategy. Therein lies a weakness, however, and the direction for improvement. The 'built' environment is almost wholly ignored, even while the lawyers creep up on military commanders at all levels. That is the lesson of Chapters 5 and 6 – that competition for boundaried geographies, though not obsolete, is the exception rather than the rule. The same innovations that are the West's hallmark evolved a strategic environment in which rights and duties must be mapped along with contour lines and water obstacles. In every government action that is other-than-war (and not necessarily other-than-military), objectives and methods are bound as much to law as they are to physical objects. When property is seen only as the thing, and not understood as the concert of preferential rights and duties associated with the thing, it is difficult to envision the ultimate objectives of military possession or presence.

This final chapter offers to better demonstrate the application of property analysis. Three cases come from the United States' near abroad, an area five-fold more important to the security of American property than is the former Soviet Union (apart from the nuclear missile threat). The country names are Guatemala, Cuba and Mexico, but most of the property disputes that arise from these neighbors are not unique to them, nor are their problems bound by the geographies that the country names distinguish. The first case, Guatemala, shows that there is still room for organizational innovation in the resolution of property conflicts. Guatemala exemplifies a state challenged by a multiplicity of owner identities originating from within and from outside its international borders. It is a place where United States geopolitical assumptions and perspectives have been overtaken both by the idealist current of foreign policy thinking and by the progressive diffusion of owner identities and particularization of power.

Cuba, the second case considered below, is a place where the United States government, non-government organizations, and hundreds of thousands of individual American citizens will be committed sooner or later. Not politics or human rights, economic theory, or military strategy will reveal the code to the Cuban puzzle as will careful consideration of property.

Discussion of the effects that Mexico's troubles will have across its northern border is also a prediction, but it serves to bring the property lessons of national security and foreign policy closer to home. The United States–Mexico example admits the possibility of internal warfare in the United States, and again, like the Cuba example, suggests why axioms of American security and military strategy are unmatched to potential, critical threats. The Mexican–American border may seem a metaphor for the waning relevance of linear warfare and decisive battles. As the example will indicate, not only are the staples of operational art in maneuver warfare less relevant, so is much of the existing American doctrine regarding insurgent and counter-insurgent war. In order to organize, to map, to navigate the challenge that turmoil in Mexico means to United States sovereignty, the key will be visualization and management of property rights.

DEMOCRATIC FORM AND THE LIST OF OWNERS

> In comparison with monarchy and other heirlooms from the cannibals and cave-dwellers, democracy is of course a great conquest, but it leaves the blind play of forces in the social relations of men untouched. (attributed to Leon Trotsky)

> Is a democracy, such as we know it, the last improvement possible in a government? Is it not possible to take a step further towards recognizing and organizing the rights of man? (Henry David Thoreau, from *Walden and Resistance to Civil Government*)

Guatemala's international borders encompass 22 officially recognized languages, dozens of religious affiliations, several distinct economic lobbies, and a rainbow of political parties. The various identities communicate poorly among each other and have mutually contentious worldviews, even while their memberships overlap. In the late 1980s, a group of Guatemalan leaders, looking at their fractured and polarized society, and wanting to effect systemic changes in the political culture, decided that a new kind of forum was needed. It had to guide sober, candid debate about national problems and not become a verbal gymnasium where a few lucky individuals let off steam, or an elegant soapbox where they could better practice demagoguery. Without appearing to be an alternative to the Guatemalan Congress it had to produce something tangible in the way of social reconciliation, and it had to attract attention and secure confidence from the broadest possible range of political interests. The resulting invention was called the Center of Strategic Studies for National Stability (ESTNA), an 'associative skills' college whose original design has become a model for conflict resolution forums in other countries.[1]

To fill the first annual class, the center directors planned a careful mix of representation from the labor movement, rural and indigenous organizations, political parties, the military, the civilian bureaucracy, local universities, and business.[2] Each organization was given a detailed explanation of the center's purpose. The separate social sectors were asked to choose their participants in any way they wished, with the guidance that the individuals chosen be representatives of their group able to articulate verbally the group's concerns. The curriculum was designed to integrate national and international economic trends and viewpoints, national security, labor, and foreign policy issues.[3]

A criticism of the center revolved around a supposed lack of conceptual depth displayed in the basic thesis upon which the center was to proceed academically. For each course, a body of workgroup coordinators, or pro tem faculty, was organized. Included were five accomplished local scholars, each supposedly guided within one of five 'factors of national power'. The five factors were geographic, economic, social, military and political. This five-part reduction of the national scene was represented symbolically in the center's five-petal blue flower logo. The symbol, like the subject organization, evoked the need to reconcile forces within these power factors. ESTNA's reduction of Guatemalan power into five discernible parts can be traced directly to Spanier's *Games Nations Play* and readings like it in which society is organized into a fixed number of abstract factors – a device requiring copious disclaimers and adjustments.[4] The same power factor reduction was expressed in a pamphlet titled 'The Thesis of National Stability' that served as the first philosophical keystone of the center.[5] As a guiding theme, 'national stability' asserted a contrast with the notion of 'national security', which was dubbed a retarding anachronism that trapped the country in the middle of the east-west conflict and presupposed an excuse for repression. When 'The Thesis of National Stability' was being written, the Cold War was coming to its unexpected end, and 'national stability' was appearing more as a slogan than as a theory. The center defended 'national stability' by reminding that it was presented not as an axiom but as a thesis and therefore something to be argued. The calculus of corporatism, paternalism, and the defense of exclusive bureaucratic estates was well understood by the center's architects. The vision of the forum model entertained three generalized precepts. First, the centers of gravity of national power, however defined, must be encouraged to interact in a balance in which no one sector is prepotent. Second, the capacity of each sector to peacefully influence other sectors must be enhanced, and third, security and welfare must ultimately be the fruit of common conviction, not the fruit of imposition.

Although ESTNA's founding literature described Guatemala's social calculus in terms of elements of power, this author ascribes the center's design to an intuitive understanding and a precise description of ownership identities and property conflicts. Property, perhaps for reasons mentioned in the introduction to this book, did not figure explicitly in the philosophical presentation of the center's purpose. Instead, the 'elements of national power' took up the explanatory space. In practice, however, the organizers looked at all of the major identities in their society that had leaders capable of articulating competitive or preferential rights. Powerful instances of otherwise unrecognized and under-addressed property clashes surfaced in the college's conference sessions. For instance, in a debate witnessed by the author, an attendee selected to represent an environmental protection group argued with an indigenous tribal leader over the right of the tribe to cut firewood. The argument involved army enforcement of laws protecting tree stands. The debate isolated and defined competing property interests in a uniquely frank way. Seemingly awkward and un-admitted alliances were exposed. The Guatemalan Army – involved by executive order (and for image purposes) in a massive tree planting effort, was aligning with environmental groups against Indian leaders whom it would otherwise be courting. Also instructive was a remark by another tribal representative on the influence that Guatemala's day-to-day reputation for violence had on the discount rate for money. Although his observation about financial markets sounded incongruous coming as it did from someone whose personal participation in banking and investments was almost nil, his was an appreciation of the essential character of the course – understanding the interrelationship of each sector's actions on the property of other sectors and of the whole society.[6]

Many observers will find Guatemala's recent electoral record to be more open and matured than that of Mexico certainly, as well as that of many other impoverished countries struggling to satisfy the model of liberal democracy required of it by the West's twentieth-century ideological victory. Credit is due in part to intense international shepherding of the Guatemalan elite. But liberty and democracy are terms that evoke a regime of diffuse ownership.

Open electoral processes are but one piece of a political structure able to spread power so that diffuse property rights might be created and maintained. Guatemala is a place where foreign critics have placed blinkered attention on the role, formation, and interplay of civilian political parties. All the while, little attention or comment has been made (except by the radical left in the form of revolutionary mantras) on property rights. The location and control of the land title registry, the status of real estate professionals, individual empowerment to protect boundaries, or the honest functioning of water courts are overlooked by political scientists and foreign service officials as political details. Can we assume that political party formation will eventually present suitable and sufficient identities to represent and protect a sufficient range of owners and claimants? It does not appear so. Guatemala has been poorly served by the invisibility of the status of property rights to political scientists and diplomats. The ESNA experiment is an odd, positive exception, but violent labor factions, inter-village warfare, and gangstering are more typical of the failure to address property rights.[7]

The dark side of human rights is also at work on Guatemala. We are not referring to violations of human rights by the Guatemalan government, either. Instead, the reference is to the cynical use of human rights as a tool to win property. Some places, as a result perhaps of earned reputations, have become the objects of a human rights industry, and as with Christian evangelism, some of the most successful human rights industrialists are no angels. Alongside nobility is the empty form. Like many Latin American lands, Guatemala has long been involved in the export of dessert or after-dinner products. These luxuries include sugar, coffee, cacao, cardamom, opium, exotic fruits, and controversy. Guatemala's place as an exporter of the last item is as linked to European and American luxury markets as are the agricultural products. In this context, the market both creates and satisfies an appetite for moral exercise. Those whose capacity for outrage is not sufficiently released on injustices close to home and who have available time, money and mental energy to devote to the questions of moral conscience, are offered a suitable outlet by responding to descriptions of injustices in a distant land. Many organizations, covering the entire gamut of sincerity and competence, have grown to service or take advantage of American and European moral dispositions by providing information and methods aimed toward solutions or purported solutions of the identified injustices. Unfortunately, many of the organizations service ends completely opposite to those advertised, feeding on the needs of well-wishers to manifest their concerns and commitments. These organizations generally go uninvestigated since in most cases the product (satisfaction of conscience or confirmation of moral self-image) is delivered at the moment of whatever act is taken by the receiver of the information. A contribution to a church or NGO, or a letter to a congressman completes the interchange. Truths regarding the object of concern or the intentions of the advertiser are minutiae. Frauds abound alongside honest dealings when it comes to the sale of human rights concern toward Guatemala. Most people find it difficult to admit having been taken in by a deceit, so this market population resists consumer-oriented investigation of the advertising. For middlemen profit-takers, Guatemala has become a golden goose whose status as an olympic violator of human rights they find it necessary to cultivate.

Guatemala's geopolitical importance to the United States is tied naturally to its location. With Belize it is the only other country touching Mexico. In the event of any Mexican–American disagreement (or of a prolonged Mexican political anarchy), Guatemala would be an obviously valuable ally. It is also a bridge for the flow of human migration and illicit drugs from the rest of Central America, South America and even Asia. However, there is a less discussed side of Guatemala's geostrategic significance. Guatemala is a place for the political far left, especially the Mexican far left, to hate. Seen from the immediate north as a quaint little counterpoint to glorious Revolutionary Mexico, Guatemala is emblematic of what socialist revolutionaries, genuine and affecting, loathe. Guatemala's own socialist revolution was nipped in the bud early in the Cold War by a CIA-sponsored coup. Guatemalan military governments henceforth sided with aggressive anti-communism; the invasion force for the Bay of Pigs debacle against Fidel Castro in 1961 was trained in Guatemala. The Mayan country did not go the way of the Aztec empire to the north, and it is probable that today strategic intentions of the far left regarding Guatemala are an ingredient in the Zapatista uprising in Mexico. These intentions can be seen in the evolving demands made by the Guatemalan guerrilla leaders' group, the URNG. In their long peace negotiations with the Guatemalan government, the URNG dropped most Marxist-Leninist rhetoric in favor of defending tribal rights. Promotion of native languages and indigenous cultural identity became new leverage points. The name Mayalan began to be heard as a threatening reference to an autonomy- or even independence-seeking Mayan territory overlapping the border of Mexico and Guatemala. Illusory though Mayalan may be, it has more chance of international recognition than Sealand. Mayalan is, in a sense, a proto-Palestine. Although it cannot be found on the map, Mayalan has a morphogenic reality, and it is a nascent ownership identity.

The URNG successfully evolved, under the pressure of need, from being a modern (and defeated) twentieth-century communist insurgent entity to being a post-modern, post-insurgency, post-Soviet, armed ombudsman. What did it do? It shepherded and fed on groups whose property claims could be successfully championed by armed litigation. It focused on property identities, the broadest being pan-Indianism, international human rights, and, when not in direct conflict, environmentalism. It did not have to field many troops, or create many Byzantine cellular support organizations. It had only to steward or endear the correct owner identities, and to maintain respect by demonstrating physical resolve through violence. It is a business with a much lower overhead than a state government, and it is much less subject to moral scruples or to international inspection of their absence.

Meanwhile, the United States government, member along with the government of Guatemala in the club of sovereigns, found its policies in Guatemala managed by the same identities that the URNG deftly tended. Bilateral alliance agreements, promises of mutual defense, recognitions of sovereign equality all fell prey to the agendas of non-state actors. The US State Department ultimately bent to insistence that Guatemala fill its market role as human rights pariah. Thus, individuals and organizations outside the US government gained control of the strategic direction of Guatemalan–American relations. Any ability of the United States government to pursue traditional geostrategic aims was effectively nullified. This may be partly due to ascendancy within the State Department of individuals who apply a moralist appraisal to foreign policy and who are sympathetic to the message of human rights groups. It is also because those who have been long tied to geopolitical thinking have been unable to make the shift that the

URNG has. The 'realists' have been unable, so far, to appreciate the strategic relevance of the non-linear math. They have not recognized how the value of land is influenced as much by the rules of its ownership as it is by location or by its natural resources. They have not respected the woman in Overland Park, Kansas, mentioned in the first chapter. Recall that her owner identities include US citizen, Kansan, Black, Dominican, owner of ten shares of Texaco, property tax payer, Republican, speedboater, female, Baptist, wife, Irish, short person, twin, lefty, kids hockey team representative, mother against drunk drivers, alcoholic, and many more. She also has her own foreign policy toward Guatemala. She can be made to feel a duty, that she will act upon, to prevent what she perceives as official acts of cruelty in a foreign country. Her interest in this matter is ably (not always honestly) represented in the marketplace that controls relevant communication with her. The United States government has an extremely small, reactive relationship to her on this subject. Sectors within the government who would formulate US national interests in conformance with perceived geopolitical advantage have almost no communication with her. When millions of similar cases are aggregated, the result is a loss of interstate strategic initiative on the part of the government. The consequences for US security may be limited in the Guatemala case, but the trend promises to transform other situations in which the same constellation of non-state identities will become involved. These actors are leaving the old geopolitics in a state of confusion and impotence.

BASEBALL, SANTERIA, AND BEACH FRONTS

> I should warn, however, that the philosophy that sovereignty is not so important is in fashion, that what they call democracy and human rights is more important, as if there could be democracy and human rights without independence and without sovereignty. (Fidel Castro, 1994)

Loss of effective political control by Fidel and Raul Castro could precipitate a state of chaos on the island of Cuba. The makeup and virulence of the disorder will depend of course on how the regime's final days play out, and judging from the expectations of published Cuba-watchers, that story might unfold in any of a hundred ways.[8]

Many predictions include violent episodes, however.[9] If violence becomes widespread or acute, chances are the United States government, alone or with international partners, will intervene to stabilize, ameliorate or fashion Cuba's transition. Other organizations based in the United States, or with significant American membership, will intervene as well. The Cuba problem would simultaneously become a growth industry for all manner of opportunist from baseball scout to cocaine distributor, to religious missionary, to foreign policy bureaucrat.

To sort out the political mess that these people will both enter and form, we can begin by reducing Cuba's ownership environment into the three parts suggested earlier in the text. The disclaimer holds that these three are not really separate or separable. Owner identities are fused both to individuals and to the rights being sought or claimed. Likewise, specific rights cannot be discussed without mention of the rules and the claimants. Nevertheless, it is helpful for presentation to divide salient issues into the three general categories – property rights and duties, owner and claimant identities, and the regime of ownership rules. The order is of little consequence.

Property rights and duties

Real estate titles. In any transition from rule by the Castros, one of the most inflammatory issues will be real property claims. The sharpest fights will be over properties owned by exiled anti-communist Cubans who, before the Communist Revolution in 1959, formed the Cuban economic and political elite.[10] Owing to their locations, many of the lost properties lend the promise of political and financial power. They are substance and symbol not only of financial worth, but of political dominance.

The history and control of land registry is distinct in Latin American countries as compared to the United States, and still more so in countries having experienced communist governments. Given the lack of a real estate profession, informality in the area of land titles will invite all kinds of conflicting claims and blatant fraud schemes. These registry problems will be a tremendous source of violence, whether the subject is return of titles to pre-revolution landlords, patenting common property formerly owned by the state, or preferences in the privatization of industries. The judicial mechanism, if there is one, will be awash with claims and counter-claims. It would be wishful thinking in the extreme to suppose that these cases, however well the relevant courts might run, will not be accompanied by violence.

Some claimants will be non-Cubans attempting to take recourse in the system of international business law to recapture equity from previously owned properties. For many commentators this question of pre-revolutionary holdings is at the forefront of the Cuba problem, but attempts at a pre-collapse property grab by the communist insiders may be its most exacerbating aspect. The Nicaraguan experience after the election of President Violeta Chamorro provides a hint regarding the potential for violence between pre-revolutionary claims against confiscated property and communist party land seizures.[11] As in Nicaragua and some East European countries, the impending ruin of the communist ownership system has caused the dictators to redistribute real estate interests. The Castros are vesting their security forces, or key leaders, with ownership slices that, if they can be translated or leveraged into equivalent rights within a capitalist framework, constitute a golden parachute. The strategy is transparent. First, the give-away might shore up support for the regime within armed institutions that may be suffering the country's economic collapse disproportionately. Second, the move offers a means to resist the political consequences of having key real estate, and the power that accompanies it, fall under control of a zealous opposition. Third, whatever the nature of the transition, a transformation of property ownership protocols may preserve political power and wealth for the Communist Party elite. Obviously, with important properties (transportation, water works, power generation, beach fronts) under possession of an armed organization, any demand for reconciliation of old claims might invite a violent defense.[12] Yet another property strategy seems to be the sale of partner shares to foreign companies, thus vesting future foreign allies in claims that, even if not secured completely, promise to establish a base for court arguments in whatever system ultimately arrives.

Tenancy. Related to real property titling are simple landlord–tenant disputes. These might be rated as exacerbating events of a relatively minor scale. However, change from a patron–communist system of tenancy rules, accompanied by an overturn of landlords and judges, will change the balance of perceived rights and duties. This will be especially true in Cuba as relatives from the United States bring with them different legal expectations and litigious energy. This is an area for which property disposition strategies can be prepared in advance – a preparation that could prove to be an important ameliorating effort.

Environmental degradation.[13] Fidel Castro's environmental record may prove as dismal as that of the other failed communist countries. Many US and transnational interest groups will lobby to have priority placed on the recuperation of damaged areas. Potential clean-up sites like the Boyeros asbestos factory near Havana or the experimental nuclear waste reprocessing center at Arroyo Naranjo strongly suggest that a multitude of agencies and organizations will find a mission in a post-Castro Cuba. Their rights and duties will conflict with those of the property claimants mentioned above. While the rights of foreign environmentalists may seem tenuous in a context of ambiguous sovereignty and system collapse, those rights will seem more valid as they become matched to political power generated in the United States and elsewhere. For this reason, and for the long-term benefit to Cuba, property interests expressed by environmental protection groups should be assigned due weight from the outset.

Lost stewardship of government installations. Under many plausible scenarios, effective control of key government lands will be lost. These properties could include large landholdings of the Cuban military such as the Ignacio Agramonte training area near Camaguey or the Siguanea training area on the Isle of Pines. Even if all Cuban military units were to divorce themselves from organized participation in any internal violence, much of the military land could be exposed to looters and squatters. It may be in the best interests of any follow-on government to insure the maintenance or orderly disposition of this land, especially if ecological recovery operations are needed.

Firearms. By all accounts there are at least several hundred thousand military small arms on the island of Cuba: almost all of them are controlled by the government. Locating weapons or control documents could become a priority for a transition government or for an intervening force.[14] These small arms may be the instruments of effective armed resistance to change away from socialism, or they could be instruments for extorting ownership slices. As discussed in Chapter 3, however, random or wholesale disarming of a population may not further defense of property rights. Careful analysis must be given to the relationship of individual private rights and the ability of privileged, isolated or outlaw groups to maintain monopolies on the possession or portation of firearms. It is very possible that widespread public possession of firearms should be encouraged as a means of empowering individual owners and as a means of enlisting adherents to a new democratic legal order.

Public health. It may turn out, as some predict, that the Cuban health care system is either not as good as has been claimed or has been severely degraded since the collapse of Warsaw Pact economic sponsorship. In addition, many specialized Cuban medical personnel will opt to leave Cuba. The United States government may perceive an obligation to undertake immediate reinforcement of the Cuban public health care system.[15] At the same time, in the minds of many Cubans, socialized medicine has been a source of national pride and perhaps a positive aspect of Castroite socialism. Visible dependence on the United States for the maintenance of public health may be an especially bitter pill. But this issue, like so many, is tied to property rights. To keep Cuban doctors, nurses and hospital administrators in Cuba, some recognition of the marketplace will be essential. Cubans may have to privatize a great deal of medical infrastructure in order to effect an equitable distribution of property shares in the health care system to health care professionals. It will be recognized sooner or later that while we might admire free universal medical care as a redeeming aspect of an otherwise unattractive socialism, the same egalitarian care is much more expensive to provide in the context of a market system. Medical professionals will seek appropriate social status, and as that status becomes measured in income, Cuba will be unable to maintain a quality health care system without paying doctors their worth.

Owner and claimant identities: Cuban stew

A superficial listing of Cuban owner identities could begin with the Communist Party of Cuba, Cuban American National Foundation, the Revolutionary Armed Forces, or the Interior Ministry. Some identities are far more nebulous, such as a racial identity or the term Cuban itself. Even 'mob' is an owner identity that will have some meaning to the extent that a leader can effectively claim control of it. Identities that seem subordinate in membership, such as a particular paramilitary unit, political faction, or religious sect, might have greater cohesive force and a more resolute leadership in relation to certain property rights than the larger group to which they seemingly belong. Among Cubans there are already dozens of interrelated and confused owner identities that will be exercised in competition over property rights. Some of the more obvious and dangerous are listed below, while some do not yet have labels.

Criminal organizations. Internal political convulsion and the attendant inability to conduct sophisticated police investigations will invigorate organized crime.[16] As discussed in Chapter 4, gangsters understand the opportunities that under-supervised territory presents. They quickly impose ownership regimes, create loyalties and obligations, and sow fear. Neither the legal political parties, rogue military units nor traditional guerrilla bands display the same efficiency and ruthlessness as does a criminal gang – or some hybrid. These groups directly and immediately focus on property rights. They deny access to their safehavens, monopolize markets and small industries, and isolate transportation means. They cultivate exclusive territorial identities. Communist Cuba boasts an unattractive record of collaboration between state security organizations and transnational criminal enterprises. The formats, contacts, and outlaw ethic are in place, if not the criminal organizations themselves. When political changes do come to the island, key members of the failing communist regime may already be under indictment in US courts for narcotics trafficking and related charges.[17]

Warlord armies. Communist Cuban military and paramilitary forces could divide and devolve into several mini-armies with disjointed but overlapping agendas, methods and membership. A single rogue army could control several hundred major weapons systems, several thousand soldiers, and significant Cuban territory.[18] Perhaps indistinguishable in morality or direction from the criminal gangs, these armies could also claim territorial definition, seek specific property rights, and invoke popular identities to enhance internal cohesiveness and influence the external balance of sympathies. A rogue army might find it easy to recruit dislocated Cubans spurred by racial fear, desire for or fear of retribution, furor over property losses, abstract ideological fanaticism, or by any combination of these and other motivators. Rejection of a United States imperialist military occupier is an obviously lucrative concept that could rally Cubans ranging from the most sincere to the most cynical. Complicating their control is the possibility that some factions will include US citizens or permanent United States residents.

Guerrilla groups. Guerrilla groups could also form, whose leadership does not stem from the Cuban military. Control of these groups could also be complicated by the membership of US citizens.[19] If the current Cuban leadership divides, and no new elite can gain effective control quickly, then United States citizens with strong Cuban affinities could arm themselves to take sides in the ensuing struggle, a struggle that could spill north over the Straits of Florida.

Migrants. Post-collapse Cuban migration could flood not only Florida, but other Caribbean islands as well. The number of migrants will probably be many times larger than during the Mariel boatlift of 1980 and may include individuals whose criminal extradition could be sought later by a post-Castro government.[20] The release of criminal prisoners from Cuban jails, whether intended as a cynical jab at the United States or just the result of abandoned wardenship, could also complicate the task of migrant control. Ironically, the fact that Florida would be the primary destination is perhaps the most important simplifying aspect of a refugee exodus. At least the major actions that can be taken by US or Florida governments will take place on the high seas or on United States soil. Political and legal concerns will be simpler than for actions that might have to be taken on Cuban soil or on other Caribbean islands.

Blacks. Observers note that Cuban racial demographics are different today than they were 35 years ago, i.e. the Cuban exile community is considered by many Cubans to be virtually all white, whereas the proportion of 'black' Cubans on the island is considered to have increased from a pre-revolutionary 20–30 per cent to perhaps as high as 50 per cent today.[21] Cuban racial categorization is poorly defined and often politically motivated. The nature of Cuban black–white racism is itself difficult to appreciate from the United States perspective. As such, the possible importance of Cuban racial differences is not entirely clear, but there is a clear warning: groups identifying internal violence with their best interests will be able to find kindling in racial fears, whether reasonable or not.

Religious identities. Castro has staged some visits by apparently politicized international church organizations, but has repressed organized religion internally.[22] A few Cuban–African cults, including the influential Santeria, Palo Monte and Abakuas groups, are said to have been courted by Castro in recent years.[23] This may cause them to support the regime a little too long toward its end, thereby causing congregants to fall away just as other religious attractions pour in from the mainland. An increase in spiritual options should prove a democratizing factor over time. Initially it may add to the possible radicalization of some sects, especially if racial identity and competition becomes a more important aspect of religious choice.[24] The Castros' present survival efforts are intended to maintain centralized economic and social control while bending selectively to market realities. In the process, the Castros have treated newly forming religious congregations inconsistently. As in pre-collapse Romania, violent repression of church formation may be among the ultimately decisive events in the regime's demise.

Regime of ownership rules

Reformation of Cuban public forces. The immediate re-establishment of internal confidence in civil police operations will be a priority for any interventionary expedition.[25] Transition of the Cuban government will depend in part on the establishment of effective and credible civilian law enforcement – a requirement that insinuates the broadest range of property rights and duties. Policing of the country must be envisioned as more than the ability to quell violent outbreaks of the peace or to apprehend criminals. Policing must mean peacefully implementing a cultural consensus regarding property rights and duties.

Prisons. Among the most troublesome properties will be the prisons. Warden cadres may be among the first to flee in order to avoid suffering acts of vengeance. They are likely to leave behind an extensive, unattended prison system and population. It will be in the best interests of the United States and Cuba to gain control as quickly as possible. Persecution of human rights monitors has contributed to an increasing number of purely political prisoners in the last few years, as well. Quivican Prison in Havana Province; Guanajay Prison in Havana Province; Aguica Prison in Matanzas Province; Villa Marista Detention Center in Havana; the Jagua Psychiatric Hospital and the Mazorra National Psychiatric Hospital all contain political prisoners identified by international human rights groups.[26] These political prisoners are likely to run an increased danger to their lives during the death throes of a collapsing regime. They and their families are also likely to have scores to settle.[27]

Foreign opportunism. Business opportunism should for the most part be welcomed. However, there will be a backlash against perceived invasion by foreign capital. More dangerous perhaps than competition presented by legal enterprises to existing legal industries is the problem of black market replacement. In those areas where goods or services are currently being offered or provided *sub rosa*, the inhibitions and pressures that favor use of violent competitive strategies will be greater. Since the Cuban economy has come to depend for survival on an extensive black market, an outlaw business ethic is already implanted. This seems to be one of the determinants of violence in other communist countries experiencing transitions toward free market democracy.

Foreign and semi-foreign business organizations will wield psychological as well as financial influence in post-Castro Cuba to a degree that is not fully appreciated. Much of this psychological influence will be positive in terms of reconciliation between the United States and Cuba or between the Cuban exile community and the island population. It is hard to imagine, for example, that Major League Baseball will not make an immediate and welcomed entrance. Such influences can be measured most readily by property indices. Stadium rights, player contracts, and broadcasting contracts will be some of the measures of mutual penetration.

Political opportunism could come in the form of internationalist support to political party organizations, e.g. Christian Democrats, Social Democrats, etc. While also welcome to infuse the electoral mechanism with seed capital and ideas, these foreign influences may be the source of additional stress on an already suffering body politic.

Castro's revolution may survive for many more years, or Cuba may slip from its communist revolutionary experience with an anticlimactic whimper. The intensity of ill-will by Cubans toward each other is difficult to measure, but some interested observers insist that a bloodbath is likely given the abuses of power and the personal atrocities committed by the communist regime. An environment of violent retribution could easily deteriorate. Grave disorder is one anticipated result when Castro and the repressive mechanisms of his personalist regime lose effective control. Many of the determinants of that disorder are already engaged while others await precipitating events. Whatever the scenario, however, the weave of Cuba's future social fabric can be envisioned in terms of who has what rights in what property, beginning with obvious property such as choice real estate and infrastructure, and membership in organizational bodies that control the rules of ownership.

Perhaps most important, such a conceptualization can guide policy planning. In the face of property-rooted violence, it behoves intelligence planners to seek with whatever precision possible, exactly who the owner-claimants are and what specific rights they might wish to defend in relation to exactly what locations. This will go a long way to finding hidden sponsors of violence, to finding areas of reconciliation, or to deciding who might best pay for security measures. Without a complete appreciation of land ownership claims and of the competing systems in which the claims might be stabilized, there can be no practical expectation of long-term success in subduing armed conflict in Cuba. There can also be no reasonable expectation that the government of the United States will be able to retain strategic initiative in competition with non-state entities able and willing to identify and service the wide variety of owner identities.

YOUR EAGLE OR MINE

'My children,' he told the assembled Indians and mestizos, 'a new dispensation comes to us this day. Are you ready to receive it? Will you be free? Will you make the effort to recover from the hated Spaniards the lands stolen from your forefathers three hundred years ago?' He then proclaimed: 'Mexicans. Long live Mexico! Death to the Gachupines!' (Miguel Hidalgo, interpreted by Alan Riding in *Distant Neighbors*)[28]

The ownership environments of Mexico and the United States are distinct but intertwined. Mexico's is passing through a period of unusually rapid change, while that of the United States, always more dynamic, shows new strains. Curiously, imbalances in the United States ownership environment correspond to Mexican strengths in a foreboding way – one that suggests a potential for organized armed violence within the borders of the United States. Like the Cuba example, what follows is speculative, and as baseball great Yogi Berra is credited to have said, 'Predicting is tough, especially when the future is involved'. The future suggested below offers, if nothing else, a vision of conflict within the borders of the United States that is of a scale exceeding public order, local law enforcement, or the localized application of federal resources. It is a scenario intended to bring the possibility of armed conflict within the known context of US society. It serves to emphasize the central significance of property ownership and of the relationship between government, protection of property rights, and political violence.

Those who know and write about Mexico know it to be one of the most powerful nations in the world – not in GDP or military formations, but in the strength of its national symbols and cohesiveness of national identity. It is the same quantity that writers like Moynihan and Schlesinger find to be eroding in the United States. The mismatch between a broadly radiated and loudly expressed sense of Mexicanness and the normally less boisterous, intermittent and context-sensitive patriotism of Americans will add to the inflammatory psychological mixture created by a mass migration of Mexicans into the United States.

Even while Mexican national identity is powerful, the privileged control of ownership within Mexico is represented by a more exclusive owner identity, the Partido Revolucionario Institucional (PRI). Within the last decade, and at an accelerated pace within the past few years, the prepotency of the PRI has been challenged. This is due in part to material overreaching and financial errors by the party that resulted in an economic tailspin. In 1994 the Mexican stock market lost about 40 per cent of its value. As a result, Mexico is living the worst internal strife since the days of the Mexican Revolution 80 years ago. Mexico may muddle through its difficulties as it has in the past, and stabilize on a lower plane of social and economic mediocrity. It is just as likely that things will get worse.

Mexican political violence was highlighted in 1994 by the flamboyant actions of the Zapatista Guerrillas in southern Mexico, and there are similar groups incubating or waiting in other parts of the country. Still, Mexico's political violence is inadequately defined as an insurgent problem. Mexico's violence follows the organizational ambiguity already described at length in this book. Narcotics trafficking is interwoven with party politics, party politics with guerrilla activities, and so on. Questions about who is conspiring with whom are poorly investigated by simply following line and block diagrams. Whether or not the Mexican is a member of a church hierarchy or a drug cartel or a government ministry is but another hint at the loyalties he will feel regarding ownership identity in a particular struggle. It is obvious, however, that the organized use of violence to secure property rights is less and less a monopoly of the Mexican state, and more and more a behavioral norm. The practical effect on United States territory of this generalized instability has not only been easily predictable, it is a matter of record. Instability in Mexico and illegal migration to the United States are related almost as the readout on a car's tachometer is related to that of its speedometer. As RPM on the tachometer go up, speed increases, albeit after a short time lag. As instability in Mexico worsens, attempts to migrate to the US will increase.

Cross-border migration is not the only perfectly predictable consequence of Mexican instability, though this is the most obvious and immediate. At the very least, American terrain will be used by contestants during a Mexican Donnybrook to organize and propagandize. In 1904 Ricardo Flores Magón, a leading Mexican anarchist, exiled himself permanently to the United States from where he pursued efforts to overthrow the Porfirio Díaz regime in Mexico. Most of Flores' contribution to the success of the Mexican Revolution was achieved while he was in the United States.[29] He died at Leavenworth Prison, but his body was later removed to Mexico City for a hero's reburial. Today the means of travel and communication make it certain that some partisans in a Mexican struggle will use United States territory as a base of operation.

Many, like Ricardo Flores, will gravitate to the political hospitality American democracy affords them, but will harbor abiding anti-American feelings at the same time.

A generalized breakdown in law and order will invigorate illicit cross-border drug trafficking as well, but this (after the direct difficulties posed by mass immigration attempts and by the activities of Mexican partisans) may be only the fourth most dangerous consequence of Mexico's troubles. The most disruptive and damaging effect of Mexican political violence, if it is prolonged, may be guerrilla warfare within the borders of the United States.

The first skirmishes, if they have not already begun, might occur over the use of Spanish or English in local organizations that determine the exercise of property rights. As soon as the use of the Spanish language is combined with public deference to Mexican national symbols to a degree that is offensive to English speakers who still have a strong emotional connection to US symbols, trouble is almost certain.

Mexicans now find it possible to remain indefinitely in United States territory without the necessity of learning English. One of the most important cultural distinctions separating Mexico from the United States – language – is changing the cultural boundaries between the two countries. In various towns and counties in the Southwest border states, native Spanish speakers represent a formidable political block, and it can be expected that, unless current trends change, native Spanish speakers (of predominantly Mexican origin) will eventually outnumber English speakers in many additional locales. The language shift will carry along with it a shift in symbolism and cultural identities that can change the balance of national cohesiveness. For instance, one will likely be able to trace the importance of Cinco de Mayo (5 May) celebrations throughout the Southwest. Changes in musical selections at official functions, the raising or displaying of Mexican flags, progressive changes in the content of school texts, and widened promotion of bilingual education in public schools are other common occurrences. Not only does none of these things constitute an illegality, none of them might ever cause a spark capable of igniting armed conflict.

However, at some time the identity of common ownership will have shifted to the point of threatening existing ownership rules and relationships. Incremental reactions against the culture shift will earn rebuke in the opinion media as being intolerant or as offenses against the rights of free speech and expression. This is especially true to the extent that Mexican national identity is tied demagogically to Hispanic identity, thereby lending the emotional weight of ethnic conflict. This scolding against anti-immigrant discrimination may seem laudable, but it will suppress visibility of an emotion that will continue to grow.

Stark contrasts will be noted between the abject poverty of new immigrants and the lot of Southwesterners who may have benefited from the free trade advantages of NAFTA. Many immigrants, led by aid groups, will pursue a strategy of alleviating economic misery by means of political organizing to demand government support. Especially inflammable could be the communities of Mexican-Americans already established in the United States, who feel they have made great efforts to succeed in the English-speaking world and who are now confronted with the possibility that the nation they left might now regain local dominance. The attitudes of some members of the Mexican-American community will be especially complex given racial overtones of the conflict, affinities to many cultural aspects of Mexicanness, and to their often-fervid patriotism toward the United States. Participation in organized violence from within this group could divide along generational lines, but even among Mexican-American youth there will be great confusion, partly because of the language barrier. Adding to this confusion will be the cross-resentments of non-Mexican legal and illegal Hispanic immigrants, most of whom will have no affinity toward Mexican symbols.

If the ignition of internal conflict is reaction against Mexicanness on the part of Anglo-Americans or multiple-generation Mexican-Americans, the United States government will be obliged to take the next fatal step toward generalizing armed violence. It will intervene to protect the rights of Mexican immigrants and of Mexican-American citizens suffering the collateral damage of racism. Many organized, armed groups of disaffected citizens will take federal intervention on behalf of immigrants as final proof that the federal government is no longer the legitimate protector of citizens' rights. Their reaction will not be spontaneous, irrational or novel. It will be a critical chapter in what is already an established grass-roots movement of rebellious expression. Particularly in the American West and Southwest, groups have been organizing whose strategy of action has been undefined, but whose dissatisfaction with the role of the federal government in their lives (focusing on property rights in most cases) has provided a latent purpose. The symbolism favored by these groups is evocative of both patriotism and territorial ferocity. The federal government can unwittingly provide a unifying course of action to armed organizations ready to deal directly with the immigrant problem. They will redouble violence against Mexicans, which in turn will provide a provocation and justification for Mexican guerrilla activity within the United States. Depending on particulars surrounding the property claims and possibilities of individual American-Indian tribes, a number of these, too, will enter the conflict. One should not, however, prejudge what side a given American Indian tribe might take. Many tribes enjoy sophisticated leadership that understands the relationship between sovereignty and real estate value and will not be lured into alliances with Mexicans on the basis of fabricated or popularized ancestral brotherhood. This is especially true since the Mexican historical record of treatment of Indian tribes like the Yaquis is no better than that of the United States. Irrespective of the postures of actual tribal leaders, the image of indigenous solidarity (perhaps exemplified by Azatlan, an even more illusory cross-border national identity than Mayalan) will gain influence for those who can manage the identity skillfully.

The Southwest of the United States has always displayed a Mexican cultural flavor that is perceived in much of the rest of the country to be not only benign but enjoyable, exotic, even brilliant. The idea that a dangerous threat to national security is brewing as a result of Mexican nationalism might not impress Americans from other parts of the United States whose direct property interests are not affected. Oddly, those Mexicans most likely to promote an aggressive expression of national identity at the cost of Uncle Sam will be able to count on spiritual solidarity, if not material support, from throughout the Western hemisphere, including from within the United States. In fact, an opportunity to promote the kind of internal disorder in the United States (that the US has for so long derided in Latin American countries) may be irresistible. News of such a predicament would be relished in many corners of the world. Seed material for some guerrilla groups may already exist in the form of Pancho Villa-type bandit groups that have been increasing markedly along the border, attacking attractive targets like the Southern Pacific Railway.

Slumping real estate values, exodus of labor able to seek options elsewhere, increasing insurance rates, disruptions in public services, collapse of municipal bond ratings, depression in tourist revenues – the list of symptoms is well known. What may not be understood is that a guerrilla movement capable of causing a property disaster can be haphazard, poorly led, without concrete or consistent ideological foundation, in want of an achievable strategic goal, and with support from only a small fraction of the total population. It does not have to move in accordance with any American military concept of strategy, even though the movement may enjoy international supporters with great-power strategy in mind. It can be improvised, rag-tag, intermittent, multiply led, irrational and still be effective. All the more so if it enjoys an engaging set of symbols, like the recovery of ancestral lands, retribution for violence committed, anti-racism, obvious economic disparities, and a cohesive owner identity associated with a place, Mexico, that promises to provide sanctuary. With these attributes, an effective guerrilla movement can survive for decades – to give sport if nothing else.

Meanwhile, back in Mexico, a number of factors could worsen conditions in the United States still further. Many Mexicans will take pleasure in the internal difficulties unfolding in the United States, even if this enjoyment competes for emotional space with the desire for economic success. Some will be enthusiastic supporters of American trouble and will find ways to fund or otherwise encourage guerrilla activity inside United States territory.

In addition, one of the consequences of a transition of political power in Cuba may be another mass migration into Mexico similar to the exodus of the Spanish Republicans after the Spanish Civil War. Unlike the wave of Cuban migrants that arrived in Miami three decades ago, the wave to Mexico will include leftists with little entrepreneurial skill, motivation or capital. Their psychology is more likely to be one of revolutionary rancor combined with Mafia-style loyalties. Some will occupy themselves with political party activities flavored by a robust anti-Americanism. Resentment toward the United States will be a strong enough emotional quantity that direct action to punish the US will be a staple release.

Salvation from organized anti-state violence within the United States must come via recognition of property rights as the central issue around which cohesive policy can be developed. Government social programs designed to redress or cure economic imbalances in the Southwest – to aid disadvantaged or marginalized populations – are destined to have a worsening effect on the conditions of violence. Such programs are rooted in the idea that internal wars are the product of unfavorable socioeconomic conditions leading to 'Perceived Relative Deprivation'. In the American Southwest, programs intended to improve the lot of immigrants will be counterproductive in the extreme since they will attract migration but will not influence either the mix of preferred owner identities (and symbols) or convince the organizers and catalysts of violent action to change their behavior. If the outcome of most redistribution programs is any guide, they will also fail to improve the long-term condition of the target population. National cohesiveness, and public cooperation to help government limit violence, must be born of a faith in government's role of protecting public and private property rights. Constricting illegal migration is important as an act of solidarity with current owners, even if legal migration is liberalized. In some locales, limited language discrimination, though it will spark some violence, will ameliorate and avoid future violence by sending a clear signal that participation in decisions regarding property rights revolves around adoption of existing cultural symbolism. The actual buying and selling of real estate to encourage specific land uses and population shifts is also an important strategy option. Attendance to some of the property complaints of currently existing armed organizations is also a preventive strategy. Finally, regulated privatization of law enforcement activities (especially those related to property protection) can anticipate and undercut vigilantism.

THE PROPERTY OF GREAT POWERS

> In these troubled circumstances, the Great Power is likely to find itself spending much more on defense than it did two generations earlier, and yet still discover that the world is a less secure environment – simply because other Powers have grown faster, and are becoming stronger.[30] (Paul Kennedy)

Before the lopsided American victory in the Persian Gulf, the academic current exemplified by Paul Kennedy's *The Rise and Fall of Great Powers* proclaimed the end of American grandeur and world leadership, prescribing a national intellectual acquiescence to a lesser position in the coming world order. As Kennedy pointed out in 1987, the theoretical bases of United States post-World War II defense strategy appeared to have eroded. Now beyond erosion, these theoretical bases seem, barring a turn of events even more abrupt and unexpected than that of the late 1980s, to be completely inapplicable.

A significant portion of Soviet leadership at some point became aware that a continuation of operative economic and technological trends threatened the core security of the empire. Fundamental changes had to be made in order to keep Russia safe from her historic nightmare of Western technological eclipse. The critical need to buy time and conserve resources in order to attempt a radical but controlled social change made Soviet foreign policy more conciliatory in its last days. Now, the prognosis for controlled change toward Western-style capitalism in the residual republics of the Soviet empire is mixed, but any return of Russia as a superpower nemesis is, in the least favorable prediction, decades away. Dissolution of the Soviet menace not only obviated many strategic preparations to oppose the Soviets, it also exposed a half-century of demographic and economic change in the rest of the world. These changes were overlooked, ignored, or under-appreciated by American strategic defense planners because of the felt need to concentrate on the main enemy. During the Cold War, and at an accelerated pace since, the security challenges facing the United States have evolved faster than the basic strategic defense theories upon which US military and diplomatic preparations, instructions and operations are based. This difference in pace between the global strategic context and United States strategic defense posture can cause the United States to waste defense money and possibly to be unprepared for real security challenges. This is not to say, as suggested by the Kennedy essay, that the United States spent beyond its means on defense, or that it needs to manage a decline in relative world power. Rather, it was America's half-century strategic rival, the Soviet Union, that passed the point of affording its military avocation. US wealth was increasing relative to its adversary's, as was America's relative ability to afford military preparedness. It must be admitted and underlined that, even if the United States remains well within its ability to afford military spending, it can easily waste money against false threats. It should interpret post-Soviet strategic dynamics so that it does not fail to spend enough against real threats.

Ray Cline's politectonics was an attempt to sell the importance of national will in applying a national strategy to oppose, on a global scale, a serious challenge to the national well-being. His theme is well-taken – resolve is an important element of power, and power is most effective when focused by a rational plan. It can be argued that the national resolve Cline sought to encourage was provided during the 1980s along with a national strategy that called for increasing American military power and a more direct challenge to Soviet expansion. This accounted in part for the defeat of the Soviet empire. However, Cline's geopolitical methodology is insufficient to fully explain either the termination of the Cold War, or the requirements of the aftermath. Geopolitics does not, in fact, analyze geography in terms of its basic value, the value of rights and duties attributable to particular peoples. Geopolitics can lead to correct answers in some contexts because absolute possession of land gives obvious advantages to its possessors. The Falklands/Malvinas War, for instance, seems to lend itself to geopolitical appraisal. Geopolitics can fail miserably when a conflict involves multiple, divided, and shared rights, fractured and overlapping identities of would-be owners, and partially competing ideologies. These complicated ownership environments are the rule, rather than the exception, in the post-Soviet world.

Francis Fukuyama may be guilty of the same geopolitical error as Ray Cline, Paul Kennedy or Colin Gray. Their writing treats historical development of the nation-state – placing politics at the top of a hierarchy of concepts. The nation-state may be only a temporally important entity, or at least may not be as important as it has been. Therefore, state sovereignty and the national armies dedicated to it, will have their importance (and their roles) adjusted accordingly. It is understandable that military planning translates the values of a nation into objectives of the nation-state as expressed or implied by the national political leadership. The military will manifest the policy of a government. But a finding that a federal civilian executive is in diminishing control of a diminishing portion of the national will forces some reflection regarding the diffusion and particularization of national interests and their effective defense. Newton's logic – internalized by Clausewitz and applied to military strategy – still rules over a wide range of military math, but the new, post-Newton science of chaos requires something beyond Clausewitz, something that responds to non-linear, temporal, non-state and partially state challenges. Seen as a changing concert of rights and duties, rather than as a fixed thing, property appears as a first key toward understanding the new strategic math.

The US military sired the ancestral Internet, but is still struggling to grasp all the Net's implications. In its infancy, the Internet was a modern communications tool for a select group of defense industry insiders. Now in adolescence, the Internet is the engine of a global electronic culture whose participation in matters of national security and strategy is yet poorly understood. The Internet serves both to complicate the security environment and to explore it. It is a decidedly 'postmodern' phenomenon in that the word 'postmodern' encapsulates the notion of going beyond the technical machinery of the Net to the profound changes it is making in the way people organize for political struggles. 'Postmodern' also gives us an option to skirt the use of two terms used elsewhere in this book – 'low intensity conflict', and 'operations other than war', since both these labels have been at times controversial and unsatisfying. 'Postmodern', while unlikely to catch on among military jargoneers, helps us scout beyond the Internet-as-machine to reconnoiter the electronic culture for any strategic danger.

It is within the realm of the 'other' threats to national security, listed in Chapter 5, that the postmodern Internet meets strategy. In the fine arts and literature, critics have been known to throw 'postmodern' around with an 'I know something you don't know' air, but there is no fixed, universal definition. There are, however, recurrent themes. People call things postmodern to suggest they go beyond whatever was, up to the time, modern – and maybe to describe rebellion against the current standards or state of the art. Postmodern art can be chaotic, disconnected, using subversive styles, a pastiche (mix of styles), or a built-in self-criticism. 'Modern' architecture, in what became known as the international style, expressed the limits of technology in monumental and efficient structures – more glass, more cement, taller buildings, shapes and sizes pressing the technical limits of the materials used. Postmodern buildings, on the other hand, incorporate symbolism and unquantifiable emotions, even including whimsicality or capriciousness. They attempt to regain character and identity lost to modernism.

The utility of the term in referring to violent conflicts is then obvious, even if the analogy is imperfect. Today, the protagonists of a violent political struggle can be very diverse, with a diffusion and overlap of goals, commitment and methods – they coordinate intermittently, implicitly, even illogically. Advanced information technologies, exemplified best by the Internet, make this all possible. The way to find Zapatistas was not to travel to the jungles of Chiapas. A look at a Swarthmore home page gives a *subcomandante's* dispatches, requests money, and has even offered the chance to send condolences to an infirm *Capitana*.[31]

The Internet provided a medium of intellectual and emotional fungibility. It allowed fleeting admixtures and translations of identities and causes. Indigenous rebels, feminists, troublemakers, and idle wireheads could participate in a cause with a limitlessly undefinable and complex population of sympathies and sympathizers. With the Internet, we can express solidarity at home, by increments, as the mood moves us, and with little personal risk. It all makes finding causes and identifying enemies easy for the online individual. It makes defining and fixing enemies far more difficult for a modern, state-sponsored military. The Internet tells us that the new security challenges may or may not be 'low intensity', may or may not be 'other than war', but they *are* postmodern. That is, by their nature they defy modern military organization. Just as the tank is confounded by urban or mountain terrain, the line-and-block diagram is confounded by fluid reshapings within the electronic culture.

CONCLUSION

> We stand at a moment in history when widening literacy, mass communications, and urbanization have produced a global political awakening. This is a fundamental event that expresses itself above all, in the intensified demand for human rights.[32]
> (Warren Christopher)

In the preceding chapters a wide variety of confrontations were used to inject the idea of property into international studies and strategy. The seizure in Mexico of Dr Alvarez Machain, the 1968 Warsaw Pact invasion of Czechoslovakia, Greenpeace's defense of the whales, Russian nationals on the Moldovan Dniester, the Falklands/Malvinas War, the abuse of Brazilian street children, founding of the Israeli state, and geosynchronous orbits were all thrown together with property rights and duties (and, subliminally, with territorial imperative) in mind. None of the examples refutes the 1980 Warren Christopher comment just quoted above. Christopher's statement has gained truth during the 15 succeeding years of continued urbanization, widening literacy, and mass communications. However, the human rights to which Christopher referred in his praise of President Carter's foreign policy soon became a narrowed and selective understanding.

Human rights policy had already fallen into the habit of seeking its mandate and establishing priorities in accordance with degrees of offense to American moral sensibilities. Even if we could claim for our human rights policies a perfect political and ideological objectivity, they remain suspect. Their departure is from the emotional perceptions of a select audience, not from the determinants of human trespass. Human rights-oriented policies taken by the United States toward some countries have been driven by levels of indignation and outrage. There is no camouflaging their sanctimony once it is obvious that they are inconsistent in their treatment of, or are oblivious to, the basic rights and duties that lead to abuses.

The inhumanities that energize American foreign policy are the violent consequences of underlying conditions, conditions that by themselves failed to generate emotional energy. Violent symptoms rather than underlying causes always seem to become the focal point of policy. By better appreciating property we can consider a broader range of those contested rights and duties that most often lead to violence. If, in all the lands where the United States regularly cites grave human rights inadequacies, one were to ask simple questions about landlord–tenant laws, title registry systems, zoning ordinances, mining stakes, paving contracts, street gang territories, paternity laws, or water courts, two judgments would be reached. First, that powerful linkages exist between violent abuses of human rights and contested property rights. Second that US intelligence collectors, analysts, policy-makers and diplomats are indifferent to details of the ownership environment.

Of all available examples used in this book, the pending collapse of Fidel Castro's regime in Cuba was chosen for greatest elaboration. History's most accomplished headache to US presidents, the Castros' final jab at America will be the nightmare of their political demise. Aside from its substantive importance as a trouble spot, however, Cuba's future presents a case study of palpable, dominant property issues. Some of the other examples were chosen exactly because the application of property theories was tenuous. Disclaimers made at the outset of the book bear repeating – almost any struggle can be described convincingly in property terms, but doing so isn't necessarily advantageous. Property, like economics, biology, or class, can be applied to the point of nonsense – or at least to the point of confusion and dullness. There are, however, some instances where property is the best device for organizing analysis. Cuba is one of them, not only because latent real estate claims overshadow the return of exiled anti-Castroites, but because competition for pieces of post-Castro Cuba will be awash with partial, overlapping identities and outlaw agendas. Transnational organized crime, criminalization of ex-soldiers, black market commercialization of excess military hardware, racial and religious superimpositions, talent draining, and every form of fraud and demagoguery will blossom. Due to Cuba's close proximity to the United States, troubles there will be covered vigorously, if superficially, by the US news media. For the interrelation of these destabilizing and threatening phenomena to be understood, however, they are best viewed as ownership struggles, even where the property involved is more subtle or intangible than possession of real estate. Without question, Cuban property competitions represent future human rights violations if no legitimate system of reconciliation is available during Cuba's coming transition period.

Ray Cline named his formula for measuring national power after plate tectonics. His liberal allusion to plate theory was an artistic bridge suggesting that big answers are valid and that problems of international conflict can be mapped on a global scale. What might a global geoproperty map look like? Freedom House, a Washington-based human rights monitoring group, produces a map that shows the status of human freedom in countries around the globe.[33] Freedom House displays in an atlas-type composition what is an admittedly subjective comparison of a mixed bag of human liberties. The map shows more than just which countries are free, partly free, and not free. With little imagination one can see that where unfree countries are in close proximity to free ones, there is potential for conflict. It is no surprise that Mexico is only partly free and that Cuba is listed as not free. A geostrategic message is delivered bell-clear by the Freedom House world map. Color-coding on the Freedom House map does not display rimlands, shatterbelts, heartlands or other spatial relationships, but instead shows differentials in rights. Because the value of global lands is not generated only by location and shape, but by the way places are owned, geostrategists can see on the Freedom House map what is invisible on those of the Spykmans and Mackinders.

Other world-scale maps could show indices of defective sovereignty or the proximity of material disparities. Although not attempted here, a world map showing differences in real property rights, the foreign impact of environmental degradation, or the transparency of land registries, would be as revealing of human conflicts as ethnic maps. Other property rights, such as minority access to public and semi-public places, corporate ownership participation, water court operations, eligibility for leadership in cooperative ownership schemes, passport and visa requirements, or child illegitimacy would all be more revealing of potential conflict than some current measures of human rights status. For example, if we rate one place as more or less humane than another because of the existence of a death penalty, that relative measure may not be reflective of political instability. The existence of a death penalty might even correlate to greater protection of other rights. Extremes in ownership, however, will always spell potential violence.

The upshot of these assertions for scholarly analysis or for strategic intelligence is obvious. However, the possibility of making a continuous weave from the global scale to the local or tactical is especially inviting. Property struggles can be mapped down to the life estate rights of tenant farmers, the right to carry a concealed weapon, the right to keep a dog off a leash, to vote on a school bond, or to carry away fallen wood. Every one of these things influences political contests, and every armed political contest will contain a mixture of these kinds of issues.

Too many property items have been overlooked in obedience to a false tension between realism and idealism in international studies. Geoproperty closes the distance between the two constructs, but it also closes the analytical distance between other themes and focal points such as:

- private and public interests in foreign political struggles;
- criminally and politically motivated uses of organized violence;
- political philosophy and military planning;

- self-determination, or nationalism, and interdependence;
- international law, international relations theory, and human rights;
- internal struggle and international conflict;
- police and military interpretations of transnational threats.

Taken together this closing of analytical distances also goes a long way to explain the changing relationship that state sovereignty has with other owner identities. State sovereignty is not going away, but it will be seen more and more for what it is – a membership agreement that observes select preferential rights in favor of an exclusive number of governing groups. As such, the dynamics of changing membership in the sovereigns' club, varying degrees of sovereignty, differing attributes, and wildly uneven power can be better understood.

Having claimed these marvelous advantages for geoproperty, what in it is immediately useful from the selfish American viewpoint? As expressed in the introduction, every cubic inch of the earth and the space around it bears some identifiable right belonging to the people of the United States. On first hearing, this statement may be redolent of just the kind of imperial arrogance that makes the rest of the world want to conspire against the only remaining superpower. Nevertheless, the assertion is eminently reasonable and entirely in concert with both realist and idealist traditions. It is not just Americans who claim property rights everywhere, it is everyone.

Violence against human or property rights no longer fits into cleanly separable categories. The coalescing of criminal arrogation of property with political arrogation is often too far advanced for us to distance 'police' responses from 'military' ones, or public safety from national security. Even the potentially big wars of the future are sure to be cluttered with extortionate and parasitic enemy strategies. To win against these, a country must be able to target discreetly with precise weapons. As has been argued, the precision of the weapons will be determined by legal as much as by technical specifications. This does not just mean that governments should develop non-lethal weapons. Violence and measures to counter it must be weighed according to their relative effect on the capacity to extort. The Anti-Ballistic Missile Treaty is a high-end example. The United States could not defend parts of its property against extortion were it tied wholly to a game of mutually assured destruction. It must be able to deter piecemeal attacks, even if those attacks boast the seemingly total threat that nuclear weapons connote.

Keying on property reminds that the job of protecting diffuse and particularized rights and duties is as often a police job as it is a military one. The force structure necessary for a successful foreign intervention must lend not only the physical strength to take and keep possession. The organization must be able to stay and police until such a time that property rights and duties can be satisfactorily resolved without the presence of a foreign military force. If policing, with all its connotations of restraint and patient occupation, is not acceptable, then initial possession is probably a wasteful, counterproductive exercise.

Threat strategies need not be the product of formal treaties or war plans. They may be organized intuitively, improvisationally, *ad hoc*, and in unspoken amalgamations and coalitions that undermine or confuse owner-claimant identities. As such, the greatest threat to a country or nation may be one against the unifying concept of what the national property includes and who the participants in that common ownership ought to be. If, for example, enough citizens of the United States were to be convinced that indeed they had stolen the American West from an innocent, weak Mexico, or from pre-colonial tribes, the United States government might find it hard to defend its sovereignty against pseudo-insurgent extortionists attacking property bit-by-bit and right-by-right under various banners of nationalism and ethnicity.

Finally, to describe the objectives, determine success and prepare strategies for environmental protection battles, relevant competitions can be described in property terms. Looking at world fisheries, we see only the beginning of environmental conflicts that will engage both formal and privatized militaries. Therein lies the meeting of legal concepts, geographical particulars, and owner identities. In the past, privatization of violent public policies might have been called privateering. Now the archaic letters of marque and reprisal may acquire new labels and new relevance. Militarized arms of NGOs and IGOs, as well as the security elements of large corporations – both tied directly to discreet property interests – will have an increasingly larger slice of the action in both international law enforcement and its violation.

The postmodern security strategy of the United States (and of other countries as well) will be successful if it admits three distinct but overlapping implications of geoproperty. First, foreign policy will, like it or not, be progressively privatized. This trend should be guided, not resisted. Second, the application of force will be increasingly constrained by legal regimes. Specialized constabulary organizations should be created in response to this trend. Finally, wars will still have to be fought. A combat military must be maintained, honed and focused on closing with and destroying enemies. We still stand at a moment in history when widening literacy, communications, and urbanization produce global political awakening. But what is fundamental about these processes cannot be analyzed ultimately as a demand for human rights; it must ultimately be analyzed as property. This is because the human ego allows us to suppose that everything, including other humans, can belong to us, whereas in the final instance there can be but one Sovereign.

NOTES

1. The Center of Strategic Studies for National Stability (Centro de Estudios Estratégicos para la Estabilidad Nacional – ESTNA) was created under the auspices of the Foundation for the Institutional Development of Guatemala (*Fundación para el Desarrollo de Guatemala* – DIG) in 1988. Much of the information about ESTNA comes from direct observations by the author and from interviews with members of the forum architects including retired Guatemalan General Héctor Gramajo, José María Argueta, and César Lechuga. In 1991, the civilian founders of ESTNA began to explore the value of exporting the ESTNA format to neighboring El Salvador. Interest among Salvadorans led to creation of the Center for Strategic Studies to Strengthen Salvadoran Democracy (Centro DEMOS) and its parent foundation, FUNDEMOS. Leaders in the Slovak Republic and other Eastern European countries have also shown serious interest in adapting the ESTNA/DEMOS model to their own situations.
2. Organizations officially represented during the first course were as follows: GUCONOFE (cooperatives union), Raphael Landívar University, The Guatemalan Congress, MEC (political party), AP-5 (political party), Cakchiquel indigenous group, Chipoj Project (indigenous development project), Quiche indigenous group, COFECOP (cooperatives federation), Bank of Guatemala, Association of Members of the 1985 National Constituent Assembly, PD (political party), MAS (political party), Chamber of Industry, DCG (political party), UNO (political party), PID (political party), FUN (political party), PSD (political party), MLN (political party), Mam indigenous group, Chamber of Commerce, PDCN (political party), Interior Ministry, APG (political party), Public Finance Union, Jutiapa Indigenous Committee, Quekchi indigenous group, UCN (political party), Guatemalan Solidarity Union, Association of Evangelical Ministries, CUSG (union confederation), ADICSE (church association), PR (political party), Ministry of Defense, Ministry of Special Affairs, CGTG (union). Centro de Estudios Estratégicos para la Estabilidad Nacional, *Programa de Clausura del Curso Inaugural*

1989–1990 (Guatemala City: Fundación para el Desarrollo Institucional de Guatemala, 1990).
3. The following partial extract of class subject titles from the 1989 course gives an idea of overall content. Constitutional History; World Political-Economic Situation; International Organizations; Regional Organizations; Economic Diagnostic of Guatemala; Security and Defense Situation of Guatemala; Guatemala As Seen From the United States; Guatemala As Seen From Europe; Reforestation; The Role of the Army in Democracy; The Army, Pressure Groups, and Political Groups in the Process of Transition; Diagnostic of National Conditions and Integral Development; Current and Permanent National Objectives. Centro de Estudios Estrategicos para la Estabilidad Nacional, *Memoria de Actividades Académicas del Curso Inaugural 1989–1990* (Guatemala: Fundación para el Desarrollo Institucional de Guatemala, 1990).
4. General Hector Gramajo, Guatemalan Minister of Defense in 1988, was the individual most credited with ESTNA's foundation. He was a graduate of the United States Army's Command and General Staff Course at Ft Leavenworth, KS and of the Inter-American Defense College, IADC, in Washington, DC. During one of these courses he was exposed to a set of lectures on the nature and measurement of national power that were based on *The Games Nations Play* and related works.
5. Héctor Alejandro Gramajo, *Tésis de la Estabilidad Nacional* (Guatemala City: Editorial del Ejército, 1989).
6. 'The achievements of the ESTNA model for developing associative skills rest with the logic and power of its curricula: a scope of analytical exercises to induce and support the interaction of all participants; the discovery of common interests; the suggestion of political action beyond the traditional collegiate association. Incredibly, for the first time in Guatemalan politics, we see previously antagonistic political strata become aware of the crisis of dissociation and the debilitating impact on civil society in the absence of modern institutions that represent and broker natural conflicts of interest.' Glen Cox, Bruce Cameron and José María Argueta, 'The Dual Crisis of New Democracy: Association and Representation in Traditional Society', Centro ESTNA, 1991. Perhaps the most notable fruit of the forum's efforts was manifested in late May of 1993 when leaders from a broad range of Guatemala's political party spectrum united to successfully oppose a usurpation of power by then President Jorge Serrano. Most of the leaders of the cooperative movement were ESTNA graduates, including outspoken members of the Guatemalan Army who also opposed President Serrano's extra-constitutional maneuver.
7. As part of the recent peace accord between the Guatemalan government and the URNG (the Guatemalan National Revolutionary Unity, the umbrella organization that represented the four main Guatemalan guerrilla factions opposing the government) the two sides came to an agreement regarding the status of indigenous peoples in Guatemala. Much of a long text entitled 'Accord on Identity and Rights of Indigenous Peoples' is devoted directly to property issues. These include regularization of land ownership by indigenous communities, use and administration of natural resources, restoration of communal lands, compensation, land purchase and legal protective mechanisms. Much of the rest of the document addresses cultural identity. In total, the accord tries to grip directly the who, what and how aspects of the ownership environment. 'Accord Reached on Indigenous Issues', Guatemala City *Diario de Centro America*, 6 April 1995, p. 6, in Spanish as translated in FBIS-LAT-95-091, 11 May 1995.
8. Edward Gonzalez and David Ronfeldt outline some of the alternative possibilities for the unfolding of the Castro regime's demise: 'The regime's efforts to pursue these models may lead to the following possible endgames, which may occur in various sequences and combinations over the short term (1 year) or medium term (1–3 years): Endgame I. The Castro regime survives over the short to medium term

by means of the current transitional model [retaining totalitarian control, but creating a dual model economy with an external foreign exchange producing sector]. Endgame II. Over the short to medium term, the regime adopts major economic reforms and muddles through with an authoritarian market-oriented model – most likely a Cuban–Chinese hybrid based on "market-Leninism". Endgame III. In the short or medium term, the regime begins to lose control and Castro halts all reform (regardless of the model); stasis and heavy repression follow. Endgame IV. In the short or medium term, popular resistance increases, Castro leaves the picture, pro-reform factions in the regime regroup, and nonviolent change takes place from above and below. This sequence leads to a new coalition-type government with elements of the internal opposition, possibly ushered in with elections and including some former exiles. Endgame V. In the short or medium term, violent change from below occurs as widespread popular unrest erupts, leading to civil war, the downfall of the Castro regime, and a seizure of power by a new set of (dictatorial? democratic?) leaders.' Edward Gonzalez and David Ronfeldt, *Storm Warnings Over Cuba* (Santa Monica, CA: RAND, 1994), p. xi. Some predictions have Fidel Castro continuing to improvise the bare bones survival of his Revolution and Marxist ideologues appear to have recovered confidence after ducking for cover while the East Europeans reported their experiences. Richard L. Harris presents an upbeat prognosis and appraisal of the contribution of Cuban Marxism in *Marxism Socialism and Democracy in Latin America* (Boulder, CO: Westview Press, 1992).
9. See generally *Transition in Cuba: New Challenges for US Policy*. This is the product of a major research project sponsored by the Office of Research, US Department of State's Bureau for Latin America and the Caribbean and the US Agency for International Development. It was undertaken by the Cuban Research Institute of the Latin America and Caribbean Center at Florida International University. It is likely to have a significant impact on US government planning regarding Cuba's future. The study poses nine possible scenarios for Cuban change. 'The first sets a baseline. It characterizes the present responses of Cuba's government and people. There is tight, repressive government control of politics, and important opening to foreign investment, booming illegal markets, and persistent economic decline.' It needs to be noted that several of the possible scenarios posit mid- to long-term survival of a communist government without a violent crisis.
10. In 1990, the University of Miami's Research Institute for Cuban Studies began a registry of expropriated properties. Andres Oppenheimer, *Castro's Final Hour: The Secret Story Behind the Coming Downfall of Communist Cuba* (New York: Simon & Schuster, 1992), p. 323.
11. Oppenheimer, *Castro's Final Hour*, p. 324. In Nicaragua, the Sandinista Army was able to maintain its political identity and physical integrity in spite of the Violeta Chamorro election win. This fact provided a coercive backstop allowing the Nicaraguan communists to resist claims of pre-revolution owners. A similar environment could exist in a post-Castro Cuba; Tim Johnson, 'Property Disputes Cloud Nicaragua's Economic Future', *The Miami Herald* (12 March 1993) . 'Many people are upset at offer of substitute property being offered for property taken by Sandinistas after the Sandinistas lost the 1990 elections. They quickly gave away 11,000 houses, farms and lots – to Sandinistas.'
12. See Kenneth Freed, 'National Agenda; Cuba's Army Becoming More Important Than Party; The Military Commands the Economy as Communists Lose Credibility. But Fidel Castro Seems Safe for Now', *Los Angeles Times*, 6 December 1994 (from The Xinhua News Agency). Freed, aside from reporting that the Cuban Army is running department stores, travel agencies, construction companies and farms, suggests that this is because the army has more professional capability and public credibility than the Cuban Communist Party.
13. For an overview of possible ecological problem areas see Jose R. Oro, *The Poisoning*

of Paradise: Environmental Pollution in the Republic of Cuba (The Endowment for Cuban American Studies, Cuban American National Foundation, ISBN: 0-918901-87-1, 1992).

14. The problem of weapons control and collection was prominent in the United States' Somalia intervention. See Robert M. Press, 'Somali Civil War is Fueled by Huge Stockpiles of Weapons', *Christian Science Monitor*, 14 October 1992, p. 1.
15. See Lizette Alvarez, 'Malnourished Cubans Flock to Hospitals: Thousands Treated for Severe Eye Disease', *Miami Herald*, 14 April 1993, p. 1.
16. 'Former Eastern European communist security personnel have created organizations suspected of coercive actions and terrorist planning (for example, Red Fist in the former German Democratic Republic); the prospect of former DGI [Cuban intelligence] free-lance activities in an unsettled region must at least be considered.' Graham H. Turbiville, 'The Cuban "Threat" in the Southern Hemisphere: Goodby to all That?', *Military Review* (December 1991), p. 87.
17. A proposed indictment of Raul Castro and the Cuban government on narcotics trafficking charges is reported in Jeff Leen and Andres Oppenheimer, 'Clinton Caught off Guard by Proposed Cuba Charges', *Miami Herald*, 9 April 1993, p. 1A; for a broad accusation regarding Cuban narcotics dealings of the Castro government see *Castro and the Narcotics Connection* (Washington, DC: Cuban American National Foundation, 1983).
18. For an unclassified review of Cuban military strength see The Combined Arms Command Threats Directorate, 'Cuban Threat Assessment', *Threats Update* (3 December 1992), p. 109.
19. A variety of Cuban political attitudes toward Cuba's transformation are sketched in Manuel Ramon De Zayas, 'Who's on First?: The Cuban Political Ballgame', *Postmodern Notes*, 1 (Spring 1991), pp. 8–26.
20. For a complete history and analysis of the 1980 Cuban boatlift, see Alex Larzelere, *The 1980 Cuban Boatlift* (Washington, DC: National Defense University Press, US Government Printing Office, 1988).
21. The CIA's *World Fact Book* places ethnic divisions as follows: mulatto = 51 per cent, white = 37 per cent, black = 11 per cent, Chinese = 1 per cent. Central Intelligence Agency, *The World Fact Book 1992* (Washington, DC: US Government Printing Office, 1993), p. 86.
22. 'Castro Meets With Methodist General Assembly Delegates', Havana Tele Rebelde and Cuba Vision Networks in Spanish, 4 April 1993, as translated in *FBIS-LAT-93-064*, 6 April 1993. Fidel talked to the assembly about the US embargo; his ministers called the embargo anti-Christian. One hundred representatives from 21 countries attended. It should be noted that the article making Cuba an atheist state was dropped from the 1992 Cuban Constitution.
23. Oppenheimer, *Castro's Final Hour*, p. 342.
24. For insight on the religious component of the Cuban political misery see Damian Fernandez, 'Revolution and Political Religion in Cuba', in *The Religious Challenge to the State*, ed. Matthew C. Moen and Lowell F. Gustaffson (Philadelphia, PA: Temple University Press, 1992).
25. A guide to the US military experience with restoring public order in Panama, as well as specific notes on military support to the police, can be found in John T. Fishel, *The Fog of Peace: Planning and Executing the Restoration of Panama* (Carlisle Barracks, PA: Strategic Studies Institute, US Army War College, 1992).
26. Human Rights Watch, 'The Persecution of Human Rights Monitors: Cuba', in *Cuba in the Nineties* (Washington, DC: Freedom House, 1990), p. 117.
27. An embarrassing sideline to the question of Cuban prisons is the ironic mission given to the United States military of maintaining thousands of Cuban would-be refugees in prison-like camps in Panama and Guantánamo. The way in which resentments held by internees in these camps will be manifested toward the United States is impossible to predict, but the message sent by the US government regarding

liberty is unmistakable. The indeterminate keeping of Cuban migrants is one of the most questionable missions ever given to, or accepted by, the US military.
28. Alan Riding, *Distant Neighbors: A Portrait of the Mexicans* (New York: Vintage Books, 1986), p. 46. *Guachupínes* was a derogatory term for the Spanish born of Mexico's ruling class. Substantially, the *Guachupín* has been replaced by the *Gringo* as a target of nationalist enmity.
29. See generally, Waldo S. Albro, *Always a Rebel: Ricardo Flores Magón and the Mexican Revolution* (Fort Worth, TX: Texas Christian University Press, 1992).
30. Paul Kennedy, *The Rise and Fall of the Great Powers: Economic Changes and Military Conflict from 1500 to 2000* (New York: Random House, 1987), p. xxiii. Kennedy's assertions must be read as products of the epoch's Westphalian mindset. The striking historical failure of Kennedy's thesis is, this author believes, in part due to the overwhelming theoretical dominance of geopolitical thought. State actor analyses all but crowded out other paradigms of ownership and power. Not only are there more 'Powers' today than just nation-states, the ascendancy of these other powers throws doubt on the validity of today's economic measurements to gauge the relative security of any polity. What, after all, is the GDP of the Zapatista Movement? How many battalions does the Pope have?
31. See generally '¡Ya Basta!' – www.ezln.org
32. Warren M. Christopher, 'Human Rights and the National Interest', in *Human Rights*, ed. Thomas Draper (New York: H.W. Wilson, 1982); the essay is a reprint of a statement by then Deputy Secretary of State Christopher before the American Bar Association on 4 August 1980. (Current Policy No. 206, United States Department of State, Bureau of Public Affairs, Office of Public Communications, Washington, DC, 1980.)
33. In addition to an annual world map, Freedom House publishes a monthly journal, *Freedom Review*, ed. Roger Kaplan, and an annual survey of political rights entitled *Freedom in the World*; see also Michael Kidron and Ronald Segal, *The New State of the World Atlas* (New York: Simon & Schuster, 1987). *The New State of the World Atlas* places attention in graphic form on many of the kinds of relationships alluded to in this book. Map titles include 'Urban Blight', 'The Longer Reach' (international mail receipts and radio ownership), 'The First Slice of the Cake', 'Religions of Rule', etc. The atlas is an attempt to display values and relationships that are overlooked in geopolitical interpretations like Chaliand and Rageau's *A Strategic Atlas* mentioned in Chapter 4 of this book. *The New State of the World Atlas* sports numerous curiosities. The Soviet Union is shown as three times less exploitative of its workforce than the United States. Other maps make equally dubious statements that the authors excuse in part by the difficulty of securing reliable and consistent international data.

Bibliography

Abel, A.H., *The American Indian as American Slaveholder and Secessionist*. Cleveland, OH: The Arthur H. Clarke Company, 1914.

Albro, W.S., *Always a Rebel: Ricardo Flores Magón and the Mexican Revolution*. Fort Worth, TX: Texas Christian University Press, 1992.

Alexander, Y. and Friedlander, R.A., eds, *Self-Determination: National, Regional, and Global Dimensions*. Boulder, CO: Westview Press, 1980.

Anderson, M., *Territory and State Formation in the Modern World*. Cambridge: Polity Press & Blackwell, 1995.

Ardrey, R., *The Territorial Imperative: A Personal Inquiry into the Animal Origins of Property and Nations*. New York: Atheneum, 1966.

Ashworth, G.J., *War and the City*. New York: Routledge, 1991.

Aspin, L., *Report on the Bottom-Up Review*. Washington, DC: US Department of Defense, 1993.

Augustine of Hippo, *The City of God*. Edited by V.J. Bourke and translated by G.G. Walsh, D.B. Zema, G. Monahan, and D.J. Honan. Garden City, NY: Doubleday, 1958.

Austin, A., *The President's War*. New York: J.B. Lippincott, 1971.

Bailyn, B., *The Ideological Origins of the American Revolution*. Cambridge, MA: Harvard University Press, 1967.

Bailyn, B., ed., *The Debate on the Constitution, Part 1*. New York: The Viking Press, 1992.

Ballentine, J., *Ballentine's Law Dictionary*. 3rd edn. San Francisco, CA: Bancroft-Whitney, 1969.

Beard, C.A., *The Idea of the National Interest*. New York: Macmillan, 1934.

Bell, M., et al., eds, *Geography and Imperialism 1820–1940*. New York: Manchester University Press, 1995.
Blainey, G., *The Causes of War*. New York: Macmillan, 1973.
Bowen, C.D., *Miracle at Philadelphia: The Story of the Constitutional Convention May to September 1787*. Boston, MA: Little, Brown, 1986.
Bracken, P. and Alcala, R.H., *Whither the RMA: Two Perspectives on Tomorrow's Army*. Carlisle, PA: Strategic Studies Institute, 1994.
Branscomb, A.W., *Who Owns Information?* New York: HarperCollins, 1994.
Brierly, J.L., *The Law of Nations: An Introduction to the International Law of Peace*. 6th edn, ed. Sir Humphrey Waldock. Oxford: Oxford University Press, 1963.
Brooks, N., *Abraham Lincoln and the Downfall of American Slavery*. New York: G.P. Putnam's Sons, 1898.
Bucholz, A., *Hans Delbruck and the German Military Establishment: War Images in Conflict*. Iowa City: University of Iowa Press, 1985.
Burke, J., *Connections: An Alternative View of Change*, BBC TV and *Time-Life* Media 1995.
Bush, G., *National Security Strategy of the United States*. Washington, DC: The White House, 1993.
Bush, V., *Modern Arms and Free Men*. New York: Simon & Schuster, 1949.
Butts, K.H., ed., *Environmental Security*. Carlisle Barracks, PA: US Army War College, 1994.
Cahn, E.S. and Hearne, D.W., eds, *Our Brother's Keeper: The Indian in White America*. New York: New American Library, 1970.
Carrigan, A., *The Palace of Justice: A Colombian Tragedy*. New York: Four Walls, Eight Windows, 1993.
Carter, F.W. and Norris, H.T., eds., *The Changing Shape of the Balkans*. Boulder, CO: Westview Press, 1996.
Castaneda, J.G., *Utopia Unarmed: The Latin American Left After the Cold War*. New York: Alfred Knopf, 1993.
CEHOPU (Centro de Estudios Históricos de Obras Públicas y Urbanismo) (Historical Study Center of Public Works and Urbanism), *La Ciudad Hispanoamericana: El Sueño de un Orden* (The Hispanoamerican City: The Dream of Order). Madrid: Ministerio de Obras Públicas y Urbanismo, 1989.
Center for Army Lessons Learned, *Operation Restore Hope: Lessons*

Learned Report, Operations Other Than War. Ft Leavenworth, KS: US Army Combined Arms Command, 1993).

Central Intelligence Agency, *The World Fact Book 1992.* Washington, DC: US Government Printing Office, 1993.

Centro de Estudios Estratégicos para la Estabilidad Nacional (Center of Strategic Studies for National Stability), *Programa de Clausura del Curso Inaugural 1989–1990* (Graduation program of the Inaugural Course). Guatemala City: Fundación para el Desarrollo Institucional de Guatemala, 1990.

Cervantes, M. de, *The Story of That Ingenious Gentleman Don Quijote De la Mancha*, trans. Burton Raffel. New York: W.W. Norton, 1995.

Chairman, Joint Chiefs of Staff, *Joint Publication 1, Joint Warfare of the US Armed Forces.* Washington, DC: Joint Chiefs of Staff, 1991.

Chaliand, G., ed., *Guerrilla Strategies: An Historical Anthology from the Long March to Afghanistan.* Berkeley: University of California Press, 1982.

Chaliand, G. and Rageau, J.-P., *A Strategic Atlas of Human Rights,* ed. Thomas Draper. New York: H.W. Wilson, 1982.

Chaliand, G. and Rageau, J.-P., *A Strategic Atlas.* 2nd edn, trans. Tony Berrett. New York: Harper & Row, 1983.

Chertikhin, V.Y. et al., *The Revolutionary Movement of Our Time and Nationalism*, trans. Vic Schneierson. Moscow: Progress Publishers, 1975.

Cline, R.S., *World Power Assessment.* Boulder, CO: Westview Press, 1975.

Clinton, W.J., *A National Security Strategy of Engagement and Enlargement.* Washington, DC: The White House, 1994.

Clinton, W.J., *National Security Strategy of Engagement and Enlargement.* Washington, DC: The White House, 1997.

Coate, R.A., ed., *US Policy and the Future of the United Nations.* New York: The Twentieth Century Fund, 1994.

Commission on Integrated Long-Term Strategy. *Discriminate Deterrence.* Washington, DC: US Government Printing Office, 1988.

Cooper, J.R., *Another View of the Revolution in Military Affair.* Carlisle, PA: Strategic Studies Institute, 1994.

Corbridge, S., *Mastering Space: Hegemony, Territory and International Economy.* New York: Routledge, 1997.

Cuban American National Foundation, *Castro and the Narcotics Connection*. Washington, DC: Cuban American National Foundation, 1983.

Cuban Research Institute of the Latin America and Caribbean Center, *Transition in Cuba: New Challenges for US Policy*. Miami: Florida International University and the Office of Research, US Department of State Bureau for Latin America and the Caribbean and The US Agency for International Development, 1995.

Davidson, R.N., *Crime and Environment*. London: Croom Helm, 1981.

Davis, M., *L.A. Was Just the Beginning – Urban Revolt in the United States: A Thousand Points of Light*. Westfield, NJ: The Open Magazine Pamphlet Series, 1992.

Davis, M., *Urban Control: The Ecology of Fear*. Westfield, NJ: The Open Magazine Pamphlet Series, 1994.

Department of the Air Force, *Basic Aerospace Doctrine of the United States Air Force*. Washington, DC: Department of the Air Force, 1992.

Department of the Army, *Field Manual 100-20, Internal Defense and Development*. Washington, DC: Department of the Army, 1974.

Department of the Army, *Field Manual 100-20, Low Intensity Conflict*. Washington, DC: Department of the Army, 1981.

Department of the Army, *Field Manual 100-20, Military Operations in Low Intensity Conflict*. Washington, DC: Department of the Army, 1990.

Department of the Army, *Field Manual 7-98, Operations in a Low Intensity Conflict*. Washington, DC: Department of the Army, 1992.

Department of the Army, *Field Manual 100-5, Operations*. Washington, DC: US Government Printing Office, 1993.

Department of Defense, *Strategic Defense Initiative: Progress and Promise*. (No publisher information or date provided.)

Department of the Navy, *Fleet Marine Force Field Manual (FMFM) 1, Warfighting*. Washington, DC: Headquarters, US Marine Corps, 1989.

Dietze, G., *In Defense of Property*. Chicago, IL: Henry Regnery Company, 1963.

Dijkink, G., *National Identity and Geopolitical Visions: Maps of*

Pride and Pain. New York: Routledge, 1997.

Dorner, P., *Land Reform and Economic Development*. Kingsport, TN: Kingsport Press, 1972.

Downs, A., *New Visions for Metropolitan America*. Washington, DC: The Brookings Institute, 1994.

Duchacek, I.D., *The Territorial Dimension of Politics Within, Among, and Across Nations*. Boulder, CO: Westview Press, 1986.

Efimenco, N.M., ed., *World Political Geography: Second Edition*. New York: Thomas Y. Crowell, 1957.

Eshleman, J.R. and Cashion, B.G., *Sociology, An Introduction*. Boston, MA: Little, Brown, 1983.

Fehrenbach, T.R., *This Kind of War: A Study in Unpreparedness*. New York: Macmillan, reprinted from US Army Command and Staff College Press, 1994.

Fishel, J.T., *The Fog of Peace: Planning and Executing the Restoration of Panama*. Carlisle Barracks, PA: Strategic Studies Institute, US Army War College, 1992.

Freedman, L., *Atlas of Global Strategy*. New York: Facts on File, 1985.

Freedom House, *Cuba in the Nineties*. Washington, DC: Freedom House, 1990.

Gonzalez, E. and Ronfeldt, D., *Storm Warnings Over Cuba*. Santa Monica, CA: RAND, 1994.

Goulden, J.C., *Truth is the First Casualty: The Gulf of Tonkin Affair – Illusion and Reality*. Chicago, IL: Rand McNally, 1969.

Gramajo, H.A., *Tésis de la Estabilidad Nacional*. Guatemala City: Editorial del Ejército, 1989.

Gray de Cerdan, N.A., *Territorio y Urbanismo: Bases de Geografía Prospectiva* (Territory and Urbanism: Bases of a Predictive Geography). Mendoza, Argentina: Consejo Nacional de Investigaciones Científicas y Técnicas, 1987.

Gray, C.S., *The Geopolitics of Superpower*. Lexington: The University of Kentucky Press, 1988.

Greenfield, G.M., ed., *Latin American Urbanization*. Westport, CT: Greenwood Publishing Group, 1994.

Guillermoprieto, A., *The Heart That Bleeds*. New York: Alfred Knopf, 1994.

Haass, R., *Intervention: The Use of American Military Force in the Post-Cold War World*. Washington, DC: Carnegie Endowment, 1994.

Halbrook, S.P., *That Every Man Be Armed: The Evolution of a Constitutional Right.* San Francisco, CA: Liberty Tree Press, 1984.

Harris, R.L., *Marxism Socialism and Democracy in Latin America.* Boulder, CO: Westview Press, 1992.

Hobsbawm, E.J., *Primitive Rebels: Studies of Archaic Forms of Social Movement in the 19th and 20th Centuries.* New York: W.W. Norton, 1959.

Hofeld, W.N., *Fundamental Legal Conceptions as Applied to Judicial Reasoning.* New Haven, CT: Yale University Press, 1919 (reissued 1964).

Holt-Jensen, A., *Geography: History and Concepts.* Totowa, NJ: Barnes & Noble Books, 1988.

Ibañez, S. and José, R., *Teoría del Estado, Geopolítica y Geoestrategia* (Theory of the State, Geopolitics and Geostrategy). Bogotá: Imprenta y Publicaciones de las Fuerzas Militares, 1985.

Instituto Panamericano de Geografía e Historia (Pan-American Institute of Geography and History), *Manual de Métodos Geográficos Para el Análisis Urbano, Chile* (Manual of Geographical Methods of Analysis, Chile). Mexico City: Comisión de Geografía, Comité de Geografíía Urbana, 1988.

International and Operational Law Division, *Operational Law Handbook.* Charlottesville, VA: The Judge Advocate General's School, 1994.

Jacobson, H.K., *Networks of Interdependence: International Organizations and the Global Political System.* New York: Alfred A. Knopf, 1979.

Jenkins, B.M., *An Urban Strategy for Guerrillas and Governments.* Santa Monica, CA: The Rand Corporation, 1972.

Johannsen, R.W., *Lincoln, the South, and Slavery: The Political Dimension.* Baton Rouge, LA: Louisiana State University Press, 1991.

Kasarda, J.H., *Third World Cities: Problems, Policies and Prospects.* Newbury Park, CA: Sage Publications, 1993.

Kelly, P., *Checkerboards and Shatterbelts: The Geopolitics of South America.* Austin: University of Texas Press, 1997.

Kennedy, P., *The Rise and Fall of the Great Powers: Economic Changes and Military Conflict from 1500 to 2000.* New York: Random House, 1987.

Kent, E.A., ed., *Law and Philosophy: Readings in Legal Philosophy*. New York: Meridith Corporation, 1970.

Kidron, M. and Segal, R., *The New State of the World Atlas*. New York: Simon & Schuster, 1987.

Kipling, R., *The Portable Kipling*, edited and Introduction by Irving Howe. New York: The Viking Press, 1982.

Knox, P.L., *Urbanization: An Introduction to Urban Geography*. Englewood Cliffs, NJ: Center for Urban and Regional Studies, Virginia Polytechnic Institute & State University, Prentice-Hall, 1994.

Kohl, J. and Litt, J., *Urban Guerrilla Warfare in Latin America*. Cambridge, MA: The MIT Press, 1974.

Kopel, D.B., *The Samurai, the Mountie, and the Cowboy: Should America Adopt the Gun Controls of Other Democracies?* Buffalo, NY: Prometheus Books, 1992.

Laqueur, W., *The Guerrilla Reader: A Historical Anthology*. Philadelphia, PA: Temple University Press, 1977.

Larzelere, A., *The 1980 Cuban Boatlift*. Washington, DC: National Defense University Press, US Government Printing Office, 1988.

Lipschutz, R.D., *When Nations Clash: Raw Materials, Ideology, and Foreign Policy*. New York: Harper & Row, 1989.

Locke, J., *Two Treatises of Government*. 2nd edn, ed. P. Laslett. Cambridge: Cambridge University Press, 1967.

Lomov, N.A., ed., *Scientific-Technical Progress and the Revolution in Military Affairs: A Soviet View*, trans. the United States Air Force. Washington, DC: US Government Printing Office, 1979.

Lowe, J.T., *Geopolitics and War: Mackinder's Philosophy of Power*. Washington, DC: University Press of America, 1981.

Lucas, N., *The Modern History of Israel*. New York: Praeger, 1975.

Lykke, A.F., Jr, ed., *Military Strategy: Theory and Application*. Carlisle Barracks, PA: US Army War College, 1989.

Mackinder, H.J., *Democratic Ideals and Reality*. New York: W.W. Norton, 1962.

Marcella, G., *Haiti Strategy: Control, Legitimacy, Sovereignty, Rule of Law, Handoffs, and Exit*. Carlisle Barracks, PA: US Army War College, 1994.

Martins, M., *Rules of Engagement for Land Forces: A Matter of Training, Not Lawyering*. Masters of Law Thesis, The Judge Advocate General's School, United States Army, 1994.

Mazaar, M.J., et al., *The Military Technical Revolution*. Washington,

DC: Center for Strategic and International Studies, 1993.

Mazaar, M.J., *The Revolution in Military Affairs: A Framework for Defense Planning*. Carlisle, PA: Strategic Studies Institute, 1994.

McCullough, D., *The Path Between the Seas: The Creation of the Panama Canal*. New York: Simon & Schuster, 1977.

Melville, T., *Guatemala: The Politics of Land Ownership*. New York: Free Press, 1971.

Mendel, W.W., *A Joint Command for Engagement Policy*. Ft Leavenworth, KS: Foreign Military Studies Office, 1994.

Metz, S. and Kievit, J., *The Revolution in Military Affairs and Conflict Short of War*. Carlisle, PA: Strategic Studies Institute, 1994.

Moen, M.C. and Gustaffson, L.F., eds, *The Religious Challenge to the State*. Philadelphia, PA: Temple University Press, 1992.

Moore, J.N., Tipson, F.S. and Turner, R.F., *National Security Law*. Durham, NC: Carolina Academic Press, 1990.

Morgenthau, H.J. and Thompson, K.W., *Politics Among Nations: the Struggle for Power and Peace*, 6th edn. New York: Alfred Knopf, 1973.

Morrison, T.J. and Hoffman, B., *The Urbanization of Insurgency*. Santa Monica, California: RAND Arroyo Center, 1994.

Moynihan, D.P., *Pandaemonium: Ethnicity in International Politics*. New York: Oxford University Press, 1993.

Murphy, D.T., *The Heroic Earth: Geopolitical Thought in Weimar Germany, 1918–1933*. Kent, OH: Kent State University Press, 1997.

Noyes, R., *The Institution of Property*. New York: Longmans, Green, 1936.

Office of Information Systems – OEIPS/TAF Program, *Patent Counts By Country/State and Year, Utility Patents, January 1993–June 1992*. Washington, DC: US Patent and Trademark Office, 1992.

Olson, G.L., *US Foreign Policy and the Third World Peasant: Land Reform in Asia and Latin America*. New York: Praeger, 1974.

Olson, W.C. and Groom, A.J.R., *International Relations Then and Now: Origins and Trends in Interpretation*. London: HarperCollins Academic, 1991.

Oppenheimer, A., *Castro's Final Hour: The Secret Story Behind the Coming Downfall of Communist Cuba*. New York: Simon & Schuster, 1992.

Oppenheimer, M., *The Urban Guerrilla*. Chicago, IL: Quadrangle Books, 1969.

Oro, J.R., *The Poisoning of Paradise: Environmental Pollution in the Republic of Cuba*. Miami: The Endowment for Cuban American Studies, Cuban American National Foundation, 1992.

Orsolini, M., *Montoneros: Sus Proyectos y Sus Planes*. Buenos Aires: Círculo Militar, 1989.

Paret, P., ed., *Makers of Modern Strategy: from Machiavelli to the Nuclear Age*. Princeton, NJ: Princeton University Press, 1986.

Paschall, R., *LIC 2000: Special Operations and Unconventional Warfare in the Next Century*. Washington, DC: Brassey's (US), 1990.

Patent and Trademark Office, *Technology Assessment and Forecast Program Brochure*. Washington, DC: US Department of Commerce, 1992.

Payne, J.L., *Labor and Politics in Peru: The System of Political Bargaining*. New Haven, CT: Yale University Press, 1965.

Powelson, J.P., *The Story of Land: A World History of Land Tenure and Agrarian Reform*. Cambridge, MA: Lincoln Institute of Land Policy, 1988.

Riding, A., *Distant Neighbors: A Portrait of the Mexicans*. New York: Vintage Books, 1986.

Rothmann, H.E., *Forging a New National Military Strategy in a Post-Cold War World: A Perspective from the Joint Staff*. Carlisle, PA: Strategic Studies Institute, 1992.

Schlesinger, A.M., Jr, *The Disuniting of America: Reflections on a Multicultural Society*. New York: W.W. Norton, 1992.

Schulze, H., *The Course of German Nationalism*. New York: Cambridge University Press, 1985.

Seton-Watson, H., *Nations and States*. Boulder, CO: Westview Press, 1977.

Shafer, B.C., *Faces of Nationalism*. New York: Harcourt Brace Jovanovich, 1972.

Sloan, G.R., *Geopolitics in United States Strategic Policy, 1890–1987*. New York: St Martin's Press, 1988.

Smith D.D., *The Third World City*. New York: Routledge, 1990.

Smith, D.H., *The Panama Canal: Its History, Activities and Organization*. Baltimore, MD: The Johns Hopkins University Press, Institute for Government Research, Service Monographs of the United States Government, 44, 1927.

Spanier, J., *Games Nations Play*, 8th edn. Washington: Congressional Quarterly, 1993.

Spykman, N.J., *The Geography of the Peace*, ed. Helen R. Nicholl. New York: Harcourt, Brace, 1944.

Spykman, N.J., *American Strategy in World Politics and the Balance of Power*. Shoe String Press, 1970.

Summers, H.G., Jr, *On Strategy: The Vietnam War in Context*. Carlisle, PA: Strategic Studies Institute, 1981.

Superior War School, *Basic Manual*. Brazil: Escola Superior de Guerra, 1992.

Svechin, A.A., *Strategy*, ed. Kent D. Lee. Minneapolis: East View Press, 1992.

Tai, H.-C., *Land Reform and Politics: A Comparative Analysis*. Berkeley: University of California Press, 1974.

Taylor, P.J., ed., *World Government*. New York: Oxford University Press, 1990.

Tennyson, A., *Alfred Tennyson Selected Poetry: Edited, with an Introduction by Douglas Smith*. New York: Random House, 1951.

The Arms Project of Human Rights Watch and Physicians for Human Rights, *Landmines: A Deadly Legacy*. New York: Human Rights Watch and Physicians for Human Rights, 1993.

The CIA and the Media: Hearings Before the House Subcommittee on Oversight, Permanent Select Committee on Intelligence, 95th Cong., 1st and 2nd Sess., 1978.

The Judge Advocate General's School, *Source Documents on International Law for Military Lawyers, Volume II, Security Arrangements*. Charlottesville, VA: The Judge Advocate General's School, US Army, 1969.

Thoreau, H.D., *Walden and Resistance to Civil Government*, 2nd edn, ed. William Rossi. New York: W.W. Norton, 1992.

Toffler, A. and Toffler, H., *War and Anti-War: Survival at the Dawn of the 21st Century*. Boston, MA: Little, Brown, 1993.

Trinquier, R., *Modern Warfare: A French View of Counterinsurgency*. New York: Praeger, 1964.

Tuan, Y.-F., *Landscapes of Fear*. Oxford: Blackwell, 1979.

Tunkin, G.I., *Theory of International Law*, trans. William E. Butler. Cambridge, MA: Harvard University Press, 1974.

Turbiville, G.H., Jr and Ward, R.H., eds, *Global Dimensions of High Intensity Crime and Low Intensity Conflict*. Chicago:

Office of International Criminal Justice and The University of Illinois at Chicago, 1995.

United States Congress, Goldwater-Nichols Department of Defense Reorganization Act of 1986, PL 99-433, 1 October 1986, Section 104.

US Government Printing Office, *Compilation of Intelligence Laws and Related Laws and Executive Orders of Interest to the National Intelligence Community*. Washington, DC: US Government Printing Office, 1993.

US Patent and Trademark Office, *All Technologies Report, January 1963–June 1992*, Washington DC: US Patent and Trademark Office, 1992.

Urbano, *Fighting in the Streets: A Manual of Urban Guerrilla Warfare*. Fort Lee, NJ: Barricade Books, 1991.

Van Doren, C., *A History of Knowledge: Past Present, and Future*. New York: Carol Publishing Group, 1991.

Von Clausewitz, C., *On War*, ed. and trans. Michael Howard and Peter Paret. Princeton, NJ: Princeton University Press, 1989.

Waldman, C., *Atlas of the North American Indian*. New York: Facts on File, 1985.

Weiner, M., ed., *International Migration and Security*. Boulder, CO: Westview Press, 1993.

Wells, H.G., *World Brain*. London: Methuen, 1938.

Wheatley, M., *Leadership and the New Science*. San Francisco, CA: Berrett-Koehler, 1992.

Wriston, W.B., *The Twilight of Sovereignty: How the Information Revolution is Transforming Our World*. New York: Charles Scribner's Sons, 1992.

Zoppo, C. and Zorgbibe, C., eds, *On Geopolitics: Classical and Nuclear*. Boston, MA: Martinus Nijhoff, 1985.

Index

Note: Information in notes is indexed as, for example: 64(n15)

acid rain: international effects, 58
agrarian reform, 174
Alvarez-Machain, Dr, 50
Amazon rain forest: destruction, 56–7
American Civil Liberties Union (ACLU), 18–19
Amnesty International, 126
animal rights, 59–60
Antarctica: sovereignty, 54
Apple® computers, 70, 102(n4)
Arab–Israeli conflict, 162
Arafat, Yasser, 186(n49)
Aspin, Les, 165, 166
Augustine, St, 55

Bacevich, A.C., 141–2, 168
Balkan Question, 27(n5)
banks: power, 126
Belize: sovereignty, 39–41, 65(n19)
Blainey, Geoffrey, 122–3, 145–6(n15)
Bodin, Jean, 32–3, 52, 64(nn8, 10)
Borge, Tomas, 86
Bosnia: intervention, 44; United States intervention, 169
Brazil: national strategy, 183–4(n22); rain forest exploitation, 57; Red Command, 107(n40)
Brezhnev Doctrine, 41–3
Brierly, J.L., 31, 64(nn8, 10)
Britain: Belize sovereignty, 40; Falkland Islands, 110, 241; global rights, 5; Northern Ireland involvement, 207
Bucholz, Arden, 163
built environment: conflicts, 86

Camarena, Enrique, 50, 51
Canada: international peace operations, 203–4
Castro, Fidel, 223, 225, 226, 230, 232, 244, 250–1(n8)

Castro, Raul, 223, 252(n17)
Chamorro, Violeta, 225, 251(n11)
chemical weapons, 133
children: urban violence, 90–1
Chile: urban conflict, 187(n61)
Christopher, Warren, 243–4
cities *see* urban areas
citizenship rights: United States, 193–5
Clausewitz, Carl Von *see* Von Clausewitz, Carl
Cline, Ray, 115–17, 143, 240–1, 245
Clinton, Bill, 157–61, 169, 202–3
Coast Guard: United States, 205–6
Coca-Cola®, 78–9
cohesiveness: definition, 145(n11)
Cold War, 153–7, 183(n16), 240–1
Colombia: constitution, 64(n15); firearms ownership rights, 73–4; narcoguerrillas, 89–90, 106(n32); Panama Canal implications, 76–8; press control, 74–5; satellites, 78; urban guerrillas, 100–1; violence, 102–3(n6)-3(n6)
common property, 18–22
communism: Cuba, 224–5; land ownership, 224–5; sovereignty views, 41–2
computers: United States superiority, 70–1
Commonwealth of Independent States (CIS): independence, 46–7
conflict: urban areas, 84–102
constitutions: Colombia, 64(n15); Russia (1993), 34–8; United States, 53–4, 72
crime: international, 126; organized, 228; urban, 84
Cuba: criminal organizations, 228; environmental degradation, 226; foreign opportunism, 231–2; future scenarios, 223–4, 244–5, 250–1(nn8, 9); guerrillas, 229; migrants to Mexico, 238; migrants to United States, 229, 252(n27); owner identities, 227–30; ownership issues,

223–32; ownership rules, 230–2;
policing, 230; prisons, 230–1; property
rights and duties, 224–7; public health,
227; racial issues, 229–30, 252(n21);
religion, 230; United States relationship,
49, 194–5, 199, 208–9, 216; warlord
armies, 228–9
Czechoslovakia: Soviet invasion
explanation, 41–3

Davis, Mike, 92
Delbruck, Hans, 163–4
developing countries: shantytowns, 93–4;
urban growth, 89, 104(n19), 105(n25)
Dietze, Gottfried, 17
Doctors Without Frontiers, 204
Douhet, Giulio, 161, 162
Downs, Anthony, 177
drug trafficking: Cuba, 228, 252(n17);
international, 51; Mexico, 234–5;
narcoguerrillas, 89–90, 106(n32); United
States countermeasures, 192–3
Duchacek, Ivo, 55–6

ecoguerrillas, 58
Ecuador: trade unions, 91–22
El Salvador: guerrilla tactics, 101, 108(n55)
elevator: urban effects, 85–6
environmental degradation: Cuba, 226
environmentalism, 56–61
Eurasia: Rimland theory, 152
exclusion zones: urban areas, 94,
107–8(n50)

Falkland Islands: British repossession, 110,
241
Febvre, Lucien, 144(n5)
firearms: ownership rights, 72–4, 103(n7),
226–7, see also weapons
fishing rights: oceans, 59
Flores Magón, Ricardo, 234
force multiplier, 205, 213(n44)
Fourth World movement, 68(n51)
Franklin, Benjamin, 54, 67(n40)
Frederick the Great, 163
Freed, Kenneth, 251(n12)
Fukuyama, Francis, 241

Genghis Khan, 121
geopolitics, 61–3, 113–15, 241; maps,
144–5(n7); political geography
distinction, 67(n49); United States,
151–2, 157–8; urban conflict, 85–6
Germany: Berlin Wall collapse, 42; Hitler
leadership, 120; military strategy, 163
Global Cultural Diversity Conference, 44–5
government: power, 66(n37)
Gramajo, Héctor, 249(n1), 250(n4)

Gray, Colin, 110, 143, 150, 241
Greenpeace: animal rights, 60
Grenada: United States invasion, 189
Guatemala: Belize relationship, 39–40,
65(n19); Center of Strategic Studies for
National Stability (ESTNA), 217–19,
249(n1), 250(nn4, 6); geopolitical
importance, 221; Guatemalan National
Revolutionary Unity (URNG), 221–3,
250(n7); human rights, 220–1;
indigenous peoples, 222, 250(n7);
Mexico relationship, 221; property
disputes, 216, 219–23; Santiago Atitlan
protest, 137; United States relationship,
221, 222–3; urban guerrillas, 99–100,
108–9(n65); urban violence, 90
guerrillas: Cuba, 229; landmine use, 133–4;
Mexicans in United States, 235–8; urban
areas, 98–102, 108(n62)
Guillen, Abraham, 99–100
Gulf War, 80, 142, 164, 184–5(n33)
Guzmán, Abimael, 138

Haass, Richard, 206, 214(n48)
Haiti: migration to United States, 127–8;
US invasion, 159–60, 184(n25), 202–3,
208, 214(n51)
Haushofer, Karl, 62
health care: Cuba, 227
Heartland Theory, 62, 113–15, 144(n6), 152
Hitler, Adolf, 120
Hobbes, Thomas, 53, 54, 66(nn35,37)
Hobsbawm, E.J., 125
Hofeld, Wesley Newcomb, 4
homeless: property rights, 18–19
human rights, 7, 22–6, 171; Guatemala,
220–1; Haiti, 214(n51); maps, 245–6,
253(n33); United Nations policy,
187(n63)

identity: owners, 3, 12–14
Ikle, Fred, 15
indigenous peoples: common interests,
68(n51)
information: intelligence gathering, 128–31,
146(n22); ownership, 146(23);
rebounding, 129; secrecy, 130
information revolution, 146(n19)
insurgency, 87
intelligence gathering, 128–31; battlefield,
137–8; news organizations, 146(n22)
Intelligence Preparation of the Battlefield
(IPB), 187(n61), 192
interagency, 202
international peace operations, 202–4
international relations: property-focused
approach, 3
Internet, 146–7(nn24, 25), 242–3

intervention: international, 38–45; United States, 206, 214(n48)
Israel: land ownership, 172–3

Japan: patents, 82; United States occupation, 170, 174–5
Jefferson, Thomas, 54, 67(n40)
Jews: Israel, 172–3
Jomini, Antoine-Henri, 161

Kaplan, Robert, 60
Keating, Paul, 44–5
Kennedy, Paul, 239–40, 253(n30)
Kieffer, John E., 144(n6)
Kissinger, Henry, 152
Kjellen, Rudolf, 62
Korea: land reform, 174, 175
Korean War: Task Force Smith, 197
Kuwait: Gulf War, 80; technology, 83

land reform, 171–7
land tenure: ownership regimes, 8
landlord–tenant relations, 10, 15, 17; Cuba, 225–6
landmines, 133–5, 147(n27)
Last, David, 203–4
Latin America: cities, 105(n27); urban rebel groups, 86–7, 90–2
law: international, 200; operational, 188–93
law enforcement: United States military, 180–1, 188–210
leadership: power, 120
legal rights: property, 6–7
legitimacy, 34–8, 211(n10), 212(n29)
Liddell Hart, Basil, 161, 162
Lincoln, Abraham, 24, 28(23)
Lipschutz, R.D., 26–7(n2)
Locke, John, 53, 66(n37)
Los Angeles: exclusion zones, 94, 107–8(n50); riots, 93, 98, 108(n59), 211–12(n18); security, 92–3, 94
low intensity conflict, 167–71
Luther, Martin, 66(n34)

MacArthur, General, 175
Mackinder, Halford, 62, 113–15, 144(nn5, 6), 150, 152
Madison, James, 26(n1)
Mahan, Alfred Thayer, 161, 162
Malvinas *see* Falkland Islands
maps: geopolitical, 144–5(n7); human rights, 245–6, 253(n33)
Marighella, Carlos, 89
Martins, Mark, 196–7
Mayalan, 222
Mazaar, Michael, 141
Mendel, William, 166–7

Mexico: Cuban migrants, 238; future scenarios, 233–9; land reform, 175–6; migration to United States, 234–8; Partido Revolucionario Institucional (PRI), 233; political violence, 234; United States relationship, 49–51, 58–9, 128, 192–3, 216–17, 233–9; Zapatista uprising, 68(n51), 234
Microsoft Windows®: property analysis analogy, 27(n3)
migration: Cuba to Mexico, 238; Cuba to United States, 229, 252(n27); Haiti to United States, 127–8; Mexico to United States, 234–8; rights, 21–2; rural–urban, 89
military: definition, 206–7; police distinction, 132, 186–7(nn56, 62), 190
military power, 145(n13); strategic, 110, 143–4(n3)
military spending: technological capability links, 83
military strategy, 5, 143–4(n3); Germany, 163; Soviet Union, 184(n33); United States, 5, 149–50, 161–7
Military Technical Revolution (MTR), 139–41
military technology, 121–2, 131–43
minorities: urban areas, 88
Mitchell, William, 161, 162
mob: political power, 125; urban control, 97–8
Moldova: property ownership problems, 47–8
Mongolia: power, 120–1
morale: definition, 145(n11)
Morgenthau, Hans, 30–1, 111

narcoguerrillas, 89–90, 106(n32)
national interests, 3, 27(n4)
national power, 110–13, 117–19, 143(n1); military element, 121–2, 145(n13)
national strategy: Brazil, 183–4(n22); definition, 149; United States, 151–61
nationalism: definition, 45; sovereignty relationship, 45–9; Soviet view, 44
Nicaragua: property disputes, 225, 251(n11)
non-governmental organizations (NGOs), 126, 204
non-rights: no-rights, 4; real estate, 11
Northern Ireland, 207
Noyes, Reinold, 6–7, 31, 171
nuclear weapons, 135

oceans: fishing rights, 59
oil: international value, 79–81
operational law: United States, 188–93, 210–11(nn3-5)

Operations Other Than War (OOTW), 165–6, 167–8, 185(n35); operational law, 188–93; policing, 201–10; psychological operations, 200–1; rules of engagement, 195–9; specialized forces, 205; US citizens, 193–5
ownership: identity, 3, 12–14, 118; rights and duties, 3–4, 9–12, 86; rules, 3–4, 14–15, 118

Palestinians, 172–3
Panama: independence, 76–7
Panama Canal: international implications, 75–8, 103(n8)
particularization: power, 123–6, 127–31
patent statistics, 82–3, 103–4(nn13, 14)
patriarchs: Romans, 33, 64(n11)
Persian Gulf War see Gulf War
Peru: real-estate value, 138
police: difference from military, 132, 186–7(nn56, 62), 190
policing: international peace operations, 201–10
politectonics, 116
political geography: geopolitics distinction, 67–8(n49)
popular sovereignty, 34–8
possibilism, 144(n5)
postmodernism, 242
Powell, Colin, 165
Powelson, John, 8–9, 186(n46)
power, 110–31; definitions, 110; elements, 113–23, 145(n10); leadership, 120; national, 110–13, 117–19, 143(n1); particularization, 123–6, 127–31; property rights, 116–17; strategic, 2, 110, 143–4(n3), 149; wealth, 120–1
press: state control, 74–5
prisons: Cuba, 230–1
propaganda, 201, 213(n33)
property: common, 18–22; ownership, 3–4, 9–14; rights, 3–4, 9–12, 138; value, 15–17, 70–5, 138
psychological operations (PSYOP): United States, 200–1

racial issues: Cuba, 229–30
Ratzel, Friedrich, 62, 113
Reagan, Ronald: national security strategy, 153–5; 'Star Wars' speech, 70, 102(nn2, 3), 156
real estate: Cuba, 224–5; non-rights, 11; ownership rights, 9–12; securitization, 95; value, 138
Red Cross, 126, 204
religion: Cuba, 230
resolve: definition, 145(n11)
Revolution in Military Affairs (RMA), 141–2
rights: protection, 131–2
rights and duties: property ownership, 3–4, 9–12
Rimland theory, 152
Romans: property law, 6, 31–2, 33–4, 64(n11)
rules: ownership, 14–15
Rules of Engagement (ROE): United States, 195–9, 211–12(n18)
Rules for the Use of Force (RUF), 211(n15)
Russia: constitution (1993), 34–8; land reform, 186(n55), see also Soviet Union
Russian Revolution, 26(n1)
Rwanda: United States involvement, 167

St Croix, 206
satellites, 78
Schulze, Hagen, 147(n25)
Sealand, 54–5
secrecy: information, 130
self-determination: limits, 32(n32); sovereignty relationship, 49–51; Soviet view, 44; United States view, 65(n20)
Sendero Luminoso (Shining Path), 104–5(n23), 138
Shalikashvili, John, 167
shantytowns, 93–4
Shining Path see Sendero Luminoso
slavery, 24
Sloan, Geoffrey, 151–2
Somalia: United States involvement, 167, 170, 197, 198–9, 204
sovereign state: definition, 67(n41)
sovereignty, 30–63, 247; definitions, 1–2, 30–4; ownership, 52–6; popular, 34–8; technology effects, 75–81
Soviet Union: Brezhnev Doctrine, 41–3; as enemy of United States, 150, 153–7, 240–1; human rights, 23; military strategy, 184(n33); property rights, 26(n1); technological inferiority, 70–1, see also Commonwealth of Independent States; Russia
space: property, 78
Spanier, John, 117
Spykman, Nicholas J., 144(n6), 150, 152, 183(n9)
squatters: rights, 21
state system: development, 52–3
strategic power, 2, 110, 143–4(n2), 149
strategy: definition, 182(n2); national, 149, 151–61
Svechin, General Major Alexandr, 184–5(n33)
technology: influences, 69–102; internal conflicts, 81–102; military, 121–2, 131–43; power element, 121;

INDEX   271

sovereignty effects, 75–81
Third World *see* developing countries
Thomas Aquinas, St, 67(n43)
trade unions: urban violence, 91–2
tribe: nation distinction, 45, 65(n26)
Tukhachevskii, Mikhail, 184–5(n33)
Tunkin, G.I., 23–4

United Nations: human rights, 187(n63); peace operations, 202–3
United States: acid rain responsibility, 58; American Revolution, 26(n1), 66(n36); cities, 105(n27); citizenship rights, 193–5; Coast Guard, 205–6; Constitution, 53–4, 72; counterdrug operations, 192–3; Cuba relationship, 229, 252(n27); firearms ownership, 72, 102(n5); foreign policy, 25–6; geopolitics, 151–2, 157–8; Goldwater–Nichols Act (1986), 153; Haitian immigrants, 127–8; homeless rights, 18–19; human rights, 24–5; immigration rights, 21–2, 127–8, 229, 236–7, 239; Indian property beliefs, 28(n10), 62; Indian/Mexican relationship, 237; intelligence gathering, 128–31, 146(n22), 192–3; interagency, 202; Joint Task Force-6, 192–5, 198; Mexican immigrants, 234–9; Mexico relationship, 49–51, 58–9, 128, 192–3, 216–17, 233–9; national power, 112–13, 117–19; national strategy, 151–61; Panama Canal, 76–7; patent records, 82, 103–4(n13); police force, 214(n53); Posse Comitatus Act, 192, 194, 195, 211(n11); sovereignty, 33; technological superiority, 70–1; urban violence, 177–8; US person definition, 146(n21), 193–5; vital or survival interests, 158–9, or survival interests, 158–9, *see also* United States, military strategy; United States, Operations Other Than War
United States, military strategy, 5, 149–50, 161–7, 247–9; Cold War, 153–7, 183(n16); Commission on Integrated Long-Term Strategy, 155–6, 183(n20); Gulf War, 80, 142, 164, 184–5(n33); Heartland Theory implications, 114–15, 144(n6); legal constraints, 180–1, 188–93; low intensity conflict, 167–71; military technology, 139–41; National Military Strategy (NMS), 166; National Security Strategy (1988), 153–7; National Security Strategy (1993), 157, 159; National Security Strategy (1994), 157, 158, 159, 202; National Security Strategy (1995), 176; Revolution in Military Affairs, 141–2; Soviet Union relationship, 150, 153–7, 240–1; Star Wars, 70, 102(nn2, 3), 156; Vietnam War, 119–20, 162–3
United States, Operations Other Than War (OOTW), 165–6, 167, 168, 185(n35), 189–210; operational law, 188–93, 210–11(nn3-5); policing role, 189–210; psychological operations (PSYOP), 200–1; Rules of Engagement (ROE), 195–9, 211–12(n18); training, 196–8, 212(nn24, 25)
Upton, Emory, 161, 162
urban areas: conflict, 84–102; definition, 87, 105(n25); developing countries, 89, 104(n19), 105(n25); exclusion zones, 94, 107–8(n50); growth models, 92, 107(n44); minorities, 88; organized crime, 89–90; ownership, 86; police/military distinction, 186–7(nn56, 62); property value, 95–6; security, 92–4; United States/Latin America comparison, 105(n27); voting patterns, 106(n30)
urban violence: control, 177–80; gangs, 91, 94–5; guerrillas, 98–102, 108(n62); mob control, 97–8; rioting, 98, 108(nn58, 59); student violence, 90–1; trade union disorder, 91–2; types, 96–8

value: property, 15–17, 70–5, 95–6
Vietnam War, 119–20, 162–3
Von Clausewitz, Carl, 140, 147–8(n32), 161–2, 163, 241
voting patterns: urban poor, 106(n30)

war: causes, 122–3; irregular, 140–2; political nature, 147–8(n32)
wealth: power, 120–11
weapons, 131–43; legality, 132–5; lethality, 135–6; nuclear, 135; police and military use, 132; precision/accuracy distinction, 147(n28); property rights effects, 138–9; proscribed, 133–5; range, 136–8, *see also* firearms
Wells, H.G., 146–7(n24)
Westphalia: Peace of, 52
Wheatley, Margaret, 148(n39)
will: definition, 145(n11)
Wohlstetter, Albert, 155
Wriston, Walter B., 146(n19)

Yugoslavia: property claims, 48–9, 65(n28)